quick
&
easy

quick
&
easy

Bath · New York · Singapore · Hong Kong · Cologne · Delhi · Melbourne

This edition published by Parragon in 2009

Parragon
Queen Street House
4 Queen Street
Bath BA1 1HE, UK

Copyright © Parragon Books Ltd 2009
Designed by Terry Jeavons & Company
Additional text written by Linda Doeser

ISBN 978-1-4075-4761-9

Printed in Indonesia

Notes for the Reader

This book uses both metric and imperial measurements. Follow the same units of measurement throughout; do not mix metric and imperial. All spoon measurements are level: teaspoons are assumed to be 5 ml, and tablespoons are assumed to be 15 ml. Unless otherwise stated, milk is assumed to be full fat, eggs and individual vegetables are medium and pepper is freshly ground black pepper.

The times given are an approximate guide only. Preparation times differ according to the techniques used by different people and the cooking times may also vary from those given. Optional ingredients, variations or serving suggestions have not been included in the calculations.

Recipes using raw or very lightly cooked eggs should be avoided by infants, the elderly, pregnant women, convalescents and anyone suffering from an illness. Pregnant and breastfeeding women are advised to avoid eating peanuts and peanut products. Sufferers from nut allergies should be aware that some of the ready-made ingredients used in the recipes in this book may contain nuts. Vegetarians should be aware that some of the ready-made ingredients, such as cheese, used in the recipes in this book may contain animal products. Always check the packaging before use.

contents

introduction

With the ever-increasing pace of modern life, finding time to feed the family without relying too heavily on ready-made convenience foods can be a daily struggle. But help is at hand in this mouth-watering collection of quick and easy recipes, guaranteed to provide you with inspiration for every meal and occasion. With step-by-step instructions, the recipes are certainly easy to follow, and although they are inspired by delicious dishes from around the world, the ingredients are widely available and most will be familiar. All of them can be prepared and cooked within an hour and many take far less time, some only minutes.

Some ingredients are the ideal choice for the busy cook – pasta, noodles, fish fillets, diced chicken and steaks, for example, require little preparation and cook very rapidly. You may need to spend more time preparing others but this is often counterbalanced by the speed with which they can be cooked. Some cooking techniques are also particularly rapid – stir-frying could legitimately be called the original fast food and both pan-frying and grilling are quick cooking methods.

There is no doubt that fresh ingredients have the most flavour, the best texture and the highest nutritional levels. However, there are shortcuts that will make cooking easier and quicker without detracting from the quality of the finished dish. In this book, any recipes that include a tomato sauce, for example, will almost always suggest using canned chopped tomatoes. Peeling and chopping fresh tomatoes isn't difficult but it's not really worth the bother, especially if they have been picked before they are fully ripe and are neither sweet nor colourful. Similarly, there is no great virtue in soaking dried beans and then boiling them for hours when you can simply open a can, drain and rinse the beans and add them straight to the dish you are preparing. Also, whilst home-made stock may be delicious, particularly for making soup, it does take quite a lot of time to make. It is therefore perfectly acceptable to use stock cubes, bouillon powder or shop-bought fresh stock. Make sure to buy a high-quality brand for maximum flavour and check the salt content on the label first.

All the recipes in this book clearly describe how the ingredients should be prepared – finely chopped, thickly sliced, diced into cubes, cut into batons, cut into strips, and so on – and it is a matter of personal choice whether you buy them ready prepared or do the work yourself. Nowadays, most supermarkets stock a wide variety of ready-prepared ingredients, such as chopped onions, diced carrots and sliced mushrooms. These ingredients undoubtedly save time but will usually be more expensive and it is worth remembering that the cut surfaces of vegetables quickly begin to lose some of their vitamins. However, there are other shortcuts you can take that aren't necessarily costly. For example, most home cooks are far from enthusiastic about scaling, cleaning and filleting whole fish as this can be fiddly and time-consuming, so you may prefer to ask your fishmonger to do this for you.

Some of the recipes in this book involve marinating ingredients. This does admittedly take time, sometimes hours, but do resist the temptation to skip this stage. Marinating adds flavour to all kinds of ingredients and also helps to tenderize meat. If you're well organized, you can mix the marinade and pour it over the chicken or meat the night before or in the morning, then cover the dish and leave it to marinate in the refrigerator. Do remember to remove it from the refrigerator about 30 minutes before you're ready to cook to bring it to room temperature. However, do not leave fish to marinate in an acid mixture – one containing citrus juice, wine or vinegar – for more than 1 hour, as, after this time, the delicate flesh reacts almost as if it has been cooked and the texture will change. In fact, 30 minutes is quite sufficient for most fish and seafood marinades and if, like most of us, you are not a well-organized cook, even meat and poultry will benefit from this brief time marinating.

Additional time may be required for cooling and chilling, so always read the recipe in advance of cooking so you can factor this into your plans. You can try to speed up cooling by putting the dish in a cool place, but do not put hot food into the refrigerator as it will affect the thermostat and could cause other food to spoil.

soups, salads & snacks

Soup is undoubtedly one of the easiest dishes to cook at home. It is always welcome and comforting and does not involve hours of stirring, straining and toiling over a hot stove. In fact, most recipes take no more than 30 minutes and are almost impossible to get wrong. Substantial soups are great served with crusty bread for easy lunches and more delicate broths make fantastic starters for both family suppers and for entertaining friends. For best results, make sure you use a good-quality stock, whether ready-made from the chiller cabinet or made with stock cubes or bouillon powder.

Salads are wonderfully versatile and may be served as a light main course, a side dish or an appetizer. They may be wholly vegetarian or feature meat, chicken, fish or seafood. The easiest and quickest salads to assemble are made from raw vegetables and fruit and may also contain other ingredients, such as nuts or cheese. A small amount of cooking is required for a number of familiar favourites, such as pasta and potato salads, and you will need to allow time for cooling. Of course, there are also time-saving salads designed to be served warm.

Home-made canapés, snacks and dips add that special extra touch when you are entertaining. Although they look impressive and are much tastier than their ready-made equivalents, they require very little effort in

the kitchen. Delightful hot snacks can be prepared in advance and cooked in minutes, while you can make dips and prepare vegetable crudités – store them in plastic bags in the refrigerator – well before the party begins.

vegetable & bean soup

ingredients

SERVES 4–6

225 g/8 oz fresh broad beans

2 tbsp olive oil

2 large garlic cloves, crushed

1 large onion, finely chopped

1 celery stalk, finely chopped

1 carrot, peeled and chopped

175 g/6 oz firm new potatoes, diced

850 ml/1½ pints vegetable stock

2 beefsteak tomatoes, peeled, deseeded and chopped

salt and pepper

1 large bunch of fresh basil, tied with kitchen string

200 g/7 oz courgette, diced

200 g/7 oz green beans, trimmed and chopped

55 g/2 oz dried vermicelli, broken into pieces, or small pasta shapes

pesto sauce

100 g/3½ oz fresh basil leaves

2 large garlic cloves

1½ tbsp pine kernels

50 ml/2 fl oz fruity extra virgin olive oil

55 g/2 oz finely grated Parmesan cheese

method

1 If the broad beans are very young and tender, they can be used as they are. If they are older, use a small, sharp knife to slit the grey outer skins, then 'pop' out the green beans.

2 Heat the olive oil in a large heavy-based saucepan over medium heat. Add the garlic, onion, celery and carrot and sauté until the onion is soft, but not brown.

3 Add the potatoes, stock and tomatoes and season with salt and pepper. Bring the stock to the boil, skimming the surface if necessary, then add the basil. Reduce the heat and cover the pan. Simmer for 15 minutes, or until the potatoes are tender.

4 Meanwhile, make the pesto sauce. Whizz the basil, garlic and pine kernels in a food processor or blender until a thick paste forms. Add the extra virgin olive oil and whizz again. Transfer to a bowl and stir in the cheese, then cover and chill until required.

5 When the potatoes are tender, stir the broad beans, courgette, green beans and vermicelli into the soup and continue simmering for 10 minutes, or until the vegetables are tender and the pasta is cooked. Taste, and adjust the seasoning if necessary. Remove and discard the bunch of basil.

6 Ladle the soup into bowls and add a spoonful of pesto sauce to each bowl.

brown lentil & pasta soup

ingredients
SERVES 4

4 slices lean bacon, cut into
   small squares
1 onion, chopped
2 garlic cloves, crushed
2 celery stalks, chopped
50 g/1¾ oz farfalline or
   spaghetti, broken into
   small pieces
400 g/14 oz canned brown
   lentils, drained
1.2 litres/2 pints hot vegetable
   stock
2 tbsp chopped fresh mint
fresh mint sprigs, to garnish

method

1 Place the bacon in a large frying pan with the onion, garlic and celery. Dry fry for 4–5 minutes, stirring, until the onion is tender and the bacon is just beginning to brown.

2 Add the pasta to the pan and cook, stirring, for 1 minute to coat the pasta in the fat.

3 Add the lentils and the stock and bring to the boil. Reduce the heat and simmer for 12–15 minutes, or until the pasta is tender but still firm to the bite.

4 Remove the pan from the heat and stir in the chopped fresh mint. Transfer the soup to warmed soup bowls, garnish with fresh mint sprigs and serve immediately.

watercress soup

ingredients

SERVES 4

2 bunches of watercress
(approx 200 g/7 oz),
thoroughly cleaned

3 tbsp butter

2 onions, chopped

225 g/8 oz potatoes, peeled
and roughly chopped

1.2 litres/2 pints vegetable
stock or water

salt and pepper

whole nutmeg, for grating
(optional)

125 ml/4 fl oz crème fraîche,
yogurt or sour cream

method

1 Remove the leaves from the stalks of the watercress and keep on one side. Roughly chop the stalks.

2 Melt the butter in a large saucepan over medium heat, add the onion and cook for 4–5 minutes until soft. Do not brown.

3 Add the potato to the pan and mix well with the onion. Add the watercress stalks and the stock. Bring to the boil, then reduce the heat, cover and simmer for 15–20 minutes until the potato is soft.

4 Add the watercress leaves and stir in to heat through. Remove from the heat and use a hand-held stick blender to process the soup until smooth. Alternatively, pour the soup into a blender, process until smooth, and return to the rinsed-out pan. Reheat and season with salt and pepper, adding a good grating of nutmeg, if using.

5 Serve in warm bowls with the crème fraîche, yogurt or sour cream spooned on top.

leek & potato soup

ingredients

SERVES 4

55 g/2 oz butter

1 onion, chopped

3 leeks, sliced

225 g/8 oz potatoes, peeled
and cut into 2-cm/3/4-inch
cubes

850 ml/1½ pints vegetable
stock

salt and pepper

150 ml/5 fl oz single cream
(optional)

2 tbsp snipped fresh chives,
to garnish

method

1 Melt the butter in a large pan over medium heat, add the prepared vegetables, and sauté gently for 2–3 minutes until soft but not brown. Pour in the stock, bring to the boil, then reduce the heat and simmer, covered, for 15 minutes.

2 Remove from the heat and blend the soup using a stick blender or food processor.

3 Reheat the soup, season with salt and pepper to taste, and serve in warm bowls, swirled with the cream, if using, and garnished with chives.

potato & pesto soup

ingredients
SERVES 4

3 slices rindless, smoked, fatty
    bacon or pancetta
450 g/1 lb floury potatoes
450 g/1 lb onions
2 tbsp olive oil
600 ml/1 pint chicken stock
600 ml/1 pint milk
100 g/3$^{1}/_{2}$ oz dried
    conchigliette
150 ml/5 fl oz double cream
chopped fresh parsley
salt and pepper
garlic bread and Parmesan
    cheese shavings, to serve

pesto sauce
55 g/2 oz finely chopped fresh
    parsley
2 garlic cloves, crushed
55 g/2 oz pine kernels,
    crushed
2 tbsp chopped fresh basil
    leaves
55 g/2 oz freshly grated
    Parmesan cheese
white pepper
150 ml/5 fl oz olive oil

method

1 To make the pesto sauce, put all of the ingredients in a blender or food processor and process for 2 minutes, or blend by hand using a mortar and pestle.

2 Finely chop the bacon, potatoes and onions. Cook the bacon in a large saucepan over medium heat for 4 minutes. Add the olive oil, potatoes and onions and cook for 12 minutes, stirring constantly.

3 Add the stock and milk to the pan, bring to the boil and simmer for 10 minutes. Add the conchigliette and simmer for a further 10–12 minutes.

4 Blend in the cream and simmer for 5 minutes. Add the chopped parsley, salt and pepper and 2 tablespoons of the pesto sauce. Transfer the soup to individual serving bowls and serve with Parmesan cheese shavings and fresh garlic bread.

broad bean & mint soup

ingredients

SERVES 4

2 tbsp olive oil

1 red onion, chopped

2 garlic cloves, crushed

450 g/1 lb diced potatoes

500 g/1 lb 2 oz broad beans,
   thawed if frozen

850 ml/1½ pints vegetable
   stock

2 tbsp freshly chopped mint

plain yogurt and fresh mint
   sprigs, to garnish

method

1 Heat the olive oil in a large saucepan. Add the onion and garlic and sauté for 2–3 minutes, until softened. Add the potatoes and cook, stirring constantly, for 5 minutes.

2 Stir in the beans and the stock. Cover and simmer gently for 30 minutes or until the beans and potatoes are tender.

3 Remove a few vegetables with a slotted spoon and set aside. Place the remainder of the soup in a food processor or blender and process to a smooth purée.

4 Return the soup to a clean saucepan and add the reserved vegetables and chopped mint. Stir thoroughly and heat through gently.

5 Ladle the soup into individual serving bowls. Garnish with swirls of plain yogurt and sprigs of fresh mint and serve immediately.

yogurt & tomato soup

ingredients

SERVES 4

4 large tomatoes

2 tbsp olive oil

1 onion, roughly chopped

1 garlic clove, chopped

300 ml/10 fl oz vegetable
   stock

2 oil-packed sun-dried
   tomatoes, chopped

1 tsp chopped fresh thyme

$1/2$ tsp ground cinnamon

salt and pepper

300 ml/10 fl oz Greek-style
   yogurt

method

1 Roughly grate the tomatoes into a bowl, discarding their skins left in your hand. Heat the oil in a saucepan, add the onion and garlic and fry for 5 minutes or until softened. Add the tomatoes to the pan and cook gently for a further 5 minutes.

2 Add the stock, sun-dried tomatoes, thyme, cinnamon, salt and pepper, bring to the boil, then simmer for 10 minutes.

3 Allow the soup to cool slightly then purée in a food processor or blender, or with a hand-held blender. Add the yogurt and mix. Adjust the seasoning if necessary.

4 If serving hot, reheat the soup gently. (Do not boil or the soup will curdle.) If serving cold, cool and then chill in the refrigerator for 3–4 hours.

sweetcorn, potato & cheese soup

ingredients
SERVES 4

55 g/2 oz butter
2 shallots, finely chopped
225 g/8 oz potatoes, peeled
   and diced
4 tbsp plain flour
2 tbsp dry white wine
300 ml/10 fl oz milk
325 g/11$\frac{1}{2}$ oz canned corn
   kernels, drained
115 g/4 oz grated Swiss
   cheese or Cheddar cheese
8–10 fresh sage leaves,
   chopped
425 ml/15 fl oz double cream
fresh sage sprigs, to garnish

croûtons
2–3 slices of day-old white
   bread
2 tbsp olive oil

method
1 To make the croûtons, cut the crusts off the bread slices, then cut the remaining bread into 5-mm/$\frac{1}{4}$-inch squares. Heat the olive oil in a heavy-based frying pan and add the bread cubes. Cook, tossing and stirring constantly, until evenly coloured. Drain the croûtons thoroughly on kitchen paper and reserve.

2 Melt the butter in a large, heavy-based saucepan. Add the shallots and cook over low heat, stirring occasionally, for 5 minutes or until softened. Add the potatoes and cook, stirring, for 2 minutes.

3 Sprinkle in the flour and cook, stirring, for 1 minute. Remove the pan from the heat and stir in the white wine, then gradually stir in the milk. Return the pan to the heat and bring to the boil, stirring constantly, then reduce the heat and simmer.

4 Stir in the corn kernels, cheese, chopped sage and cream and heat through gently until the cheese has just melted. Ladle the soup into warmed bowls, scatter over the croûtons, garnish with fresh sage sprigs and serve.

vegetable & noodle soup

ingredients

SERVES 4

2 tbsp vegetable or peanut oil

1 onion, sliced

2 garlic cloves, chopped finely

1 large carrot, cut into thin
  sticks

1 courgette, cut into thin sticks

115 g/4 oz head of broccoli,
  cut into florets

1 litre/1³/₄ pints vegetable
  stock

400 ml/14 fl oz coconut milk

3–4 tbsp Thai soy sauce

2 tbsp Thai red curry paste

55 g/2 oz wide rice noodles

115 g/4 oz mung or soy
  beansprouts

4 tbsp chopped fresh
  coriander

method

1 Heat the oil in a wok or large frying pan and stir-fry the onion and garlic for 2–3 minutes. Add the carrot, courgette and broccoli and stir-fry for 3–4 minutes, until just tender.

2 Pour in the stock and coconut milk and bring to the boil. Add the soy sauce, curry paste and noodles and simmer for 2–3 minutes, until the noodles have swelled. Stir in the beansprouts and coriander and serve immediately.

hot-&-sour soup

ingredients

SERVES 4

6 dried shiitake mushrooms

115 g/4 oz rice vermicelli
  noodles

4 small fresh green chillies,
  deseeded and chopped

6 tbsp rice wine vinegar

850 ml/1½ pints vegetable
  stock

2 lemon grass stalks, snapped
  in half

115 g/4 oz canned water
  chestnuts, drained, rinsed
  and halved

6 tbsp Thai soy sauce

juice of 1 lime

1 tbsp jaggery or soft light
  brown sugar

3 spring onions, chopped,
  to garnish

method

1 Place the dried mushrooms in a bowl and pour in enough hot water to cover. Set aside to soak for 1 hour. Place the noodles in another bowl and pour in enough hot water to cover. Set aside to soak for 10 minutes. Combine the chillies and rice wine vinegar in a third bowl and set aside.

2 Drain the mushrooms and noodles. Bring the stock to the boil in a large saucepan. Add the mushrooms, noodles, lemon grass, water chestnuts, soy sauce, lime juice and sugar and bring to the boil.

3 Stir in the chilli and vinegar mixture and cook for 1–2 minutes. Remove and discard the lemon grass. Ladle the soup into warmed bowls and serve hot, garnished with the spring onions.

chicken & pasta broth

ingredients

SERVES 6

350 g/12 oz boneless chicken
    breasts
2 tbsp corn oil
1 onion, diced
250 g/9 oz carrots, diced
250 g/9 oz cauliflower florets
850 ml/1½ pints chicken
    stock
2 tsp dried mixed herbs
125 g/4¹/₂ oz dried small pasta
    shapes
salt and pepper
freshly grated Parmesan
    cheese, for sprinkling
    (optional)
fresh crusty bread, to serve

method

1 Using a sharp knife, finely dice the chicken, discarding any skin.

2 Heat the corn oil in a large saucepan and quickly cook the chicken, onion, carrots and cauliflower until they are lightly coloured.

3 Stir in the chicken stock and dried mixed herbs and bring to the boil.

4 Add the pasta shapes to the pan and return to the boil. Cover the pan and simmer the broth for 10 minutes, stirring occasionally to prevent the pasta sticking together.

5 Season the broth with salt and pepper and sprinkle with grated Parmesan cheese, if using. Serve with crusty bread.

chicken & broccoli soup

ingredients

SERVES 4–6

225 g/8 oz head broccoli
salt and pepper
55 g/2 oz unsalted butter
1 onion, chopped
225 g/8 oz basmati rice
225 g/8 oz skinless, boneless
    chicken breast, cut into
    thin slivers
25 g/1 oz plain wholewheat
    flour
300 ml/10 fl oz milk
500 ml/18 fl oz chicken stock
55 g/2 oz sweetcorn kernels

method

1 Break the broccoli into small florets and cook in a saucepan of lightly salted boiling water for 3 minutes, drain, then plunge into cold water and set aside.

2 Melt the butter in a pan over medium heat, add the onion, rice and chicken, and cook for 5 minutes, stirring frequently.

3 Remove the pan from the heat and stir in the flour. Return to the heat and cook for 2 minutes, stirring constantly. Stir in the milk and then the stock. Bring to the boil, stirring constantly, then reduce the heat and simmer for 10 minutes.

4 Drain the broccoli and add to the pan with the sweetcorn, salt and pepper. Simmer for a further 5 minutes, or until the rice is tender, then serve.

chicken & tarragon soup

ingredients

SERVES 4

55 g/2 oz unsalted butter
1 large onion, chopped
300 g/10½ oz cooked skinless
    chicken, shredded finely
600 ml/1 pint chicken stock
salt and pepper
1 tbsp chopped fresh tarragon
150 ml/5 fl oz double cream
fresh tarragon leaves,
    to garnish
deep-fried croûtons, to serve

method

1 Melt the butter in a large saucepan and fry the onion for 3 minutes.

2 Add the chicken to the pan with half of the chicken stock. Bring to the boil, then reduce the heat and simmer for 20 minutes. Let cool, then process until smooth in a blender or food processor.

3 Add the remainder of the stock and season with salt and pepper.

4 Add the chopped tarragon, then transfer the soup to individual serving bowls and stir in the cream.

5 Garnish the soup with fresh tarragon and serve with deep-fried croûtons.

spicy beef & noodle soup

ingredients

SERVES 4

1 litre/1³/₄ pints beef stock

150 ml/5 fl oz vegetable or
    peanut oil

85 g/3 oz rice vermicelli
    noodles

2 shallots, sliced thinly

2 garlic cloves, crushed

2.5-cm/1-inch piece fresh root
    ginger, sliced thinly

225-g/8-oz piece fillet steak,
    cut into thin strips

2 tbsp Thai green curry paste

2 tbsp Thai soy sauce

1 tbsp fish sauce

chopped fresh coriander,
    to garnish

method

1 Pour the stock into a large saucepan and bring to the boil. Meanwhile, heat the oil in a wok or large frying pan. Add a third of the noodles and cook for 10–20 seconds, until they have puffed up. Lift out of the oil with tongs, drain on kitchen paper and set aside. Discard all but 2 tablespoons of the oil.

2 Add the shallots, garlic and ginger to the wok or frying pan and stir-fry for 1 minute. Add the beef and curry paste and stir-fry for a further 3–4 minutes, until tender.

3 Add the beef mixture, the uncooked noodles, soy sauce and fish sauce to the pan of stock and simmer for 2–3 minutes, until the noodles have swelled. Serve hot, garnished with the chopped coriander and the reserved crispy noodles.

fishermen's soup

ingredients

SERVES 6

900 g/2 lb fillets of mixed
   white fish and shellfish,
   such as cod, flounder,
   halibut, monkfish, sea
   bass, whiting and peeled
   prawns

150 ml/5 fl oz olive oil

2 large onions, sliced

2 celery sticks, thinly sliced

2 garlic cloves, chopped

150 ml/5 fl oz white wine

4 canned tomatoes, chopped

pared rind of 1 orange

1 tsp chopped fresh thyme

2 tbsp chopped fresh parsley

2 bay leaves

salt and pepper

lemon wedges, to serve

croûtons, to garnish

method

1 Cut the fish into fairly large, thick serving portions, discarding any skin. Heat the oil in a large saucepan, add the onion, celery and garlic and fry for 5 minutes or until softened.

2 Add the fish and prawns to the pan, then add the wine, tomatoes, pared orange rind, thyme, parsley, bay leaves, salt, pepper and enough cold water to cover. Bring to the boil, then simmer, uncovered, for 15 minutes.

3 Serve the soup hot with lemon wedges, garnished with croûtons.

prawn laksa

ingredients

SERVES 4

400 g/14 oz canned coconut milk

300 ml/10 fl oz vegetable stock

50 g/1¾ oz vermicelli rice noodles

1 red pepper, deseeded and cut into strips

225 g/8 oz canned bamboo shoots, drained and rinsed

5-cm/2-inch piece fresh root ginger, sliced thinly

3 spring onions, chopped

1 tbsp Thai red curry paste

2 tbsp fish sauce

1 tsp jaggery or soft light brown sugar

6 sprigs fresh Thai basil

12 cooked prawns, in their shells

method

1 Pour the coconut milk and stock into a saucepan and bring slowly to the boil. Add the remaining ingredients, except the prawns, and simmer gently for 4–5 minutes, until the noodles are cooked.

2 Add the prawns and simmer for a further 1–2 minutes, until heated through. Ladle the soup into small, warmed bowls, dividing the prawns equally between them, and serve immediately.

corn & crab soup

ingredients

SERVES 4

2 tbsp vegetable or peanut oil

4 garlic cloves, chopped finely

5 shallots, chopped finely

2 lemon grass stalks, chopped finely

2.5-cm/1-inch piece fresh root ginger, chopped finely

1 litre/1³/₄ pints chicken stock

400 g/14 oz canned coconut milk

225 g/8 oz frozen sweetcorn kernels

350 g/12 oz canned crabmeat, drained and shredded

2 tbsp fish sauce

juice of 1 lime

1 tsp jaggery or soft light brown sugar

bunch of fresh coriander, chopped, to garnish

method

1 Heat the oil in a large frying pan and sauté the garlic, shallots, lemon grass and ginger over low heat, stirring occasionally, for 2–3 minutes, until softened. Add the stock and coconut milk and bring to the boil. Add the corn, reduce the heat and simmer gently for 3–4 minutes.

2 Add the crabmeat, fish sauce, lime juice and sugar and simmer gently for 1 minute. Ladle into warmed bowls, garnish with the chopped coriander and serve at once.

quick clam chowder

ingredients

SERVES 4

2 tsp corn oil

115 g/4 oz rindless lean
    bacon, diced

2 tbsp butter

1 onion, chopped

2 celery stalks, chopped

2 potatoes, chopped

salt and pepper

2 leeks, sliced

400 g/14 oz canned chopped
    tomatoes

3 tbsp chopped fresh parsley

1.2 litres/2 pints fish stock

550 g/1 lb 4 oz canned clams,
    drained and rinsed

method

1 Heat the oil in a heavy-based saucepan. Add the bacon and cook over medium heat, stirring, for 5 minutes or until the fat runs and it begins to crisp. Remove from the pan, drain on kitchen paper and reserve.

2 Melt the butter in the pan. Add the onion, celery and potatoes with a pinch of salt. Cover and cook over low heat, stirring occasionally, for 10 minutes, or until soft.

3 Stir in the leeks, the tomatoes and their juices, and 2 tablespoons of the parsley. Pour in the stock, bring to the boil, reduce the heat and simmer for 10–15 minutes, or until the vegetables are tender. Season to taste with salt and pepper and stir in the clams.

4 Heat the soup gently for 2–3 minutes, then ladle into warmed bowls, garnish with the remaining parsley and reserved bacon, and serve.

green bean salad with feta cheese

ingredients

SERVES 4

350 g/12 oz green beans

1 red onion, chopped

3–4 tbsp chopped fresh
    coriander

2 radishes, thinly sliced

75 g/2³/₄ oz feta cheese
    drained weight, crumbled

1 tsp chopped fresh oregano,
    plus extra leaves to garnish
    (optional), or ¹/₂ tsp dried

pepper

2 tbsp red wine or fruit vinegar

80 ml/3 fl oz extra virgin olive
    oil

3 ripe tomatoes, cut into
    wedges

slices of crusty bread, to serve

method

1 Bring about 5 cm/2 inches of water to the boil in the bottom of a steamer. Add the beans to the top part of the steamer, cover and steam for 5 minutes, or until just tender.

2 Place the beans in a large bowl and add the onion, coriander, radishes and feta cheese.

3 Sprinkle the oregano over the salad, then season with pepper. Mix the vinegar and oil together in a small bowl and pour over the salad. Toss gently to mix well.

4 Transfer to a serving platter, surround with the tomato wedges and serve at once with slices of crusty bread, or cover and chill until ready to serve.

roasted pepper salad

ingredients

SERVES 8

3 red peppers

3 yellow peppers

5 tbsp Spanish extra virgin
   olive oil

2 tbsp dry sherry vinegar or
   lemon juice

2 garlic cloves, crushed

pinch of sugar

salt and pepper

1 tbsp capers

8 small black Spanish olives

2 tbsp chopped fresh
   marjoram, plus extra sprigs
   to garnish

method

1 Preheat the grill to high. Place the peppers on a wire rack or grill pan and cook under the grill for 10 minutes, until their skins have blackened and blistered, turning them frequently.

2 Remove the roasted peppers from the heat, and either put them in a bowl and immediately cover tightly with a clean, damp tea towel or put them in a plastic bag. The steam helps to soften the skins and makes it easier to remove them. Let stand for about 15 minutes, until cool enough to handle.

3 Holding one pepper at a time over a clean bowl, use a sharp knife to make a small hole in the base and gently squeeze out the juices and reserve them. Still holding the pepper over the bowl, carefully peel off the blackened skin with your fingers, or a knife, and discard it. Cut the peppers in half and remove the stem, core and seeds, then cut each pepper into neat thin strips. Arrange the pepper strips on a serving dish.

4 To the reserved pepper juices add the olive oil, sherry vinegar, garlic, sugar, salt and pepper. Whisk together until combined. Drizzle the dressing evenly over the salad.

5 Sprinkle the capers, olives and chopped marjoram over the salad, garnish with marjoram sprigs and serve at room temperature.

avocado salad with lime dressing

ingredients

SERVES 4

60 g/2¼ oz mixed red and
    green lettuce leaves
60 g/2¼ oz wild rocket
4 spring onions, finely diced
5 tomatoes, sliced
25 g/1 oz walnuts, toasted and
    chopped
2 avocados
1 tbsp lemon juice

lime dressing

1 tbsp lime juice
1 tsp French mustard
1 tbsp sour cream
1 tbsp chopped fresh parsley
    or coriander
3 tbsp extra virgin olive oil
pinch of sugar
salt and pepper

method

1 Wash and drain the lettuce and rocket, if necessary. Shred all the leaves and arrange in the bottom of a large salad bowl. Add the spring onions, tomatoes and walnuts.

2 Stone, peel and thinly slice or dice the avocados. Brush with the lemon juice to prevent discoloration, then transfer to the salad bowl. Gently mix together.

3 To make the dressing, put all the dressing ingredients in a screw-top jar and shake well. Drizzle over the salad and serve immediately.

orange & fennel salad

ingredients

SERVES 4

4 large, juicy oranges

1 large fennel bulb, sliced very
   thinly

1 mild white onion, sliced
   finely

2 tbsp extra virgin olive oil

12 plump black olives, stoned
   and sliced thinly

1 fresh red chilli, deseeded
   and sliced very thinly
   (optional)

finely chopped fresh parsley

French bread, to serve

method

1 Finely grate the rind from the oranges into a bowl; set aside. Using a small serrated knife, remove all the white pith from the oranges, working over a bowl to catch the juices. Cut the oranges horizontally into thin slices.

2 Toss the orange slices with the fennel and onion slices. Whisk the oil into the reserved orange juice, then spoon over the oranges. Sprinkle the olive slices over the top, add the chilli, if using, then sprinkle with the orange rind and parsley.

3 Serve with slices of French bread.

greek salad

ingredients
SERVES 4

4 tomatoes, cut into wedges

1 onion, sliced

$1/2$ cucumber, sliced

225 g/8 oz kalamata olives,
    stoned

225 g/8 oz feta cheese, cubed

2 tbsp fresh coriander leaves

fresh flat-leaf parsley sprigs,
    to garnish

pitta bread, to serve

dressing

5 tbsp extra virgin olive oil

2 tbsp white wine vinegar

1 tbsp lemon juice

$1/2$ tsp sugar

1 tbsp chopped fresh
    coriander

salt and pepper

method

1 To make the dressing, put all the ingredients for the dressing into a large bowl and mix well together.

2 Add the tomatoes, onion, cucumber, olives, cheese and coriander. Toss all the ingredients together, then divide between individual serving bowls. Garnish with parsley sprigs and serve with pitta bread.

herby potato salad

ingredients

SERVES 4

500 g/1 lb 2 oz new potatoes

salt and pepper

16 vine-ripened cherry
   tomatoes, halved

55 g/2 oz black olives, stoned
   and roughly chopped

4 spring onions, finely sliced

2 tbsp chopped fresh mint

2 tbsp chopped fresh parsley

2 tbsp chopped fresh
   coriander

juice of 1 lemon

3 tbsp extra virgin olive oil

method

1 Cook the potatoes in a saucepan of lightly salted boiling water for 15 minutes, or until tender. Drain, then cool slightly before peeling off the skins. Cut into halves or quarters, depending on the size of the potato. Then combine with the tomatoes, olives, spring onions and herbs in a salad bowl.

2 Mix the lemon juice and oil together in a small bowl or jug and pour over the potato salad. Season to taste with salt and pepper before serving.

pasta salad with chargrilled peppers

ingredients
SERVES 4

1 red pepper

1 orange pepper

280 g/10 oz dried conchiglie

5 tbsp extra virgin olive oil

2 tbsp lemon juice

2 tbsp pesto

1 garlic clove

3 tbsp shredded fresh basil
    leaves

salt and pepper

method
1 Put the whole peppers on a baking sheet and place under a preheated grill, turning frequently, for 15 minutes, until charred all over. Remove with tongs and place in a bowl. Cover with clingfilm and set aside.

2 Meanwhile, bring a large saucepan of lightly salted water to the boil. Add the pasta, bring back to the boil and cook for 8–10 minutes, until tender but still firm to the bite.

3 Combine the olive oil, lemon juice, pesto and garlic in a bowl, whisking well to mix. Drain the pasta, add it to the pesto mixture while still hot and toss well. Set aside.

4 When the peppers are cool enough to handle, peel off the skins, then cut open and remove the seeds. Roughly chop the flesh and add it to the pasta with the basil. Season to taste with salt and pepper and toss well. Serve at room temperature.

three-colour salad

ingredients

SERVES 4

280 g/10 oz buffalo
      mozzarella, drained and
      thinly sliced

8 plum tomatoes, sliced

salt and pepper

20 fresh basil leaves

125 ml/4 fl oz extra virgin
      olive oil

method

1 Arrange the cheese and tomato slices on 4 individual serving plates and season to taste with salt. Set aside in a cool place for 30 minutes.

2 Sprinkle the basil leaves over the salad and drizzle with the olive oil. Season with pepper and serve immediately.

sweet potato & mozzarella salad

ingredients
SERVES 4

2 sweet potatoes, peeled and
    cut into chunks

2 tbsp olive oil

pepper

2 garlic cloves, crushed

1 large aubergine, sliced

2 red peppers, deseeded and
    sliced

200 g/7 oz mixed salad leaves

2 x 150 g/5^{1}/$_{2}$ oz mozzarella
    cheeses, drained and
    sliced

wholewheat bread, to serve

dressing

1 tbsp balsamic vinegar

1 garlic clove, crushed

3 tbsp olive oil

1 small shallot, finely chopped

2 tbsp chopped mixed fresh
    herbs, such as tarragon,
    chervil and basil

pepper

method

1 Put the sweet potato chunks into a roasting tin with the oil, pepper to taste and garlic and toss to combine. Roast in a preheated oven, 190°C/375°F/Gas Mark 5, for 30 minutes, or until soft and slightly charred.

2 Meanwhile, preheat the grill to high. Arrange the aubergine and pepper slices on the grill pan and cook under the preheated grill, turning occasionally, for 10 minutes, or until soft and slightly charred.

3 To make the dressing, whisk the balsamic vinegar, garlic and oil together in a small bowl and stir in the shallot and herbs. Season to taste with pepper.

4 To serve, divide the salad leaves between 4 serving plates and arrange the sweet potato, aubergine, peppers and mozzarella on top. Drizzle with the dressing and serve with wholewheat bread.

pasta salad with nuts & gorgonzola

ingredients

SERVES 4

225 g/8 oz dried farfalle

2 tbsp walnut oil

4 tbsp safflower oil

2 tbsp balsamic vinegar

salt and pepper

280 g/10 oz mixed salad
  leaves

225 g/8 oz Gorgonzola cheese,
  diced

115 g/4 oz walnuts, halved
  and toasted

method

1 Bring a large, heavy-based saucepan of lightly salted water to the boil. Add the pasta, return to the boil and cook for 8–10 minutes, or until tender but still firm to the bite. Drain, refresh in a bowl of cold water and drain again.

2 Mix the walnut oil, safflower oil and vinegar together in a measuring cup, whisking well, and season with salt and pepper.

3 Arrange the salad leaves in a large serving bowl. Top with the pasta, Gorgonzola cheese and walnuts. Pour the dressing over the salad, toss lightly and serve.

warm red lentil salad with goat's cheese

ingredients
SERVES 4

2 tbsp olive oil

2 tsp cumin seeds

2 garlic cloves, crushed

2 tsp grated fresh root ginger

300 g/10$\frac{1}{2}$ oz split red lentils

700 ml/1$\frac{1}{4}$ pints vegetable
  stock

2 tbsp chopped fresh mint

2 tbsp chopped fresh
  coriander

2 red onions, thinly sliced

200 g/7 oz baby spinach
  leaves

1 tsp hazelnut oil

150 g/5$\frac{1}{2}$ oz soft goat's
  cheese

4 tbsp Greek-style yogurt

pepper

1 lemon, cut into quarters,
  to garnish

toasted rye bread, to serve

method

1 Heat half the olive oil in a large saucepan over medium heat, add the cumin seeds, garlic and ginger and cook for 2 minutes, stirring constantly.

2 Stir in the lentils, then add the stock, a ladleful at a time, until it is all absorbed, stirring constantly – this will take about 20 minutes. Remove from the heat and stir in the herbs.

3 Meanwhile, heat the remaining olive oil in a frying pan over medium heat, add the onions and cook, stirring frequently, for 10 minutes, or until soft and lightly browned.

4 Toss the spinach in the hazelnut oil in a bowl, then divide between 4 serving plates.

5 Mash the goat's cheese with the yogurt in a small bowl and season with pepper.

6 Divide the lentils between the serving plates and top with the onions and goat's cheese mixture. Garnish with lemon quarters and serve with toasted rye bread.

cajun chicken salad

ingredients

SERVES 4

4 skinless, boneless chicken
    breasts, about 140 g/5 oz
    each

4 tsp Cajun seasoning

2 tsp corn oil (optional)

1 ripe mango, peeled, stoned
    and cut into thick slices

200 g/7 oz mixed salad leaves

1 red onion, thinly sliced and
    cut in half

175 g/6 oz cooked beetroot,
    diced

85 g/3 oz radishes, sliced

55 g/2 oz walnut halves

4 tbsp walnut oil

1–2 tsp Dijon mustard

1 tbsp lemon juice

salt and pepper

2 tbsp sesame seeds

method

1 Make 3 diagonal slashes across each chicken breast. Put the chicken into a shallow dish and sprinkle all over with the Cajun seasoning. Cover and chill for at least 30 minutes.

2 When ready to cook, brush a griddle pan with the corn oil, if using. Heat over high heat until very hot and a few drops of water sprinkled into the pan sizzle immediately. Add the chicken and cook for 7–8 minutes on each side, or until thoroughly cooked. If still slightly pink in the centre, cook a little longer. Remove the chicken and set aside.

3 Add the mango slices to the pan and cook for 2 minutes on each side. Remove from the pan and set aside.

4 Meanwhile, arrange the salad leaves in a salad bowl, reserving a few for a garnish, and sprinkle over the onion, beetroot, radishes and walnut halves.

5 Put the walnut oil, mustard, lemon juice, salt and pepper in a screw-top jar and shake until well blended. Pour over the salad and sprinkle with the sesame seeds.

6 Arrange the mango and the salad on a serving plate, top with the chicken breast and garnish with a few of the salad leaves.

spicy chicken salad

ingredients

SERVES 4

2 skinless, boneless chicken
   breast portions, about
   125 g/4½ oz each
2 tbsp butter
1 fresh red chilli, deseeded
   and chopped
1 tbsp honey
½ tsp ground cumin
2 tbsp chopped fresh
   coriander
600 g/1 lb 5 oz diced potatoes
50 g/1¾ oz French beans,
   halved
1 red pepper, deseeded and
   cut into thin strips
2 tomatoes, deseeded and
   diced

dressing
2 tbsp olive oil
pinch of chilli powder
1 tbsp garlic wine vinegar
pinch of caster sugar
1 tbsp chopped fresh
   coriander

method

1 Cut the chicken into thin strips. Melt the butter in a heavy saucepan and add the chicken strips, fresh red chilli, honey and cumin. Cook for 10 minutes, turning until cooked through. Transfer the mixture to a bowl and cool, then stir in the chopped coriander.

2 Meanwhile, cook the diced potatoes in a saucepan of boiling water for 10 minutes, until they are tender. Drain and cool.

3 Blanch the French beans in a saucepan of boiling water for 3 minutes. Drain well and leave to cool. Combine the French beans and potatoes in a mixing bowl. Add the pepper strips and tomatoes to the potato mixture. Stir in the chicken mixture.

4 In a small bowl, whisk the dressing ingredients together and pour the dressing over the salad, tossing well. Transfer the spicy chicken salad to a serving bowl or large platter and serve immediately.

indonesian chicken salad

ingredients

SERVES 4

1.25 kg/2 lb 12 oz waxy potatoes, cut into small dice

300 g/10½ oz fresh pineapple, peeled and diced

2 carrots, grated

175 g/6 oz beansprouts

1 bunch of spring onions, sliced

1 large courgette, cut into thin sticks

3 celery stalks, cut into thin sticks

175 g/6 oz unsalted peanuts

2 cooked skinless, boneless chicken breast portions, about 125 g/4½ oz each, sliced

dressing

6 tbsp crunchy peanut butter

6 tbsp olive oil

2 tbsp light soy sauce

1 fresh red chilli, deseeded and chopped

2 tsp sesame oil

4 tsp lime juice

method

1 Cook the diced potatoes in a saucepan of boiling water for about 10 minutes, or until tender. Drain them thoroughly in a colander and cool, then transfer to a salad bowl.

2 Add the diced pineapple, grated carrots, beansprouts, spring onions, courgette and celery sticks, peanuts and sliced chicken to the bowl of potatoes. Toss thoroughly to mix all the salad ingredients together.

3 To make the dressing, put the peanut butter in a small mixing bowl and gradually whisk in the olive oil and light soy sauce with a fork or a balloon whisk. Stir in the chilli, sesame oil and lime juice. Mix well until combined.

4 Pour the spicy dressing over the salad and toss lightly to coat all of the ingredients. Serve the potato and chicken salad immediately.

grilled beef salad

ingredients

SERVES 4

50 g/1¾ oz dried oyster
    mushrooms

600 g/1 lb 5 oz rump steak

1 red pepper, deseeded and
    thinly sliced

55 g/2 oz roasted cashew nuts

red and green lettuce leaves

fresh mint leaves, to garnish

dressing

2 tbsp sesame oil

2 tbsp Thai fish sauce

2 tbsp sweet sherry

2 tbsp oyster sauce

1 tbsp lime juice

1 fresh red chilli, deseeded
    and finely chopped

method

1 Put the mushrooms in a heatproof bowl, cover with boiling water and let stand for 20 minutes. Drain, then cut into slices.

2 Preheat the grill to medium or heat a ridged griddle pan. To make the dressing, place all the ingredients in a bowl and whisk to combine.

3 Cook the steak under the preheated grill or on the hot griddle pan, turning once, for 5 minutes, or until browned on both sides but still rare in the centre. Cook the steak longer if desired.

4 Slice the steak into thin strips and place in a bowl with the mushrooms, pepper and nuts. Add the dressing and toss together.

5 Arrange the lettuce on a large serving platter and place the beef mixture on top. Garnish with mint leaves. Serve at room temperature.

peppered beef salad

ingredients

SERVES 4

4 x 115-g/4-oz fillet steaks

2 tbsp black peppercorns, crushed

1 tsp Chinese five spice powder

115 g/4 oz beansprouts

2.5-cm/1-inch piece fresh root ginger, chopped finely

4 shallots, sliced finely

1 red pepper, deseeded and sliced thinly

3 tbsp Thai soy sauce

2 fresh red chillies, deseeded and sliced

1/2 lemon grass stalk, chopped finely

3 tbsp vegetable or peanut oil

1 tbsp sesame oil

method

1 Wash the steaks and pat dry on kitchen paper. Mix the peppercorns with the five spice powder and press onto all sides of the steaks. Cook on a griddle pan or under a grill for 2–3 minutes each side, or until cooked to your liking.

2 Meanwhile mix the beansprouts, half the ginger, the shallots and pepper together and divide between 4 plates. Mix the remaining ginger, soy sauce, chillies, lemon grass and oils together.

3 Slice the beef and arrange on the vegetables. Drizzle with the dressing and serve immediately.

mixed antipasto meat platter

ingredients

SERVES 4

1 cantaloupe melon

55 g/2 oz Italian salami, thinly sliced

8 slices prosciutto

8 slices bresaola

8 slices mortadella

4 plum tomatoes, thinly sliced

4 fresh figs, quartered

115 g/4 oz black olives, stoned and sliced

2 tbsp shredded fresh basil leaves

4 tbsp extra virgin olive oil, plus extra for serving

pepper

method

1 Cut the melon in half, scoop out and discard the seeds, then cut the flesh into 8 wedges. Arrange the wedges on one half of a large serving platter.

2 Arrange the salami, prosciutto, bresaola and mortadella in loose folds on the other half of the platter. Arrange the tomato slices and fig quarters along the centre of the platter.

3 Sprinkle the olives over the meat. Sprinkle the basil over the tomatoes and drizzle with olive oil. Season to taste with pepper, then serve with extra olive oil.

parma ham & figs

ingredients

SERVES 4

175 g/6 oz Parma ham, thinly
   sliced
pepper
4 fresh figs
1 lime
2 fresh basil sprigs

method

1 Using a sharp knife, trim the visible fat from the slices of Parma ham and discard. Arrange the Parma ham on 4 large serving plates, loosely folding it so that it falls into decorative shapes. Season to taste with pepper.

2 Using a sharp knife, cut each fig lengthways into 4 wedges. Arrange a fig on each serving plate. Cut the lime into 6 wedges, place a wedge on each plate and reserve the others. Remove the leaves from the basil sprigs and divide between the plates. Cover with clingfilm and chill in the refrigerator until ready to serve.

3 Just before serving, remove the plates from the refrigerator and squeeze the juice from the remaining lime wedges over the ham.

salad niçoise

ingredients

SERVES 4

2 tuna steaks, about
    2 cm/³/₄ inch thick

olive oil

salt and pepper

250 g/9 oz French beans,
    trimmed

2 hearts of lettuce, leaves
    separated

3 large hard-boiled eggs,
    cut into quarters

2 juicy vine-ripened tomatoes,
    cut into wedges

50 g/1³/₄ oz anchovy fillets in
    oil, drained

55 g/2 oz black olives

torn fresh basil leaves,
    to garnish

garlic vinaigrette

125 ml/4 fl oz olive or other
    vegetable oil

3 tbsp white wine vinegar or
    lemon juice

1 tsp Dijon mustard

¹/₂ tsp caster sugar

salt and pepper

method

1 To make the garlic vinaigrette, put all the ingredients in a screw-top jar, secure the lid and shake well until an emulsion forms. Taste and adjust the seasoning if necessary.

2 Heat a ridged griddle pan over a high heat until you can feel the heat rising from the surface. Brush the tuna steaks with oil, then place, oiled-side down, on the hot pan and chargrill for 2 minutes.

3 Lightly brush the top side of the tuna steaks with a little more oil. Use a pair of tongs to turn the tuna steaks over, then season to taste. Continue chargilling for a further 2 minutes for rare or up to 4 minutes for well done. Let cool.

4 Meanwhile, bring a saucepan of salted water to the boil. Add the beans and return to the boil, then boil for 3 minutes, or until tender-crisp. Drain the beans and immediately transfer them to a large bowl. Pour over the garlic vinaigrette and stir together, then set aside to cool.

5 To serve, line a platter with lettuce leaves. Lift the beans out of the bowl, leaving the excess dressing behind, and pile them in the centre of the platter. Break the tuna into large flakes and arrange it over the beans.

6 Put the hard-boiled eggs and tomatoes around the edge and arrange the anchovy fillets, olives and basil on the salad. Drizzle over the remaining dressing and serve.

tuna & tomato salad with ginger dressing

ingredients
SERVES 4

handful of shredded Chinese
    cabbage
3 tbsp rice wine or dry sherry
2 tbsp Thai fish sauce
1 tbsp finely shredded fresh
    root ginger
1 garlic clove, finely chopped
1/2 small fresh red Thai chilli,
    finely chopped
2 tsp brown sugar
2 tbsp lime juice
400 g/14 oz fresh tuna steak
corn oil, for brushing
125 g/4 1/2 oz cherry tomatoes
fresh mint leaves and mint
    sprigs, coarsely chopped,
    to garnish

method
1 Place a small pile of shredded cabbage on a large serving plate. Place the rice wine or dry sherry, fish sauce, ginger, garlic, chilli, sugar and 1 tablespoon of lime juice in a screw-top jar and shake well to combine.

2 Using a sharp knife, cut the tuna into strips of an even thickness. Sprinkle with the remaining lime juice.

3 Brush a wide frying pan or ridged griddle pan with oil and heat until very hot. Arrange the tuna strips in the pan and cook until just firm and light golden, turning them over once. Remove the tuna strips from the pan and reserve.

4 Add the tomatoes to the pan and cook over high heat until lightly browned. Spoon the tuna and tomatoes over the cabbage, then spoon over the dressing. Garnish with fresh mint and serve warm.

salmon & avocado salad

ingredients

SERVES 4

450 g/1 lb new potatoes
4 salmon steaks, about
        115 g/4 oz each
1 avocado
juice of 1/2 lemon
55 g/2 oz baby spinach leaves
125 g/41/2 oz mixed small
        salad leaves, including
        watercress
4 tomatoes, cut into quarters
55 g/2 oz chopped walnuts

dressing
3 tbsp unsweetened clear
        apple juice
1 tsp balsamic vinegar
pepper

method

1 Cut the new potatoes into bite-sized pieces, put into a saucepan and cover with cold water. Bring to the boil, then reduce the heat, cover and simmer for 10–15 minutes, or until just tender. Drain and keep warm.

2 Meanwhile, preheat the grill to medium. Cook the salmon steaks under the preheated grill for 10–15 minutes, depending on the thickness of the steaks, turning halfway through cooking. Remove from the grill and keep warm.

3 While the potatoes and salmon are cooking, cut the avocado in half, remove and discard the stone and peel the flesh. Cut the avocado flesh into slices and coat in the lemon juice to prevent discoloration.

4 Toss the spinach leaves and mixed salad leaves together in a large serving bowl until combined. Arrange the greens and the tomato quarters on individual serving plates.

5 Remove and discard the skin and any bones from the salmon. Flake the salmon and divide between the plates along with the potatoes. Sprinkle the walnuts over the salads.

6 To make the dressing, mix the apple juice and vinegar together in a small bowl or jug and season well with pepper. Drizzle over the salads and serve immediately.

mackerel & potato salad

ingredients

SERVES 4

125 g/4½ oz new potatoes, scrubbed and diced

225 g/8 oz mackerel fillets, skinned

1.2 litres/2 pints water

1 bay leaf

1 slice of lemon

1 eating apple, cored and diced

1 shallot, thinly sliced

3 tbsp white wine vinegar

1 tsp sunflower oil

1½ tsp caster sugar

¼ tsp Dijon mustard

salt and pepper

to serve

2 tbsp low-fat plain yogurt

¼ cucumber, thinly sliced

1 bunch of watercress

1 tbsp snipped fresh chives

method

1 Steam the potatoes over a saucepan of simmering water for 10 minutes, or until tender.

2 Meanwhile, cut the mackerel into bite-size pieces. Bring the water to the boil in a large, shallow saucepan, then reduce the heat so that it is just simmering and add the fish pieces, bay leaf and lemon. Poach for 3 minutes, or until the flesh of the fish is opaque. Remove with a slotted spoon and transfer to a serving dish.

3 Drain the potatoes and transfer to a large bowl. Add the apple and shallot and mix well, then spoon the mixture over the fish.

4 Mix the vinegar, oil, sugar and mustard together in a jug, season to taste with salt and pepper, and whisk thoroughly. Pour the dressing over the potato mixture. Cover and chill in the refrigerator for up to 6 hours.

5 To serve, spread the yogurt over the salad, then arrange the cucumber decoratively on top. Add sprigs of watercress and sprinkle with the chives.

prawn & papaya salad

ingredients

SERVES 4

1 papaya, peeled
350 g/12 oz large cooked
    prawns, peeled
assorted baby salad leaves

dressing

4 spring onions, chopped
    finely
2 fresh red chillies, deseeded
    and chopped finely
1 tsp fish sauce
1 tbsp vegetable or peanut oil
juice of 1 lime
1 tsp jaggery or soft light
    brown sugar

method

1 Scoop the seeds out of the papaya and slice thinly. Stir gently together with the prawns.

2 Mix the spring onions, chillies, fish sauce, oil, lime juice and sugar together.

3 Arrange the salad leaves in a bowl and top with the papaya and prawns. Pour the dressing over the salad and serve immediately.

prawn cocktail

ingredients

SERVES 4

1/2 iceberg lettuce, finely
    shredded
150 ml/5 fl oz mayonnaise
2 tbsp single cream
2 tbsp tomato ketchup
few drops of Tabasco sauce,
    or to taste
juice of 1/2 lemon, or to taste
salt and pepper
175 g/6 oz cooked peeled
    prawns
paprika, for sprinkling
4 cooked prawns, in their
    shells, and 4 lemon slices,
    to garnish
thin buttered brown bread
    slices (optional), to serve

method

1 Divide the lettuce between 4 small serving dishes (traditionally, stemmed glass ones, but any small dishes will be fine).

2 Mix the mayonnaise, cream and tomato ketchup together in a bowl. Add the Tabasco sauce and lemon juice and season well with salt and pepper.

3 Divide the peeled prawns equally between the dishes and pour over the dressing. Cover and chill in the refrigerator for 30 minutes.

4 Sprinkle a little paprika over the cocktails and garnish each dish with a prawn and a lemon slice. Serve the cocktails with slices of brown bread and butter.

sautéed garlic mushrooms

ingredients

SERVES 6

450 g/1 lb white mushrooms

5 tbsp Spanish olive oil

2 garlic cloves, finely chopped

squeeze of lemon juice

salt and pepper

4 tbsp chopped fresh flat-leaf
    parsley

crusty bread, to serve

method

1 Wipe or brush clean the mushrooms, then trim off the stalks close to the caps. Cut any large mushrooms in half or into quarters. Heat the olive oil in a large, heavy-based frying pan, add the garlic and cook for 30 seconds–1 minute, or until lightly browned. Add the mushrooms and sauté over high heat, stirring most of the time, until the mushrooms have absorbed all the oil in the pan.

2 Reduce the heat to low. When the juices have come out of the mushrooms, increase the heat again, and sauté for 4–5 minutes, stirring most of the time, until the juices have almost evaporated. Add a squeeze of lemon juice and season to taste with salt and pepper. Stir in the chopped parsley and cook for a further minute.

3 Transfer the sautéed mushrooms to a warmed serving dish and serve piping hot or warm. Accompany with chunks or slices of crusty bread for mopping up the garlic cooking juices.

courgette fritters with yogurt dip

ingredients

SERVES 4

2–3 courgettes, about
   400 g/14 oz
1 garlic clove, crushed
3 spring onions, finely sliced
125 g/4$\frac{1}{2}$ oz feta cheese,
   crumbled
2 tbsp finely chopped fresh
   parsley
2 tbsp finely chopped fresh
   mint
1 tbsp finely chopped fresh dill
$\frac{1}{2}$ tsp freshly grated nutmeg
2 tbsp plain flour
pepper
2 eggs
2 tbsp olive oil
1 lemon, cut into quarters,
   to garnish

yogurt dip

250 g/9 oz strained plain
   yogurt
$\frac{1}{4}$ cucumber, diced
1 tbsp finely chopped fresh dill
pepper

method

1 Grate the courgettes straight onto a clean tea towel and cover with another. Pat well and set aside for 10 minutes until the courgettes are dry.

2 Meanwhile, to make the dip, mix the yogurt, cucumber, dill and pepper in a serving bowl. Cover and chill.

3 Tip the courgettes into a large mixing bowl. Stir in the garlic, spring onions, cheese, herbs, nutmeg, flour and pepper. Beat the eggs in a separate bowl and stir into the courgette mixture – the batter will be quite lumpy and uneven but this is fine.

4 Heat the oil in a large, wide frying pan over medium heat. Drop 4 tablespoonfuls of the batter into the pan, with space in between, and cook for 2–3 minutes on each side. Remove, drain on kitchen paper and keep warm. Cook the second batch of fritters in the same way. (There should be 8 fritters in total.)

5 Serve the fritters hot with the dip, garnished with lemon quarters.

sweet potato, mint & feta patties

ingredients

SERVES 4

600 g/1 lb 5 oz sweet potatoes, peeled and grated

1 egg, lightly beaten

50 g/1¾ oz plain flour

70 g/2½ oz butter, melted

100 g/3½ oz feta cheese, crumbled

3 tbsp chopped fresh mint

salt and pepper

1 tbsp vegetable oil

4 tbsp sour cream

2 tbsp chopped fresh parsley, to garnish

method

1 Mix the grated sweet potato with the egg, flour, melted butter, feta and mint until well combined. Season the mixture to taste with salt and pepper.

2 Heat the oil in a large non-stick frying pan over medium heat. Spoon large tablespoons of the mixture into patties, flattening slightly, and cook on both sides in batches until golden brown.

3 Slide the patties onto a baking sheet covered with parchment paper and bake in a preheated oven, 160°C/325°F/Gas Mark 2½, for 15 minutes, or until crisp. Place 2 patties on each plate, top with a tablespoon of sour cream and garnish with a little chopped parsley. Serve at once.

falafel with tahini sauce

ingredients

SERVES 4

450 g/1 lb canned cannellini
    beans, drained
350 g/12 oz canned
    chickpeas, drained
1 onion, finely chopped
2 garlic cloves, chopped
1 small fresh red chilli,
    deseeded and chopped
1 tsp baking powder
25 g/1 oz fresh parsley,
    chopped, plus extra sprigs
    to garnish
pinch of cayenne
2 tbsp water
salt and pepper
vegetable oil, for deep-frying
pitta bread, thick plain yogurt
    or yogurt dip and lemon
    wedges, to serve

tahini sauce

200 ml/7 fl oz tahini
1 garlic clove, chopped
1–2 tbsp water
2–3 tsp lemon juice, to taste

method

1 To make the tahini sauce, put the tahini and garlic in a bowl. Gradually stir in the water until a fairly smooth consistency is reached, then stir in the lemon juice. Add more water or lemon juice, if necessary. Cover with clingfilm and chill in the refrigerator until required.

2 To make the falafel, rinse and drain the beans and chickpeas. Put them in a food processor with the onion, garlic, chilli, baking powder, chopped parsley and cayenne pepper. Process to a coarse paste, then add the water and season with plenty of salt and pepper. Process again briefly.

3 Heat about 6 cm/2$1/2$ inches of oil in a deep-fat fryer, large, heavy-based saucepan or wok over high heat. Deep-fry rounded tablespoonfuls of the mixture in batches for 2–2$1/2$ minutes until golden and crispy on the outside. Remove with a slotted spoon and drain well on kitchen paper. Serve hot or cold, garnished with parsley sprigs and accompanied by the tahini sauce, pitta bread, yogurt or yogurt dip and lemon wedges.

crispy spring rolls

ingredients

SERVES 4

2 tbsp vegetable or peanut oil

6 spring onions, cut into
    5-cm/2-inch lengths

1 fresh green chilli, deseeded
    and chopped

1 carrot, cut into thin sticks

1 courgette, cut into thin sticks

$1/2$ red pepper, deseeded and
    thinly sliced

115 g/4 oz beansprouts

115 g/4 oz canned bamboo
    shoots, drained and rinsed

3 tbsp Thai soy sauce

1–2 tbsp chilli sauce

8 egg roll skins

vegetable or peanut oil,
    for deep-frying

method

1 Heat the oil in a wok and stir-fry the spring onions and chilli for 30 seconds. Add the carrot, courgette and red pepper and stir-fry for 1 minute more. Remove the wok from the heat and stir in the beansprouts, bamboo shoots, soy sauce and chilli sauce. Taste and add more soy sauce or chilli sauce if necessary.

2 Place an egg roll skin on a work surface and spoon some of the vegetable mixture diagonally across the centre. Roll one corner over the filling and flip the sides of the skin over the top to enclose the filling. Continue to roll up to make an enclosed package. Repeat with the remaining skins and filling to make 8 egg rolls.

3 Heat the oil for deep-frying in a wok or large frying pan. Deep-fry the egg rolls, 3–4 at a time, until they are crisp and golden brown. Remove with a slotted spoon, drain on kitchen paper while you cook the remainder, then serve immediately.

thai tofu cakes with chilli dip

ingredients

SERVES 8

300 g/10½ oz firm tofu, drained weight, coarsely grated

1 lemon grass stalk, outer layer discarded, finely chopped

2 garlic cloves, chopped

2.5-cm/1-inch piece fresh root ginger, grated

2 kaffir lime leaves, finely chopped (optional)

2 shallots, finely chopped

2 fresh red chillies, deseeded and finely chopped

4 tbsp chopped fresh coriander

90 g/3¼ oz plain flour, plus extra for flouring

½ tsp salt

corn oil, for cooking

chilli dip

3 tbsp white distilled vinegar or rice wine vinegar

2 spring onions, finely sliced

1 tbsp caster sugar

2 fresh chillies, finely chopped

2 tbsp chopped fresh coriander

pinch of salt

method

1 To make the chilli dip, mix all the ingredients together in a small serving bowl and set aside.

2 Mix the tofu with the lemon grass, garlic, ginger, lime leaves, if using, shallots, chillies and coriander in a mixing bowl. Stir in the flour and salt to make a coarse, sticky paste. Cover and chill in the refrigerator for 1 hour to let the mixture firm up slightly.

3 Form the mixture into 8 large walnut-size balls and, using floured hands, flatten into circles. Heat enough oil to cover the bottom of a large, heavy-based frying pan over medium heat. Cook the cakes in 2 batches, turning halfway through, for 4–6 minutes, or until golden brown. Drain on kitchen paper and serve warm with the chilli dip.

devilled eggs

ingredients

SERVES 16

8 large eggs

2 whole pimientos from a jar
or can

8 green olives

5 tbsp mayonnaise

8 drops Tabasco sauce

large pinch cayenne pepper

salt and pepper

paprika, for dusting

sprigs of fresh dill, to garnish

method

1 To cook the eggs, put them in a saucepan, cover with cold water and slowly bring to the boil. Immediately reduce the heat to very low, cover and simmer gently for 10 minutes. As soon as the eggs are cooked, drain and put under cold running water to prevent a black ring from forming round the yolk. Gently tap the eggs to crack the shells and set aside until cold. When cold, remove the shells.

2 Using a stainless steel knife, halve the eggs lengthways, then carefully remove the yolks. Put the yolks in a nylon sieve set over a bowl and rub through, then mash them with a wooden spoon or fork. If necessary, rinse the egg whites under cold water and dry very carefully.

3 Drain the pimientos on kitchen paper, then chop them finely, reserving a few strips. Finely chop the olives, reserving 16 larger pieces to garnish. Add the chopped pimientos and chopped olives to the mashed egg yolks. Add the mayonnaise, mix well together, then add the Tabasco sauce, cayenne pepper and salt and pepper to taste.

4 Use a teaspoon to spoon the prepared filling into each egg half. Arrange the eggs on a serving plate. Add a small strip of the reserved pimientos and a piece of olive to the top of each stuffed egg. Dust with a little paprika and garnish with dill sprigs.

lime-drizzled prawns

ingredients

SERVES 6

4 limes

12 raw jumbo prawns, in their
   shells

3 tbsp Spanish olive oil

2 garlic cloves, finely chopped

splash of fino sherry

salt and pepper

4 tbsp chopped fresh flat-leaf
   parsley

method

1 Grate the rind and squeeze the juice from 2 of the limes. Cut the remaining 2 limes into wedges and set aside for later.

2 To prepare the prawns, remove the heads and legs, leaving the shells and tails intact. Using a sharp knife, make a shallow slit along the back of each prawn, then pull out the dark vein and discard. Rinse the prawns under cold water and dry on kitchen paper.

3 Heat the olive oil in a large, heavy-based frying pan, then add the garlic and cook for 30 seconds. Add the prawns and cook for 5 minutes, stirring from time to time, or until they turn pink and start to curl. Mix in the lime rind and juice, add a splash of sherry to moisten, then stir well together.

4 Transfer the cooked prawns to a serving dish, season with salt and pepper and sprinkle with the parsley. Serve piping hot, accompanied by the reserved lime wedges for squeezing over the prawns.

calamari

ingredients
SERVES 6

450 g/1 lb prepared squid
plain flour, for coating
sunflower oil, for deep-frying
salt
lemon wedges, to garnish
garlic mayonnaise, to serve

method

1 Slice the squid into 1-cm/¹/₂-inch rings and halve the tentacles if large. Rinse under cold running water and dry well with kitchen paper. Dust the squid rings with flour so that they are lightly coated.

2 Heat the oil in a deep-fat fryer, large heavy-based saucepan, or wok to 180–190°C/350–375°F, or until a cube of bread browns in 30 seconds. Deep-fry the squid rings in small batches for 2–3 minutes, or until golden brown and crisp all over, turning several times (if you deep-fry too many squid rings at one time, the oil temperature will drop and they will be soggy). Do not overcook as the squid will become tough and rubbery rather than moist and tender.

3 Remove with a slotted spoon and drain well on kitchen paper. Keep warm in a low oven while you deep-fry the remaining squid rings.

4 Sprinkle the fried squid rings with salt and serve piping hot, garnished with lemon wedges for squeezing over. Accompany with a bowl of garlic mayonnaise for dipping.

guacamole

ingredients

SERVES 4

2 large, ripe avocados

juice of 1 lime, or to taste

2 tsp olive oil

1/2 onion, finely chopped

1 fresh green chilli, such as
    poblano, deseeded and
    finely chopped

1 garlic clove, crushed

1/4 tsp ground cumin

1 tbsp chopped fresh
    coriander, plus extra leaves
    to garnish (optional)

salt and pepper

method

1 Cut the avocados in half lengthways and twist the 2 halves in opposite directions to separate. Stab the stone with the point of a sharp knife and lift out.

2 Peel, then coarsely chop, the avocado halves and place in a non-metallic bowl. Squeeze over the lime juice and add the oil.

3 Mash the avocados with a fork until the desired consistency is reached – either chunky or smooth. Blend in the onion, chilli, garlic, cumin and chopped coriander, then season with salt and pepper.

4 Transfer to a serving dish and serve at once, to avoid discoloration, garnished with the coriander leaves, if liked.

aubergine dip ·

ingredients

SERVES 6–8

olive oil

1 large aubergine, about
    400 g/14 oz, sliced

2 spring onions, chopped
    finely

1 large garlic clove, crushed

2 tbsp finely chopped fresh
    parsley

salt and pepper

smoked sweet Spanish
    paprika, to garnish

French bread, to serve

method

1 Heat 4 tablespoons of oil in a large frying pan over medium–high heat. Add the aubergine slices and cook on both sides until soft and starting to brown. Remove from the pan and set aside to cool. The slices will release the oil again as they cool.

2 Heat another tablespoon of oil in the frying pan. Add the spring onions and garlic and cook for 3 minutes, or until the spring onions become soft. Remove from the heat and set aside with the aubergine slices to cool.

3 Transfer the cooled spring onions, garlic and aubergine slices to a food processor and process just until a coarse purée forms. Transfer to a serving bowl and stir in the parsley. Taste and adjust the seasoning, if necessary. Serve at once, or cover and chill until 15 minutes before required. Sprinkle with paprika and serve with slices of French bread.

tapenade

ingredients

**MAKES ABOUT
300 G/10½ OZ**

250 g/9 oz black olives, such
as Nyons or Niçoise,
stoned

3 anchovy fillets in oil, drained

1 large garlic clove, halved,
with the green centre
removed if necessary

2 tbsp pine kernels

½ tbsp capers in brine, rinsed

125 ml/4 fl oz extra virgin olive
oil

freshly squeezed lemon or
orange juice, to taste

pepper

garlic croûtes

12 slices French bread, about
5 mm/¼ inch thick

extra virgin olive oil

2 garlic cloves, peeled and
halved

method

1 Put the olives, anchovy fillets, garlic, pine kernels and capers in a food processor or blender and whizz until well blended. With the motor still running, pour the olive oil through the feed tube and continue blending until a loose paste forms.

2 Add the lemon juice and pepper to taste. It shouldn't need any salt because of the saltiness of the anchovies. Cover and chill until required.

3 To make the garlic croûtes, preheat the grill to high. Place the bread slices on the grill rack and toast 1 side for 1–2 minutes, or until golden brown. Flip the bread slices over, lightly brush the untoasted side with olive oil, then toast for 1–2 minutes.

4 Rub 1 side of each bread slice with the garlic cloves while it is still hot, then set aside and cool completely. Store in an airtight container for up to 2 days.

5 Serve the tapenade with the garlic croûtes.

moorish broad bean dip

ingredients

SERVES 6

500 g/1 lb 2 oz shelled fresh
   or frozen broad beans

5 tbsp olive oil

1 garlic clove, finely chopped

1 onion, finely chopped

1 tsp ground cumin

1 tbsp lemon juice

175 ml/6 fl oz water

1 tbsp chopped fresh mint

salt and pepper

paprika, to garnish

raw vegetables, crusty bread
   or breadsticks, to serve

method

1 If using fresh broad beans, bring a large saucepan of lightly salted water to the boil. Add the beans, then reduce the heat and simmer, covered, for 7 minutes. Drain well, then refresh under cold running water and drain again. Remove and discard the outer skins. If using frozen beans, thaw completely, then remove and discard the outer skins.

2 Heat 1 tablespoon of the olive oil in a frying pan. Add the garlic, onion and cumin and cook over low heat, stirring occasionally, until the onion is softened and translucent. Add the broad beans and cook, stirring frequently, for 5 minutes.

3 Remove the frying pan from the heat and transfer the mixture to a food processor or blender. Add the lemon juice, the remaining olive oil, water and mint and process to a paste. Season to taste with salt and pepper.

4 Scrape the paste back into the frying pan and heat gently until warm. Transfer to individual serving bowls and dust lightly with paprika. Serve with dippers of your choice.

chicken

Chicken is a great choice for family meals because it is astonishingly versatile and it goes well with such a wide variety of other ingredients – it tastes as good in a creamy sauce as it does in a spicy curry. In addition, it can be cooked in lots of different ways – for example, grilled, roasted, pan-fried or poached – and is as appetizing in risotto as it is on kebab skewers. It's always a popular option and is ideal for adding variety to the family menu.

For health reasons, it is important that chicken is cooked all the way through. Timings vary depending on the cooking method and cut of chicken, but an approximate guide is given in each recipe. To test whether the chicken is fully cooked, pierce the thickest part with the point of a sharp knife – the chicken is ready if the juices run clear, but it will require further cooking if there are any traces of pink. It is not a good idea to attempt to speed up the cooking process by increasing the heat as this is likely to cause the meat to dry out in a thoroughly unappetizing way.

Chicken does cook much more quickly if a boneless cut is diced, sliced or cut into strips, making it ideal for stir-fries and pasta sauces. Flattening a whole breast portion by covering it with clingfilm and beating it to an even thickness with the side of rolling pin also enables it to be cooked more

speedily. If a recipe suggests marinating chicken before cooking, it is worth doing this even if time is short because chicken readily absorbs the flavours of spices, herbs and sauces and this will also help to keep the chicken moist.

chicken with basil & pine kernel pesto

ingredients

SERVES 4

2 tbsp vegetable oil

4 skinless, boneless
    chicken breasts

350 g/12 oz dried farfalle

salt and pepper

sprig of fresh basil, to garnish

pesto

100 g/3½ oz shredded
    fresh basil

125 ml/4 fl oz extra virgin olive
    oil

3 tbsp pine kernels

3 garlic cloves, crushed

55 g/2 oz freshly grated
    Parmesan cheese

2 tbsp freshly grated romano
    cheese

method

1 To make the pesto, place the basil, olive oil, pine kernels, garlic and a generous pinch of salt in a food processor or blender and process until smooth. Scrape the mixture into a bowl and stir in the cheeses.

2 Heat the vegetable oil in a frying pan over medium heat. Fry the chicken breasts, turning once, for 8–10 minutes, or until the juices are no longer pink. Cut into small cubes.

3 Cook the pasta in plenty of lightly salted boiling water until tender but still firm to the bite. Drain and transfer to a warmed serving dish. Add the chicken and pesto, then season with pepper. Toss well to mix.

4 Garnish with a basil sprig and serve warm.

fettuccine with chicken & onion cream sauce

ingredients

SERVES 4

1 tbsp olive oil

2 tbsp butter

1 garlic clove, chopped
   very finely

4 boneless, skinless chicken
   breasts

salt and pepper

1 onion, chopped finely

1 chicken stock cube,
   crumbled

125 ml/4 fl oz water

300 ml/10 fl oz double cream

175 ml/6 fl oz milk

6 spring onions, green part
   included, sliced diagonally

35 g/1¼ oz freshly grated
   Parmesan

450 g/1 lb dried fettuccine

chopped fresh flat-leaf parsley,
   to garnish

fresh crusty bread, to serve

method

1 Heat the oil and butter with the garlic in a large frying pan over medium–low heat. Cook the garlic until just beginning to colour. Add the chicken breasts and raise the heat to medium. Cook for 4–5 minutes on each side, or until the juices are no longer pink. Season with salt and pepper. Remove from the heat. Lift out the chicken breasts, leaving the oil in the pan. Slice the breasts diagonally into thin strips and set aside.

2 Reheat the oil in the pan. Add the onion and gently cook for 5 minutes, or until soft. Add the crumbled stock cube and the water. Bring to the boil, then simmer over medium–low heat for 10 minutes. Stir in the cream, milk, spring onions and Parmesan. Simmer until heated through and slightly thickened.

3 Cook the fettucine in boiling salted water until al dente. Drain and transfer to a warm serving dish. Layer the chicken slices over the pasta. Pour on the sauce, then garnish with parsley and serve. Serve with fresh crusty bread.

spaghetti with parsley chicken

ingredients

SERVES 4

1 tbsp olive oil

thinly pared rind of 1 lemon,
　　cut into julienne strips

1 tsp finely chopped fresh root
　　ginger

1 tsp sugar

salt

250 ml/8 fl oz chicken stock

250 g/9 oz dried spaghetti

4 tbsp butter

225 g/8 oz skinless, boneless
　　chicken breasts, diced

1 red onion, finely chopped

leaves from 2 bunches of
　　flat-leaf parsley

method

1 Heat the olive oil in a heavy-based saucepan. Add the lemon rind and cook over low heat, stirring frequently, for 5 minutes. Stir in the ginger and sugar, season with salt and cook, stirring constantly, for a further 2 minutes. Pour in the chicken stock, bring to the boil, then cook for 5 minutes, or until the liquid has reduced by half.

2 Meanwhile, bring a large heavy-based saucepan of lightly salted water to the boil. Add the pasta, return to the boil and cook for 8–10 minutes, or until tender but still firm to the bite.

3 Meanwhile, melt half the butter in a frying pan. Add the chicken and onion and cook, stirring frequently, for 5 minutes, or until the chicken is light brown all over. Stir in the lemon and ginger mixture and cook for 1 minute. Stir in the parsley leaves and cook, stirring constantly, for a further 3 minutes.

4 Drain the pasta and transfer to a warmed serving dish, then add the remaining butter and toss well. Add the chicken sauce, toss again and serve.

pasta with chicken & feta

ingredients

SERVES 4

2 tbsp olive oil

450 g/1 lb skinless, boneless chicken breasts, cut into thin strips

6 spring onions, chopped

225 g/8 oz feta cheese, diced

4 tbsp chopped fresh chives

salt and pepper

450 g/1 lb dried garganelli

tomato focaccia, to serve

method

1 Heat the olive oil in a heavy-based frying pan. Add the chicken and cook over medium heat, stirring frequently, for 5–8 minutes, or until golden all over and cooked through. Add the spring onions and cook for 2 minutes. Stir the feta cheese into the pan with half the chives and season with salt and pepper.

2 Meanwhile, bring a large heavy-based saucepan of lightly salted water to the boil. Add the pasta, return to the boil and cook for 8–10 minutes, or until tender but still firm to the bite. Drain well, then transfer to a warmed serving dish.

3 Spoon the chicken mixture onto the pasta, toss lightly and serve immediately, garnished with the remaining chives and accompanied by tomato focaccia.

fruity chicken fusilli

ingredients

SERVES 4

450 g/1 lb skinless, boneless
　　chicken, diced
1 tsp ground turmeric
1/4 tsp ground cinnamon
1/4 tsp ground cumin
1/4 tsp ground cardamom
pinch of cayenne pepper
2 tbsp peanut oil
1 onion, finely chopped
2 garlic cloves, finely chopped
375 ml/12 fl oz chicken stock
salt
2 tbsp raisins
1 ripe mango, peeled, stoned
　　and diced
280 g/10 oz dried fusilli
2 tbsp chopped fresh
　　coriander, to garnish

method

1 Place the chicken in a shallow dish. Sprinkle with the turmeric, cinnamon, cumin, cardamom and cayenne and toss well to coat. Cover with clingfilm and let stand in the refrigerator for 30 minutes.

2 Heat the peanut oil in a heavy-based frying pan. Add the onion and garlic and cook over low heat, stirring occasionally, for 5 minutes, or until softened. Add the spiced chicken and cook, stirring frequently, for 5 minutes, or until golden brown all over. Pour in the chicken stock and season with salt. Bring to the boil, add the raisins and mango, partially cover, and simmer for 25 minutes.

3 Meanwhile, bring a large heavy-based saucepan of lightly salted water to the boil. Add the pasta, return to the boil and cook for 8–10 minutes, or until tender but still firm to the bite. Drain and transfer to a warmed serving dish. Add the chicken mixture, toss lightly and serve, garnished with the coriander.

sweet-&-sour chicken

ingredients

SERVES 4–6

450 g/1 lb lean chicken meat,
   cubed
5 tbsp vegetable or peanut oil
1/2 tsp finely chopped garlic
1/2 tsp finely chopped
   fresh ginger
1 green pepper, roughly
   chopped
1 onion, roughly chopped
1 carrot, finely sliced
1 tsp sesame oil
1 tbsp finely chopped
   spring onions

marinade
2 tsp light soy sauce
1 tsp Shaoxing rice wine
pinch of white pepper
1/2 tsp salt
dash of sesame oil

sauce
8 tbsp rice vinegar
4 tbsp sugar
2 tsp light soy sauce
6 tbsp tomato ketchup

method

1 Place all the marinade ingredients in a bowl and marinate the chicken cubes for at least 20 minutes.

2 To prepare the sauce, heat the vinegar in a saucepan and add the sugar, light soy sauce and tomato ketchup. Stir to dissolve the sugar, then set aside.

3 In a preheated wok or deep saucepan, heat 3 tablespoons of the oil and stir-fry the chicken until it starts to turn golden brown. Remove and set aside.

4 In the clean wok or deep saucepan, heat the remaining oil and cook the garlic and ginger until fragrant. Add the vegetables and cook for 2 minutes. Add the chicken and cook for 1 minute or until the chicken is thoroughly cooked. Finally add the sauce and sesame oil, then stir in the spring onions and serve.

chicken with cashew nuts

ingredients

SERVES 4–6

450 g/1 lb boneless chicken meat, cut into bite-sized pieces

3 dried Chinese mushrooms, soaked in warm water for 20 minutes

2 tbsp vegetable or peanut oil

4 slices of fresh ginger

1 tsp finely chopped garlic

1 red pepper, cut into 2.5-cm/1-inch squares

1 tbsp light soy sauce

85 g/3 oz cashew nuts, roasted

marinade

3 tbsp light soy sauce

1 tsp Shaoxing rice wine

pinch of sugar

$^1/_2$ tsp salt

method

1 Combine all the ingredients for the marinade in a bowl and marinate the chicken, covered, for at least 20 minutes.

2 Squeeze any excess water from the mushrooms and finely slice, discarding any tough stems. Reserve the soaking water.

3 In a preheated wok or deep saucepan, heat 1 tablespoon of the oil. Add the ginger and stir-fry until fragrant. Stir in the chicken and cook for 2 minutes, or until it begins to turn brown. Before the chicken is cooked through, remove and set aside.

4 In the clean wok or deep saucepan, heat the remaining oil and stir-fry the garlic until fragrant. Add the mushrooms and red pepper and stir-fry for 1 minute. Add about 2 tablespoons of the mushroom soaking water and cook for about 2 minutes, or until the water has evaporated. Return the chicken to the wok, then add the light soy sauce and cashew nuts and stir-fry for 2 minutes, or until the chicken is thoroughly cooked through.

chicken fried rice

ingredients

SERVES 4

$^1/_2$ tbsp sesame oil

6 shallots, peeled and cut
    into quarters

450 g/1 lb cooked, cubed
    chicken meat

3 tbsp soy sauce

2 carrots, diced

1 celery stick, diced

1 red pepper, diced

175 g/6 oz fresh peas

100 g/3$^1/_2$ oz canned
    sweetcorn

275 g/9$^3/_4$ oz cooked
    long-grain rice

2 large eggs, scrambled

method

1 Heat the oil in a large frying pan over a medium heat. Add the shallots and fry until soft, then add the chicken and 2 tablespoons of the soy sauce and stir-fry for 5–6 minutes.

2 Stir in the carrots, celery, red pepper, peas and sweetcorn and stir-fry for a further 5 minutes. Add the rice and stir thoroughly.

3 Finally, stir in the scrambled eggs and the remaining tablespoon of soy sauce. Serve immediately.

chicken chow mein

ingredients

SERVES 4

250 g/9 oz dried medium
   Chinese egg noodles
2 tbsp sunflower oil
280 g/10 oz cooked chicken
   breasts, shredded
1 garlic clove, finely chopped
1 red pepper, deseeded and
   thinly sliced
100 g/3½ oz shiitake
   mushrooms, sliced
6 spring onions, sliced
100 g/3½ oz beansprouts
3 tbsp soy sauce
1 tbsp sesame oil

method

1 Place the noodles in a large bowl or dish and break them up slightly. Pour enough boiling water over the noodles to cover and set aside while preparing the other ingredients.

2 Preheat a wok over a medium heat. Add the sunflower oil and swirl it around to coat the sides of the wok. When the oil is hot, add the shredded chicken, garlic, pepper, mushrooms, spring onions and beansprouts to the wok and stir-fry for about 5 minutes.

3 Drain the noodles thoroughly then add them to the wok, toss well and stir-fry for a further 5 minutes. Drizzle over the soy sauce and sesame oil and toss until thoroughly combined.

4 Transfer to warmed serving bowls and serve immediately.

yaki soba

ingredients

SERVES 2

400 g/14 oz ramen noodles

1 onion, finely sliced

200 g/7 oz beansprouts

1 red pepper, deseeded and
    finely shredded

1 boneless, skin-on cooked
    chicken breast, about
    150 g/5½ oz, cooked
    and sliced

12 cooked peeled prawns

1 tbsp oil

2 tbsp shoyu (Japanese soy
    sauce)

½ tbsp mirin

1 tsp sesame oil

1 tsp roasted sesame seeds

2 spring onions, finely sliced

method

1 Cook the noodles according to the packet instructions, drain well, and tip into a bowl.

2 Mix the onion, beansprouts, red pepper, chicken and prawns together in a separate bowl. Stir through the noodles.

3 Preheat a wok over high heat. Add the oil and heat until very hot. Add the noodle mixture and stir-fry for 4 minutes, or until golden, then add the shoyu, mirin and sesame oil and toss together.

4 Divide the mixture between 2 plates, sprinkle with the sesame seeds and spring onions and serve at once.

gong bau chicken

ingredients

SERVES 4

2 boneless chicken breasts,
    with or without skin, cut
    into 1-cm/^{1}/$_2$-inch cubes
1 tbsp vegetable or peanut oil
10 dried red chillies or more,
    to taste, snipped into 2 or
    3 pieces
1 tsp Szechuan peppercorns
3 garlic cloves, finely sliced
2.5-cm/1-inch piece of fresh
    root ginger, finely sliced
1 tbsp coarsely chopped
    spring onion, white
    part only
85 g/3 oz peanuts, roasted

marinade
2 tsp light soy sauce
1 tsp Shaoxing rice wine
^{1}/$_2$ tsp sugar

sauce
1 tsp light soy sauce
1 tsp dark soy sauce
1 tsp black Chinese rice
    vinegar
a few drops of sesame oil
2 tbsp chicken stock
1 tsp sugar

method

1 Combine all the ingredients for the marinade in a bowl and marinate the chicken, covered, for at least 20 minutes. Mix together all the ingredients for the sauce and set aside.

2 In a preheated wok or deep saucepan, heat the oil and stir-fry the chillies and peppercorns until crisp and fragrant. Toss in the chicken pieces. When they begin to turn white, add the garlic, ginger and spring onion. Stir-fry for about 5 minutes, or until the chicken is cooked.

3 Pour in the sauce, and when everything is well mixed, stir in the peanuts. Serve at once.

shredded chicken & mixed mushrooms

ingredients

SERVES 4

2 tbsp vegetable or peanut oil

2 skinless, boneless chicken breasts

1 red onion, sliced

2 garlic cloves, chopped finely

2.5-cm/1-inch piece fresh root ginger, grated

115 g/4 oz baby white mushrooms

115 g/4 oz shiitake mushrooms, halved

115 g/4 oz chestnut mushrooms, sliced

2–3 tbsp green curry paste

2 tbsp Thai soy sauce

4 tbsp chopped fresh parsley

boiled noodles or rice, to serve

method

1 Heat the oil in a wok and cook the chicken on all sides until lightly browned and cooked through. Remove with a slotted spoon, shred into even-size pieces and set aside.

2 Pour off any excess oil, then stir-fry the onion, garlic and ginger for 1–2 minutes, or until softened. Add all the mushrooms and stir-fry for 2–3 minutes, until they start to brown.

3 Add the curry paste, soy sauce and shredded chicken to the wok and stir-fry for 1–2 minutes. Stir in the parsley and serve immediately with boiled noodles or rice.

five-spice chicken with vegetables

ingredients

SERVES 4

2 tbsp sesame oil

1 garlic clove, chopped

3 spring onions, trimmed
    and sliced

1 tbsp cornflour

2 tbsp rice wine

4 skinless chicken breasts, cut
    into strips

1 tbsp Chinese five-spice
    powder

1 tbsp grated fresh root ginger

125 ml/4 fl oz chicken stock

100 g/3^1/$_2$ oz baby corn cobs,
    sliced

300 g/10^1/$_2$ oz beansprouts

finely chopped spring onions,
    to garnish, optional

freshly cooked jasmine rice,
    to serve

method

1 Heat the oil in a preheated wok or large frying pan. Add the garlic and spring onions and stir-fry over medium–high heat for 1 minute.

2 In a bowl, mix together the cornflour and rice wine, then add the mixture to the pan. Stir-fry for 1 minute, then add the chicken, five-spice powder, ginger and chicken stock and cook for another 4 minutes. Add the corn cobs and cook for 2 minutes, then add the beansprouts and cook for another minute.

3 Remove from the heat, garnish with chopped spring onions, if using, and serve with freshly cooked jasmine rice.

chicken & ginger stir-fry

ingredients

SERVES 4

3 tbsp vegetable oil

700 g/1 lb 9 oz lean skinless,
   boneless chicken breasts,
   cut into 5-cm/2-inch strips

3 garlic cloves, crushed

1 tsp pomegranate seeds,
   crushed

4-cm/1$\frac{1}{2}$-inch piece fresh root
   ginger, cut into strips

$\frac{1}{2}$ tsp turmeric

1 tsp garam masala

2 fresh green chillies, sliced

$\frac{1}{2}$ tsp salt

4 tbsp lemon juice

grated rind of 1 lemon

6 tbsp chopped fresh
   coriander, plus extra
   to garnish

125 ml/4 fl oz chicken stock

naan bread, to serve

method

1 Heat the oil in a preheated wok or large frying pan. Add the chicken and stir-fry until golden brown all over. Remove from the wok and set aside.

2 Add the garlic, pomegranate seeds and ginger to the wok and stir-fry in the oil for 1 minute, taking care not to let the garlic burn.

3 Stir in the turmeric, garam masala and chillies and fry for 30 seconds.

4 Return the chicken to the wok and add the salt, lemon juice, lemon rind, coriander and stock. Stir the chicken well to make sure it is coated in the sauce.

5 Bring the mixture to the boil, then reduce the heat and simmer for 10–15 minutes, or until the chicken is thoroughly cooked. Garnish with chopped coriander and serve with warm naan bread.

chicken with pak choi

ingredients

SERVES 4

175 g/6 oz broccoli

1 tbsp peanut oil

2.5-cm/1-inch piece fresh root
ginger, finely grated

1 fresh red Thai chilli,
deseeded and chopped

2 garlic cloves, crushed

1 red onion, cut into wedges

450 g/1 lb skinless, boneless
chicken breast, cut into
thin strips

175 g/6 oz pak choi, shredded

115 g/4 oz baby corn, halved

1 tbsp light soy sauce

1 tbsp Thai fish sauce

1 tbsp chopped fresh
coriander

1 tbsp toasted sesame seeds

method

1 Break the broccoli into small florets and cook in a saucepan of lightly salted boiling water for 3 minutes. Drain and set aside.

2 Heat a wok over high heat until almost smoking, add the oil, then add the ginger, chilli and garlic. Stir-fry for 1 minute. Add the onion and chicken and stir-fry for a further 3–4 minutes, or until the chicken is sealed on all sides.

3 Add the remaining vegetables to the wok, including the broccoli, and stir-fry for 3–4 minutes, or until tender.

4 Add the soy and Thai fish sauces to the wok and stir-fry for a further 1–2 minutes, then serve at once, sprinkled with the coriander and sesame seeds.

chicken with yellow curry sauce

ingredients

SERVES 4

spice paste

6 tbsp Thai yellow curry paste

150 ml/5 fl oz plain yogurt

400 ml/14 fl oz water

handful of fresh coriander,
    chopped, plus extra to
    garnish

handful of fresh Thai basil
    leaves, shredded, plus
    extra to garnish

stir-fry

2 tbsp vegetable or peanut oil

2 onions, cut into thin wedges

2 garlic cloves, chopped finely

2 skinless, boneless chicken
    breasts, cut into strips

175 g/6 oz baby corn, halved
    lengthways

method

1 To make the spice paste, stir-fry the yellow curry paste in a wok for 2–3 minutes, then stir in the yogurt, water and herbs. Bring to the boil, then simmer for 2–3 minutes.

2 Meanwhile, heat the oil in a wok and stir-fry the onions and garlic for 2–3 minutes. Add the chicken and baby corn and stir-fry for 3–4 minutes, until the meat and baby corn are tender.

3 Stir in the spice paste and bring to the boil. Simmer for 2–3 minutes, until heated through. Serve immediately, garnished with the extra coriander and basil.

ginger chicken with noodles

ingredients

SERVES 4

2 tbsp vegetable or peanut oil

1 onion, sliced

2 garlic cloves, chopped finely

5-cm/2-inch piece fresh root
    ginger, sliced thinly

2 carrots, sliced thinly

4 skinless, boneless chicken
    breasts, cut into cubes

300 ml/10 fl oz chicken stock

4 tbsp Thai soy sauce

225 g/8 oz canned bamboo
    shoots, drained and rinsed

75 g/2¾ oz flat rice noodles

4 spring onions, chopped,
    and 4 tbsp chopped fresh
    coriander, to garnish

method

1 Heat the oil in a wok and stir-fry the onion, garlic, ginger and carrots for 1–2 minutes, until softened. Add the chicken and stir-fry for 3–4 minutes, until the chicken is cooked through and lightly browned.

2 Add the stock, soy sauce and bamboo shoots to the wok and gradually bring to the boil. Simmer for 2–3 minutes. Meanwhile, soak the noodles in boiling water for 6–8 minutes. Drain well. Garnish with the spring onions and coriander and serve immediately, with the chicken stir-fry.

rice noodles with chicken, prawns & tofu

ingredients

SERVES 4

225 g/8 oz rice noodles

90 g/3¼ oz peanuts, roughly chopped, plus extra to garnish

2 tbsp lime juice

1 tbsp caster sugar

6 tbsp Thai fish sauce

1 tsp hot chilli sauce, or to taste

250 g/9 oz firm tofu (drained weight), cubed

vegetable oil, for deep-frying

3 tbsp peanut oil

1 garlic clove, crushed

1 onion, finely sliced

1 red pepper, deseeded and thinly sliced

250 g/9 oz skinless, boneless chicken breast, cut into thin strips

85 g/3 oz beansprouts

125 g/4½ oz mangetout

175 g/6 oz cooked peeled prawns, cut in half lengthways

3 eggs, beaten

lemon wedges, 4 finely chopped spring onions, and 1 tbsp chopped fresh basil, to garnish

method

1 Soak the noodles in a bowl of warm water for about 20 minutes, or until soft. Drain thoroughly in a colander and set aside. Mix the peanuts, lime juice, sugar, fish sauce and hot chilli sauce together in a small bowl and set aside.

2 Rinse the tofu in cold water, place between layers of kitchen paper and pat dry. Heat the oil for deep-frying in a large frying pan or wok. Deep-fry the tofu over medium heat for 2 minutes until light brown and crisp. Remove from the heat, lift the tofu out with a slotted spoon and drain thoroughly on kitchen paper.

3 Heat another large frying pan or preheated wok and add the peanut oil, garlic, onion, red pepper and chicken strips. Cook for 2–3 minutes. Stir in the beansprouts and mangetout and cook for 1 minute, then add the prawns, noodles, eggs and tofu and stir-fry for 4–5 minutes. Finally, add the peanut and lime juice mixture and cook for 3–4 minutes. Transfer to warmed dishes, garnish with the lemon, spring onions, peanuts and basil and serve immediately.

balti chicken

ingredients

SERVES 6

3 tbsp ghee or vegetable oil

2 large onions, sliced

3 tomatoes, sliced

1/2 tsp kalonji seeds

4 black peppercorns

2 cardamom pods

1 cinnamon stick

1 tsp chilli powder

1 tsp garam masala

1 tsp garlic purée

1 tsp ginger purée

salt

700 g/1 lb 9 oz skinless,
   boneless chicken breasts
   or thighs, diced

2 tbsp plain yogurt

2 tbsp chopped fresh
   coriander, plus extra to
   garnish

2 fresh green chillies,
   deseeded and finely
   chopped

2 tbsp lime juice

naan bread, to serve

method

1 Heat the ghee in a large, heavy-based frying pan. Add the onions and cook over low heat, stirring occasionally, for 10 minutes, or until golden. Add the sliced tomatoes, kalonji seeds, peppercorns, cardamoms, cinnamon stick, chilli powder, garam masala, garlic purée and ginger purée and season with salt. Cook, stirring constantly, for 5 minutes.

2 Add the chicken and cook, stirring constantly, for 5 minutes, or until well coated in the spice paste. Stir in the yogurt. Cover and simmer, stirring occasionally, for 10 minutes.

3 Stir in the chopped coriander, chillies and lime juice. Transfer to a warmed serving dish, sprinkle with more chopped coriander and serve immediately with naan bread.

chicken pasanda

ingredients

SERVES 4

4 cardamom pods

6 black peppercorns

1/2 cinnamon stick

1/2 tsp cumin seeds

2 tsp garam masala

1 tsp chilli powder

1 tsp grated fresh root ginger

1 garlic clove, very finely
    chopped

4 tbsp thick plain yogurt

pinch of salt

675 g/1 lb 8 oz skinless,
    boneless chicken, diced

5 tbsp peanut oil

2 onions, finely chopped

3 fresh green chillies,
    deseeded and chopped

2 tbsp chopped fresh
    coriander

125 ml/4 fl oz single cream

fresh coriander sprigs,
    to garnish

method

1 Place the cardamom pods in a non-metallic dish with the peppercorns, cinnamon, cumin, garam masala, chilli powder, ginger, garlic, yogurt and salt. Add the chicken pieces and stir well to coat. Cover and marinate in the refrigerator for 2–3 hours.

2 Heat the oil in a preheated wok. Add the onions and cook over low heat, stirring occasionally, for 5 minutes, or until softened, then add the chicken pieces and marinade and cook over medium heat, stirring, for 15 minutes, or until the chicken is cooked through.

3 Stir in the fresh chillies and coriander and pour in the cream. Heat through gently, but do not let it boil. Garnish with fresh coriander and serve immediately.

thai red chicken curry

ingredients

SERVES 4

6 garlic cloves, chopped

2 fresh red chillies, chopped

2 tbsp chopped fresh
    lemon grass

1 tsp finely grated lime rind

1 tbsp chopped fresh kaffir
    lime leaves

1 tbsp Thai red curry paste

1 tbsp coriander seeds,
    toasted and crushed

1 tbsp chilli oil

4 skinless, boneless chicken
    breasts, sliced

300 ml/10 fl oz coconut milk

300 ml/10 fl oz chicken stock

1 tbsp soy sauce

55 g/2 oz shelled unsalted
    peanuts, toasted and
    ground

3 spring onions,
    diagonally sliced

1 red pepper, deseeded
    and sliced

3 Thai aubergines, sliced

2 tbsp chopped fresh Thai
    basil or fresh coriander

fresh coriander, to garnish

freshly cooked jasmine rice,
    to serve

method

1 Place the garlic, chillies, lemon grass, lime rind, lime leaves, curry paste and coriander seeds in a food processor and process until the mixture is smooth.

2 Heat the oil in a preheated wok or large frying pan over high heat. Add the chicken and the garlic mixture and stir-fry for 5 minutes. Add the coconut milk, stock and soy sauce and bring to the boil. Reduce the heat and cook, stirring, for a further 3 minutes. Stir in the ground peanuts and simmer for 20 minutes.

3 Add the spring onions, pepper and aubergines and simmer, stirring occasionally, for a further 10 minutes. Remove from the heat, stir in the basil and garnish with coriander. Serve immediately with freshly cooked jasmine rice.

red hot chilli chicken

ingredients

SERVES 4

1 tbsp curry paste

2 fresh green chillies, chopped

5 dried red chillies

2 tbsp tomato purée

2 garlic cloves, chopped

1 tsp chilli powder

pinch of sugar

pinch of salt

2 tbsp peanut or corn oil

1/2 tsp cumin seeds

1 onion, chopped

2 curry leaves

1 tsp ground cumin

1 tsp ground coriander

1/2 tsp ground turmeric

400 g/14 oz canned chopped
    tomatoes

150 ml/5 fl oz chicken stock

4 skinless, boneless chicken
    breasts

1 tsp garam masala

freshly cooked rice and plain
    yogurt garnished with
    mint sprigs and diced
    cucumber, to serve

method

1 To make the chilli paste, place the curry paste, fresh and dried chillies, tomato purée, garlic, chilli powder and sugar in a blender or food processor with the salt. Process to a smooth paste.

2 Heat the oil in a large, heavy-based saucepan. Add the cumin seeds and cook over medium heat, stirring constantly, for 2 minutes, or until they begin to pop and release their aroma. Add the onion and curry leaves and cook, stirring, for 5 minutes.

3 Add the chilli paste, cook for 2 minutes, then stir in the ground cumin, coriander and turmeric and cook for a further 2 minutes.

4 Add the tomatoes and their juices and the stock. Bring to the boil, then reduce the heat and simmer for 5 minutes. Add the chicken and garam masala, cover, and simmer gently for 20 minutes, or until the chicken is cooked through and tender. Serve immediately with freshly cooked rice and yogurt garnished with mint sprigs and diced cucumber.

creamy chicken curry with lemon rice

ingredients

SERVES 4

2 tbsp vegetable oil

4 skinless, boneless chicken
   breasts, 800 g/1 lb 12 oz
   in total, cut into 2.5-cm/
   1-inch pieces

1½ tsp cumin seeds

1 large onion, grated

2 fresh green chillies, finely
   chopped

2 large garlic cloves, grated

1 tbsp grated fresh root ginger

1 tsp ground turmeric

1 tsp ground coriander

1 tsp garam masala

300 ml/10 fl oz coconut milk

250 ml/9 fl oz canned
   chopped tomatoes

2 tsp lemon juice

salt

2 tbsp chopped fresh
   coriander, to garnish

lemon rice

350 g/12 oz basmati rice,
   rinsed

1.2 litres/2 pints water

juice and grated rind of
   1 lemon

3 cloves

method

1 Heat the oil in a large, heavy-based saucepan over medium heat. Add the chicken and cook for 5–8 minutes, turning frequently, until lightly browned and cooked through. Remove from the pan and set aside. Add the cumin seeds and cook until they start to darken and sizzle. Stir in the onion, partially cover and cook over medium–low heat, stirring frequently, for 10 minutes, or until soft and golden. Add the chillies, garlic, ginger, turmeric, ground coriander and garam masala and cook for 1 minute.

2 Return the chicken to the pan and stir in the coconut milk and tomatoes. Partially cover and cook over medium heat for 15 minutes until the sauce has reduced and thickened. Stir in the lemon juice and season with salt.

3 Meanwhile, put the rice into a saucepan and cover with the water. Add the lemon juice and cloves. Bring to the boil, then reduce the heat, cover and simmer over very low heat for 15 minutes, or until the rice is tender and all the water has been absorbed. Remove the pan from the heat and stir in the lemon rind. Let the rice stand, covered, for 5 minutes.

4 Serve the curry with the lemon rice, sprinkled with fresh coriander.

chicken & peanut curry

ingredients

SERVES 4

1 tbsp vegetable or peanut oil

2 red onions, sliced

2 tbsp Penang curry paste

400 ml/14 fl oz coconut milk

150 ml/5 fl oz chicken stock

4 kaffir lime leaves, torn
coarsely

1 lemon grass stalk, chopped
finely

6 skinless, boneless chicken
thighs, chopped

1 tbsp fish sauce

2 tbsp Thai soy sauce

1 tsp jaggery or soft, light
brown sugar

50 g/1¾ oz unsalted peanuts,
roasted and chopped, plus
extra to garnish

175 g/6 oz fresh pineapple,
chopped coarsely

15-cm/6-inch piece
cucumber, peeled,
deseeded and sliced
thickly, plus extra
to garnish

method

1 Heat the oil in a wok and stir-fry the onions for 1 minute. Add the curry paste and stir-fry for 1–2 minutes.

2 Pour in the coconut milk and stock. Add the lime leaves and lemon grass and simmer for 1 minute. Add the chicken and gradually bring to the boil. Simmer for 8–10 minutes, until the chicken is tender.

3 Stir in the fish sauce, soy sauce and sugar, and simmer for 1–2 minutes. Stir in the peanuts, pineapple and cucumber, and cook for 30 seconds. Serve immediately, sprinkled with the extra nuts and cucumber.

green chicken curry

ingredients

SERVES 4

1 tbsp vegetable or peanut oil
1 onion, sliced
1 garlic clove, chopped finely
2–3 tbsp Thai green curry
    paste
400 ml/14 fl oz coconut milk
150 ml/5 fl oz chicken stock
4 kaffir lime leaves
4 skinless, boneless chicken
    breasts, cut into cubes
1 tbsp fish sauce
2 tbsp Thai soy sauce
grated rind and juice of
    1/2 lime
1 tsp jaggery or soft light
    brown sugar
4 tbsp chopped fresh
    coriander, to garnish
freshly cooked rice, to serve

method

1 Heat the oil in a wok or large frying pan and stir-fry the onion and garlic for 1–2 minutes, until starting to soften. Add the curry paste and stir-fry for 1–2 minutes.

2 Add the coconut milk, stock and lime leaves, bring to the boil and add the chicken. Reduce the heat and simmer gently for 15–20 minutes, until the chicken is tender.

3 Add the fish sauce, soy sauce, lime rind and juice and sugar. Cook for 2–3 minutes, until the sugar has dissolved. Garnish with chopped coriander and serve immediately, with rice.

spiced coriander chicken

ingredients

SERVES 4

4 skinless, boneless chicken
   breasts
2 garlic cloves
1 fresh green chilli, deseeded
2-cm/3/4-inch piece fresh root
   ginger
4 tbsp chopped coriander
finely grated rind of 1 lime
3 tbsp lime juice
2 tbsp light soy sauce
1 tbsp caster sugar
175 ml/6 fl oz coconut milk

to garnish
finely chopped coriander
cucumber slices
radish slices
1/2 fresh red chilli, deseeded
   and sliced into rings
freshly cooked rice, to serve

method

1 Using a sharp knife, cut 3 deep slashes into the skinned side of each chicken breast. Place the breasts in a single layer in a non-metallic dish.

2 Place the garlic, chilli, ginger, coriander, lime rind and juice, soy sauce, sugar and coconut milk in a food processor and process to a smooth paste.

3 Spread the paste over both sides of the chicken breasts, coating them evenly. Cover with clingfilm and marinate in the refrigerator for 1 hour.

4 Preheat the grill to medium. Lift the chicken from the marinade, then drain off the excess and place on a grill pan. Cook under the hot grill for 12–15 minutes, or until thoroughly and evenly cooked.

5 Meanwhile, place the remaining marinade in a saucepan and bring to the boil. Reduce the heat and simmer for several minutes. Transfer the chicken breasts to serving plates and pour over the cooked marinade. Garnish with chopped coriander, cucumber slices, radish slices and chilli rings and serve with rice.

lime chicken with mint

ingredients

SERVES 6

3 tbsp finely chopped
    fresh mint
4 tbsp honey
4 tbsp lime juice
salt and pepper
12 boneless chicken thighs
mixed salad, to serve

s a u c e
150 ml/5 fl oz low-fat thick
    plain yogurt
1 tbsp finely chopped
    fresh mint
2 tsp finely grated lime rind

method

1 Mix the mint, honey and lime juice in a large bowl and season with salt and pepper. Use cocktail sticks to keep the chicken thighs in neat shapes and add the chicken to the marinade, turning to coat evenly.

2 Cover with clingfilm and marinate the chicken in the refrigerator for at least 30 minutes. Remove the chicken from the marinade and drain. Set aside the marinade.

3 Preheat the grill to medium. Place the chicken on a grill rack and cook under the hot grill for 15–18 minutes, or until the chicken is tender and the juices run clear when the tip of a knife is inserted into the thickest part of the meat, turning the chicken frequently and basting with the marinade.

4 Meanwhile, combine all the sauce ingredients in a bowl. Remove the cocktail sticks and serve the chicken with a mixed salad and the sauce, for dipping.

grilled chicken with lemon

ingredients

SERVES 4

4 chicken quarters

grated rind and juice of
    2 lemons

4 tbsp olive oil

2 garlic cloves, crushed

2 sprigs fresh thyme, plus
    extra to garnish

salt and pepper

method

1 Prick the skin of the chicken quarters all over with a fork. Put the chicken pieces in a dish, add the lemon juice, oil, garlic, thyme, salt and pepper, and mix well. Cover and marinate in the refrigerator for at least 2 hours.

2 To cook the chicken, preheat the barbecue or grill. Put the chicken on the barbecue rack or in a griddle pan and baste with the marinade. Cook for 30–40 minutes, basting and turning occasionally, until the chicken is tender. (To test if the chicken is cooked, pierce the thickest part of the chicken pieces with a skewer. If the juices run clear, it is ready.) Serve hot, garnished with thyme sprigs and the grated lemon rind.

sticky lime chicken

ingredients

SERVES 4

4 part-boned, skinless chicken breasts, about 140 g/5 oz each

grated rind and juice of 1 lime

1 tbsp honey

1 tbsp olive oil

1 garlic clove, chopped (optional)

1 tbsp chopped fresh thyme

pepper

boiled new potatoes and lightly cooked seasonal vegetables, to serve

method

1 Arrange the chicken breasts in a shallow roasting pan.

2 Put the lime rind and juice, honey, oil, garlic, if using, and thyme in a small bowl and combine thoroughly. Spoon the mixture evenly over the chicken breasts and season with pepper.

3 Roast the chicken in a preheated oven, 190°C/ 375°F/Gas Mark 5, basting every 10 minutes, for 35–40 minutes, or until the chicken is tender and the juices run clear when a skewer is inserted into the thickest part of the meat. If the juices still run pink, return the chicken to the oven and cook for a further 5 minutes, then test again. As the chicken cooks, the liquid in the pan thickens to give a tasty, sticky coating.

4 Serve with boiled new potatoes and lightly cooked seasonal vegetables.

chicken pinwheels with blue cheese & herbs

ingredients

SERVES 4

2 tbsp pine kernels, lightly
   toasted
2 tbsp chopped fresh parsley
2 tbsp chopped fresh thyme
1 garlic clove, chopped
1 tbsp grated lemon rind
salt and pepper
4 large, skinless chicken
   breasts
250 g/9 oz blue cheese, such
   as Stilton, crumbled
twists of lemon and sprigs of
   fresh thyme, to garnish
fresh green and red salad
   leaves, to serve

method

1 Put the pine kernels into a food processor with the parsley, thyme, garlic and lemon rind. Season with salt and pepper.

2 Pound the chicken breasts lightly to flatten them. Spread them on one side with the pine kernel mixture, then top with the cheese. Roll them up from one short end to the other, so that the filling is enclosed. Wrap the rolls individually in foil and seal well. Transfer to a steamer, or a metal colander placed over a pan of boiling water, cover tightly and steam for 10–12 minutes, or until cooked through.

3 Arrange the salad leaves on a large serving platter. Remove the chicken from the heat, discard the foil, and cut the chicken rolls into slices. Arrange the slices over the salad leaves, garnish with twists of lemon and sprigs of thyme and serve.

chicken rolls with cheese & pine kernels

ingredients

SERVES 6

3 slices white bread, crusts removed

6 skinless, boneless chicken breasts, about 175 g/6 oz each

2 shallots, finely chopped

2 garlic cloves, finely chopped

2 tbsp finely chopped fresh flat-leaf parsley

2 tbsp freshly grated Parmesan cheese

55 g/2 oz pine kernels

pinch of ground mace

salt and pepper

tarragon-flavoured oil or olive oil, for brushing

a few sprigs of fresh flat-leaf parsley, to garnish

method

1 Tear the bread into pieces, place in a bowl and add cold water to cover. Set aside to soak for 10 minutes.

2 Meanwhile, place the chicken breasts between 2 sheets of clingfilm and pound gently with a meat mallet or the side of a rolling pin to flatten.

3 Drain the bread and squeeze out the excess liquid. Mix together the bread, shallots, garlic, parsley, Parmesan, pine kernels and mace in a bowl. Season with salt and pepper.

4 Spread the filling evenly over the chicken breasts and roll up. Secure each roll with a wooden cocktail stick. Brush with the oil and grill, turning frequently and brushing with more oil as necessary, for 25–30 minutes, or until cooked through and tender. Serve at once, garnished with parsley.

chicken kiev

ingredients

SERVES 4

4 tbsp butter, softened

1 garlic clove, finely chopped

1 tbsp finely chopped fresh parsley

1 tbsp finely chopped fresh oregano

salt and pepper

4 skinless, boneless chicken breasts

85 g/3 oz fresh white or wholewheat breadcrumbs

3 tbsp freshly grated Parmesan cheese

1 egg, beaten

250 ml/9 fl oz vegetable oil, for deep-frying

slices of lemon and flat-leaf parsley sprigs, to garnish

freshly cooked new potatoes and selection of cooked vegetables, to serve

method

1 Place the butter and garlic in a bowl and mix together well. Stir in the chopped herbs and season well with salt and pepper. Pound the chicken breasts to flatten them to an even thickness, then place a tablespoon of herb butter in the centre of each one. Fold in the sides to enclose the butter, then secure with wooden cocktail sticks.

2 Combine the breadcrumbs and grated Parmesan on a plate. Dip the chicken parcels into the beaten egg, then coat in the breadcrumb mixture. Transfer to a plate, cover and chill for 30 minutes. Remove from the refrigerator and coat in the egg and then the breadcrumb mixture for a second time.

3 Pour the oil into a deep-fryer to a depth that will cover the chicken parcels. Heat until it reaches 180–190°C/350–375°F, or until a cube of bread browns in 30 seconds. Transfer the chicken to the hot oil and deep-fry for 5 minutes, or until cooked through. Lift out the chicken and drain on kitchen paper.

4 Divide the chicken between 4 serving plates, garnish with lemon slices and parsley sprigs and serve with new potatoes and a selection of vegetables.

roasted chicken with sun-blush tomato pesto

ingredients

SERVES 4

4 skinless, boneless chicken
   breasts, about 800 g/
   1 lb 12 oz in total
1 tbsp olive oil
salt and pepper
2 tbsp pine kernels, lightly
   toasted, to garnish

sun-blush tomato
   pesto
125 g/4¹/₂ oz sun-blush
   tomatoes in oil (drained
   weight), chopped
2 garlic cloves, crushed
4 tbsp pine kernels, lightly
   toasted
150 ml/5 fl oz extra virgin
   olive oil

method

1 To make the sun-blush tomato pesto, put the tomatoes, garlic, pine kernels and oil into a food processor and process to a coarse paste.

2 Arrange the chicken in a large, ovenproof dish or roasting pan. Brush each breast with the oil, then place a tablespoon of red pesto over each breast. Using the back of a spoon, spread the pesto so that it covers the top of each breast. (Store the remaining pesto in an airtight container in the refrigerator for up to 1 week.)

3 Roast the chicken in a preheated oven, 200°C/400°F/Gas Mark 6, for 30 minutes, or until tender and the juices run clear when a skewer is inserted into the thickest part of the meat.

4 Serve sprinkled with toasted pine kernels.

pesto & ricotta chicken with tomato vinaigrette

ingredients

SERVES 4

1 tbsp pesto sauce

115 g/4 oz ricotta cheese

4 x 175 g/6 oz boneless
    chicken breasts

1 tbsp olive oil

pepper

salad leaves, to garnish

tomato vinaigrette

100 ml/3$\frac{1}{2}$ fl oz olive oil

1 bunch fresh chives

500 g/1 lb 2 oz tomatoes,
    peeled, deseeded and
    chopped

juice and finely grated rind
    of 1 lime

salt and pepper

method

1 Mix together the pesto and ricotta in a small bowl until well combined. Using a sharp knife, cut a deep slit in the side of each chicken breast to make a pocket. Spoon the ricotta mixture into the pockets and re-shape the chicken breasts to enclose it. Place the chicken on a plate, cover and chill for 30 minutes.

2 To make the vinaigrette, pour the olive oil into a blender or food processor, add the chives and process until smooth. Scrape the mixture into a bowl and stir in the tomatoes and the lime juice and rind. Season with salt and pepper.

3 Brush the chicken with the olive oil and season with pepper. Cook on a fairly hot barbecue for about 8 minutes on each side, or until cooked through and tender. Transfer to serving plates, spoon over the vinaigrette and serve immediately, garnished with salad leaves.

chicken with saffron mash

ingredients

SERVES 4

550 g/1 lb 4 oz floury
   potatoes, cut into chunks
1 garlic clove, peeled
1 tsp saffron threads, crushed
1.2 litres/2 pints chicken or
   vegetable stock
4 skinless, boneless chicken
   breasts, trimmed of all
   visible fat
2 tbsp olive oil
1 tbsp lemon juice
1 tbsp chopped fresh thyme
1 tbsp chopped fresh
   coriander
1 tbsp coriander seeds,
   crushed
100 ml/3½ fl oz hot
   skimmed milk
salt and pepper
fresh thyme sprigs, to garnish

method

1 Put the potatoes, garlic and saffron in a large heavy-based saucepan, add the stock and bring to the boil. Cover and simmer for 20 minutes, or until tender.

2 Meanwhile, brush the chicken breasts all over with half the olive oil and all of the lemon juice. Sprinkle with the fresh thyme and coriander and the crushed coriander seeds. Heat a griddle pan, add the chicken and cook over medium–high heat for 5 minutes on each side, or until the juices run clear when the meat is pierced with the tip of a sharp knife. Alternatively, cook the chicken breasts under a preheated medium–hot grill for 5 minutes on each side, or until cooked through.

3 Drain the potatoes and return the contents of the strainer to the pan. Add the remaining olive oil and the milk, season with salt and pepper and mash until smooth. Divide the saffron mash between 4 large, warmed serving plates, top with a piece of chicken and garnish with a few sprigs of fresh thyme. Serve.

tarragon chicken

ingredients

SERVES 4

4 skinless, boneless chicken
    breasts, about 175 g/
    6 oz each
salt and pepper
125 ml/4 fl oz dry white wine
250–300 ml/9–10 fl oz
    chicken stock
1 garlic clove, finely chopped
1 tbsp dried tarragon
175 ml/6 fl oz double cream
1 tbsp chopped fresh tarragon
fresh tarragon sprigs,
    to garnish

method

1 Season the chicken with salt and pepper and place in a single layer in a large, heavy-based frying pan. Pour in the wine and just enough chicken stock to cover, and add the garlic and dried tarragon. Bring to the boil, reduce the heat and cook gently for 10 minutes, or until the chicken is tender and cooked through.

2 Remove the chicken with a slotted spoon or tongs, cover and keep warm. Strain the poaching liquid into a clean frying pan and skim off any fat from the surface. Bring to the boil and cook for 12–15 minutes, or until reduced by about two-thirds.

3 Stir in the cream, return to the boil and cook until reduced by about half. Stir in the fresh tarragon. Slice the chicken breasts and arrange on warmed plates. Spoon over the sauce, garnish with tarragon sprigs and serve immediately.

chicken with goat's cheese & basil

ingredients

SERVES 4

4 skinned chicken breast
    fillets
100 g/3½ oz soft goat's
    cheese
small bunch fresh basil
salt and pepper
2 tbsp olive oil

method

1 Using a sharp knife, slit along one long edge of each chicken breast, then carefully open out each breast to make a small pocket. Divide the cheese equally between the pockets and tuck three or four basil leaves in each. Close the openings and season the breasts with salt and pepper.

2 Heat the oil in a frying pan, add the chicken breasts and fry gently for 15–20 minutes, turning several times, until golden and tender.

3 Serve warm, garnished with a sprig of basil.

chicken with walnut sauce

ingredients

SERVES 4

4–8 skinned chicken pieces

1/2 lemon, cut into wedges

3 tbsp olive oil

150 ml/5 fl oz dry white wine

300 ml/10 fl oz chicken stock

1 bay leaf

salt and pepper

100 g/3 1/2 oz walnut pieces

2 garlic cloves

150 ml/5 fl oz Greek-style
   yogurt

chopped fresh flat-leaf parsley,
   to garnish

rice or pilaf and pitta bread,
   to serve

method

1 Rub the chicken pieces with the lemon. Heat the oil in a large frying pan, add the chicken pieces and fry quickly until lightly browned on all sides.

2 Pour the wine into the pan and bring to the boil. Add the stock, bay leaf, salt and pepper and simmer for about 20 minutes, turning several times, until the chicken is tender.

3 Meanwhile, put the walnuts and garlic in a food processor and blend to form a fairly smooth purée.

4 When the chicken is cooked, transfer to a warmed serving dish and keep warm. Stir the walnut mixture and yogurt into the pan juices and heat gently for about 5 minutes until the sauce is quite thick. (Do not boil or the sauce will curdle.) Season with salt and pepper.

5 Pour the walnut sauce over the chicken pieces and serve hot with rice or pilaf and pitta bread. Garnish with chopped fresh parsley.

paprika chicken on a bed of onions & ham

ingredients

SERVES 4

150 ml/5 fl oz freshly
    squeezed lemon juice

4 chicken breast fillets,
    skin on

1–1¹/₂ tsp mild or hot Spanish
    paprika, to taste

salt and pepper

about 2 tbsp olive oil

70 g/2¹/₂ oz serrano ham or
    prosciutto, diced

4 large onions, sliced thinly

125 ml/4 fl oz dry white wine

125 ml/4 fl oz chicken stock

fresh thyme or chopped fresh
    parsley, to garnish

method

1 Pour the lemon juice over the chicken breasts in a non-metallic bowl and marinate in the refrigerator overnight.

2 Remove the chicken from the marinade and pat dry. Rub the skins with the paprika and season to taste. Heat 2 tablespoons of the oil in a large, lidded frying pan over medium–high heat. Add the chicken breasts, skin-sides down, and cook for 5 minutes or until the skins are golden; remove from the pan.

3 Stir the ham into the fat remaining in the pan, cover and cook for about 2 minutes until it renders any fat. Add the onions and cook for about 5 minutes, stirring occasionally and adding a little extra oil if necessary, until the onions are soft but not brown.

4 Add the wine and stock and bring to the boil, stirring. Return the chicken breasts to the pan and season to taste. Reduce the heat, cover and simmer for 20 minutes or until the chicken is cooked and the juices run clear. Remove and set aside in a warm oven.

5 Bring the sauce to the boil and let it bubble while the juices reduce. Taste and adjust the seasoning. Divide the onion mixture between 4 warmed plates and arrange a chicken breast on top of each. Garnish with herbs to serve.

chicken with garlic

ingredients

SERVES 4–6

4 tbsp plain flour

Spanish paprika, either hot or
    smoked sweet, to taste

salt and pepper

1 large chicken, about
    1.75 kg/3 lb 14 oz, cut into
    8 pieces, rinsed, and
    patted dry

4–6 tbsp olive oil

24 large garlic cloves,
    peeled and halved

450 ml/16 fl oz chicken stock

4 tbsp dry white wine,
    such as white Rioja

2 sprigs fresh parsley,

1 bay leaf and 1 sprig fresh
    thyme, tied together

fresh parsley and thyme
    leaves, to garnish

method

1 Sift the flour onto a large plate and season with paprika and salt and pepper to taste. Dredge the chicken pieces with the flour on both sides, shaking off the excess.

2 Heat 4 tablespoons of the oil in a large, deep frying pan or flameproof casserole over medium heat. Add the garlic pieces and cook, stirring frequently, for about 2 minutes to flavour the oil. Remove with a slotted spoon and set aside to drain on kitchen paper.

3 Cook the chicken pieces, skin-side down, in a single layer, in batches if necessary, to avoid overcrowding the frying pan, adding a little extra oil if necessary. Cook for 5 minutes until the skin is golden brown. Turn over and cook for 5 minutes longer.

4 Pour off any excess oil. Return the garlic and chicken pieces to the frying pan and add the chicken stock, wine and herbs. Bring to the boil, then reduce the heat, cover, and simmer for 20–25 minutes, until the chicken is cooked through and the garlic very soft. Remove the chicken pieces and keep warm.

5 Bring the cooking liquid to the boil, with the garlic and herbs, and boil until reduced to about 300 ml/10 fl oz. Discard the herbs. Spoon the sauce and the garlic cloves over the chicken pieces. Garnish with the parsley and thyme and serve.

lemon grass chicken skewers

ingredients

SERVES 4

2 long or 4 short lemon grass stems

2 large skinless, boneless chicken breasts, about 400 g/14 oz in total

1 small egg white

1 carrot, finely grated

1 small fresh red chilli, deseeded and chopped

2 tbsp snipped fresh garlic chives

2 tbsp chopped coriander

salt and pepper

1 tbsp corn oil

coriander sprigs and lime slices, to garnish

mixed salad leaves, to serve

method

1 If the lemon grass stems are long, cut them in half across the centre to make 4 short lengths. Cut each stem in half lengthways, so that you have 8 sticks.

2 Coarsely chop the chicken pieces and place them in a food processor with the egg white. Process to a smooth paste, then add the carrot, chilli, chives, coriander and salt and pepper to taste. Process for a few seconds to mix well. Transfer the mixture to a large bowl. Cover and chill in the refrigerator for 15 minutes.

3 Preheat the grill to medium. Divide the mixture into 8 equal-size portions and use your hands to shape the mixture around the lemon grass 'skewers'.

4 Brush the skewers with oil and cook under the hot grill for 4–6 minutes, turning them occasionally, until golden brown and thoroughly cooked. Alternatively, barbecue over medium–hot coals.

5 Transfer to serving plates. Garnish with coriander sprigs and lime slices and serve hot with salad leaves.

chicken kebabs with yogurt sauce

ingredients

SERVES 4

300 ml/10 fl oz Greek-style
   yogurt
2 garlic cloves, crushed
juice of 1/2 lemon
1 tbsp chopped fresh herbs
   such as oregano, dill,
   tarragon or parsley
salt and pepper
4 large skinned, boned
   chicken breasts
corn oil, for oiling
8 firm stems of fresh
   rosemary, optional
lemon wedges, to garnish
shredded romaine lettuce
   and rice, to serve

method

1 To make the sauce, put the yogurt, garlic, lemon juice, herbs, salt and pepper in a large bowl and mix well together.

2 Cut the chicken breasts into chunks measuring about 4 cm/1 1/2 inches square. Add to the yogurt mixture and toss well together until the chicken pieces are coated. Cover and marinate in the refrigerator for about 1 hour. If you are using wooden skewers, soak them in cold water for 30 minutes before use.

3 Preheat the grill. Thread the pieces of chicken onto 8 flat, oiled metal kebab skewers, wooden skewers or rosemary stems and place on an oiled grill pan.

4 Cook the kebabs under the grill for about 15 minutes, turning and basting with the remaining marinade occasionally, until lightly browned and tender.

5 Pour the remaining marinade into a saucepan and heat gently but do not boil. Serve the kebabs with shredded lettuce on a bed of rice, and garnish with lemon wedges. Accompany with the yogurt sauce.

chicken satay

ingredients

SERVES 4

2 tbsp vegetable or peanut oil

1 tbsp sesame oil

juice of 1/2 lime

2 skinless, boneless chicken
  breasts, cut into small
  cubes

dip

2 tbsp vegetable or peanut oil

1 small onion, chopped finely

1 small fresh green chilli,
  deseeded and chopped

1 garlic clove, chopped finely

115 g/4 oz crunchy peanut
  butter

6–8 tbsp water

juice of 1/2 lime

method

1 Combine both the oils and the lime juice in a non-metallic dish. Add the chicken cubes, cover with clingfilm and chill for 1 hour. Soak 8–12 wooden skewers in cold water for 30 minutes before use, to prevent burning.

2 To make the dip, heat the oil in a frying pan and sauté the onion, chilli and garlic over low heat, stirring occasionally, for about 5 minutes, until just softened. Add the peanut butter, water and lime juice and simmer gently, stirring constantly, until the peanut butter has softened enough to make a dip – you may need to add a little extra water to make a thinner consistency.

3 Meanwhile, drain the chicken cubes and thread them onto the wooden skewers. Put under a hot grill or on a barbecue, turning frequently, for about 10 minutes, until cooked and browned. Serve hot with the warm dip.

gingered chicken kebabs

ingredients

SERVES 4

3 skinless, boneless chicken breasts, cut into small cubes

juice of 1 lime

2.5-cm/1-inch piece root ginger, peeled and chopped

1 fresh red chilli, deseeded and sliced

2 tbsp vegetable or peanut oil

1 onion, sliced

2 garlic cloves, chopped

1 aubergine, cut into chunks

2 courgettes, cut into thick slices

1 red pepper, deseeded and cut into squares

2 tbsp Thai red curry paste

2 tbsp Thai soy sauce

1 tsp jaggery or soft light brown sugar

boiled rice, with chopped coriander, to serve

method

1 Put the chicken cubes in a shallow dish. Mix the lime, ginger and chilli together and pour over the chicken pieces. Stir gently to coat. Cover and chill in the refrigerator for at least 3 hours to marinate.

2 Soak 8–12 wooden skewers in cold water for 30 minutes before use, to prevent burning.

3 Thread the chicken pieces onto the soaked wooden skewers and cook under a hot grill for 3–4 minutes, turning frequently, until they are cooked through.

4 Meanwhile, heat the oil in a wok or large frying pan and sauté the onion and garlic for 1–2 minutes, until softened, but not browned. Add the aubergine, courgettes and pepper and cook for 3–4 minutes, until cooked but still firm. Add the curry paste, soy sauce and sugar and cook for 1 minute.

5 Serve hot with boiled rice, stirred through with chopped coriander.

moroccan chicken

ingredients

SERVES 4

4 skinless, boneless chicken
　　breasts, about 140 g/5 oz
　　each
salt and pepper
toasted flat breads, to serve

m a r i n a d e
3 tbsp olive oil
4 tbsp lemon juice
2 tbsp chopped fresh parsley
2 tbsp chopped fresh
　　coriander
1 garlic clove, finely chopped
1 tsp ground coriander
1/2 tsp ground cumin
1 tsp sweet paprika
pinch of chilli powder

s a l a d
200 g/7 oz raw carrots
200 g/7 oz raw white cabbage
100 g/3 1/2 oz sprouting beans
50 g/1 3/4 oz alfalfa sprouts
50 g/1 3/4 oz sultanas
50 g/1 3/4 oz raisins
1 tbsp lemon juice

method

1 Mix together the oil, lemon juice, parsley, fresh coriander, garlic, ground coriander, cumin, paprika and chilli powder in a large, shallow, non-metallic dish.

2 Using a sharp knife, score the chicken breasts 3–4 times. Add the chicken to the dish, turning to coat. Cover with clingfilm and marinate in a cool place, turning occasionally, for 2–3 hours.

3 Drain the chicken, reserving the marinade. Barbecue over hot coals, brushing occasionally with the reserved marinade, for 20–30 minutes, or until tender and cooked through. Season with salt and pepper.

4 Meanwhile, to make the salad, trim and peel the carrots, then grate them into a large salad bowl. Trim the white cabbage, then shred it finely. Transfer it to a large colander and rinse under cold running water. Drain well, then add it to the carrots. Put the sprouting beans and alfalfa sprouts into the colander and rinse well, then drain and add to the salad. Rinse and drain the sultanas and raisins and add them to the bowl. Pour in the lemon juice and toss the salad into it.

5 Serve the Moroccan chicken with the salad and toasted flat breads.

chicken fajitas

ingredients

SERVES 4

3 tbsp olive oil, plus extra
    for drizzling
3 tbsp maple syrup or honey
1 tbsp red wine vinegar
2 garlic cloves, crushed
2 tsp dried oregano
1–2 tsp dried red pepper
    flakes
salt and pepper
4 skinless, boneless chicken
    breasts
2 red peppers, deseeded and
    cut into 2.5-cm/1-inch
    strips
8 flour tortillas, warmed

method

1 Place the oil, maple syrup, vinegar, garlic, oregano, pepper flakes, salt and pepper in a large, shallow plate or bowl and mix together.

2 Slice the chicken across the grain into slices 2.5 cm/1 inch thick. Toss in the marinade until well coated. Cover and chill in the refrigerator for 2–3 hours, turning occasionally.

3 Heat a griddle pan until hot. Lift the chicken slices from the marinade with a slotted spoon, lay on the griddle pan and cook over medium–high heat for 3–4 minutes on each side, or until cooked through. Remove the chicken to a warmed serving plate and keep warm.

4 Add the peppers, skin-side down, to the griddle pan and cook for 2 minutes on each side. Transfer to the serving plate.

5 Serve at once with the warmed tortillas to be used as wraps.

chicken tacos from puebla

ingredients

SERVES 4

8 soft corn tortillas

2 tsp vegetable oil

225–350 g/8–12 oz leftover
    cooked chicken, diced
    or shredded

salt and pepper

225 g/8 oz canned refried
    beans, warmed with 2 tbsp
    water to thin

$1/4$ tsp ground cumin

$1/4$ tsp dried oregano

1 avocado, stoned, peeled,
    sliced and tossed with lime
    juice

salsa of your choice

1 canned chipotle chilli in
    adobo marinade, chopped,
    or bottled chipotle salsa

175 ml/6 fl oz sour cream

$1/2$ onion, chopped

handful of lettuce leaves

5 radishes, diced

method

1 Heat the tortillas through, in an unoiled non-stick frying pan, in a stack, alternating the tortillas from the top to the bottom so that they warm evenly. Wrap in foil or a clean tea towel to keep them warm.

2 Heat the oil in a frying pan. Add the chicken and heat through. Season with salt and pepper.

3 Combine the warmed refried beans with the cumin and oregano.

4 Spread one tortilla with the refried beans, then top with a spoonful of the chicken, a slice or two of avocado, a little salsa, chipotle to taste, a spoonful of sour cream and a sprinkling of onion, lettuce and radishes. Season with salt and pepper, then roll up as tightly as you can. Repeat with the remaining tortillas and serve at once.

bacon-wrapped chicken burgers

ingredients

SERVES 4

450 g/1 lb fresh chicken
   mince
1 onion, grated
2 garlic cloves, crushed
55 g/2 oz pine kernels, toasted
55 g/2 oz Gruyère cheese,
   grated
2 tbsp fresh snipped chives
salt and pepper
2 tbsp wholewheat flour
8 lean bacon slices
1–2 tbsp corn oil
crusty rolls, chopped lettuce
   and red onion rings,
   to serve
mayonnaise and snipped
   chives, to garnish

method

1 Place the chicken mince, onion, garlic, pine kernels, cheese, chives and salt and pepper in a food processor. Using the pulse button, blend the mixture together using short sharp bursts. Scrape out onto a board and shape into 4 even-size burgers. Coat in the flour, then cover and chill for 1 hour.

2 Wrap each burger with 2 bacon slices, securing in place with a wooden cocktail stick.

3 Heat a heavy-based frying pan and add the oil. When hot, add the burgers and cook over medium heat for 5–6 minutes on each side, or until thoroughly cooked through.

4 Serve the burgers immediately in crusty rolls on a bed of lettuce and red onion rings and topped with mayonnaise and chives.

chicken tagine

ingredients

SERVES 4

1 tbsp olive oil

1 onion, cut into small wedges

2–4 garlic cloves, sliced

450 g/1 lb skinless, boneless
  chicken breast, diced

1 tsp ground cumin

2 cinnamon sticks, lightly
  bruised

1 tbsp plain wholewheat flour

225 g/8 oz aubergine, diced

1 red pepper, deseeded and
  chopped

85 g/3 oz white mushrooms,
  sliced

1 tbsp tomato purée

600 ml/1 pint chicken stock

280 g/10 oz canned
  chickpeas, drained and
  rinsed

55 g/2 oz no-soak dried
  apricots, chopped

salt and pepper

1 tbsp chopped fresh
  coriander

method

1 Heat the oil in a large saucepan over medium heat, add the onion and garlic and cook for 3 minutes, stirring frequently. Add the chicken and cook, stirring constantly, for a further 5 minutes, or until sealed on all sides. Add the cumin and cinnamon sticks to the pan halfway through sealing the chicken.

2 Sprinkle in the flour and cook, stirring constantly, for 2 minutes. Add the aubergine, red pepper and mushrooms and cook for a further 2 minutes, stirring constantly.

3 Blend the tomato purée with the stock, stir into the pan and bring to the boil. Reduce the heat and add the chickpeas and apricots. Cover and simmer for 15–20 minutes, or until the chicken is tender.

4 Season with salt and pepper and serve at once, sprinkled with coriander.

chicken risotto with saffron

ingredients

SERVES 4

125 g/4¹/₂ oz butter

900 g/2 lb skinless, boneless
   chicken breasts,
   thinly sliced

1 large onion, chopped

500 g/1 lb 2 oz Arborio rice

150 ml/5 fl oz white wine

1 tsp crumbled saffron threads

1.4 litres/2¹/₂ pints simmering
   chicken stock

salt and pepper

55 g/2 oz freshly grated
   Parmesan cheese

method

1 Heat 55 g/2 oz of the butter in a deep saucepan, add the chicken and onion and cook, stirring frequently, for 8 minutes, or until golden brown. Add the rice and mix to coat in the butter. Cook, stirring constantly for 2–3 minutes, or until the grains are translucent. Add the wine and cook, stirring constantly, for 1 minute until reduced.

2 Mix the saffron with 4 tablespoons of the hot stock. Add the liquid to the rice and cook, stirring constantly, until it is absorbed. Gradually add the remaining hot stock, a ladleful at a time. Stir constantly and add more liquid as the rice absorbs each addition. Cook for 20 minutes, or until all the liquid is absorbed and the rice is creamy. Season with salt and pepper.

3 Remove the risotto from the heat and add the remaining butter. Mix well, then stir in the Parmesan until it melts. Spoon the risotto onto warmed plates and serve at once.

chicken, mushroom & cashew risotto

ingredients

SERVES 4

55 g/2 oz butter

1 onion, chopped

250 g/9 oz skinless, boneless
    chicken breasts, diced

350 g/12 oz Arborio rice

1 tsp ground turmeric

150 ml/5 fl oz white wine

1.4 litres/2½ pints simmering
    chicken stock

75 g/2¾ oz chestnut
    mushrooms, sliced

50 g/1¾ oz cashews, halved

salt and pepper

wild rocket, fresh Parmesan
    cheese shavings, and
    fresh basil leaves,
    to garnish

method

1 Melt the butter in a large saucepan over medium heat. Add the onion and cook, stirring occasionally, for 5 minutes, or until softened. Add the chicken and cook, stirring frequently, for a further 5 minutes. Reduce the heat, add the rice and mix to coat in butter. Cook, stirring constantly, for 2–3 minutes, or until the grains are translucent. Stir in the turmeric, then add the wine. Cook, stirring constantly, for 1 minute until reduced.

2 Gradually add the hot stock, a ladleful at a time. Stir constantly and add more liquid as the rice absorbs each addition. Increase the heat to medium so that the liquid bubbles. Cook for 20 minutes, or until all the liquid is absorbed and the rice is creamy. About 3 minutes before the end of the cooking time, stir in the mushrooms and cashews. Season with salt and pepper.

3 Arrange the rocket leaves on 4 individual serving plates. Remove the risotto from the heat and spoon it over the rocket. Sprinkle over the Parmesan shavings and basil leaves and serve.

chicken & duck paella with orange

ingredients

SERVES 4–6

1/2 tsp saffron threads

2 tbsp hot water

175 g/6 oz skinless, boneless chicken breast

4 large skinless, boneless duck breasts

salt and pepper

2 tbsp olive oil

1 large onion, chopped

2 garlic cloves, crushed

1 tsp paprika

225 g/8 oz tomato wedges

1 orange pepper, grilled, peeled, deseeded and chopped

175 g/6 oz canned red kidney beans (drained weight)

375 g/13 oz paella rice

1 tbsp chopped fresh flat-leaf parsley, plus extra sprigs to garnish

1 tbsp freshly grated orange rind

2 tbsp orange juice

100 ml/3 1/2 fl oz white wine

1.2 litres/2 pints simmering chicken stock

orange wedges, to garnish

method

1 Put the saffron threads and water in a small bowl and infuse for a few minutes.

2 Cut the chicken and duck into bite-size chunks and season. Heat the oil in a paella pan and cook the chicken and duck over medium–high heat, stirring, until golden all over. Transfer to a bowl and set aside.

3 Add the onion and cook over medium heat, stirring, until softened. Add the garlic, paprika and saffron and its soaking liquid and cook, stirring constantly, for 1 minute. Add the tomato wedges, orange pepper and beans and cook, stirring, for a further 2 minutes.

4 Add the rice and parsley and cook, stirring, for 1 minute. Add the orange rind and juice, the wine and most of the hot stock. Bring to the boil, then simmer, uncovered, for 10 minutes. Do not stir during cooking, but shake the pan once or twice, and when adding ingredients. Return the chicken and duck to the pan and season. Cook for 10–15 minutes, or until the rice grains are plump and cooked, adding a little more stock if necessary.

5 When all the liquid has been absorbed and you detect a faint toasty aroma coming from the rice, remove from the heat. Cover with foil and stand for 5 minutes. Garnish with parsley sprigs and orange wedges to serve.

jambalaya

ingredients

SERVES 4

400 g/14 oz skinless, boneless
   chicken breast, diced

1 red onion, diced

1 garlic clove, crushed

600 ml/1 pint chicken stock

400 g/14 oz canned chopped
   tomatoes in tomato juice

280 g/10 oz brown rice

1–2 tsp hot chilli powder

1/2 tsp paprika

1 tsp dried oregano

1 red pepper, deseeded
   and diced

1 yellow pepper, deseeded
   and diced

85 g/3 oz frozen sweetcorn
   kernels

85 g/3 oz frozen peas

3 tbsp chopped fresh parsley

pepper

crisp salad leaves, to serve
   (optional)

method

1 Put the chicken, onion, garlic, stock, tomatoes and rice into a large, heavy-based saucepan. Add the chilli powder, paprika and oregano and stir well. Bring to the boil, then reduce the heat, cover and simmer for 25 minutes.

2 Add the red and yellow peppers, sweetcorn and peas to the rice mixture and return to the boil. Reduce the heat, cover and simmer for a further 10 minutes, or until the rice is just tender (brown rice retains a 'nutty' texture when cooked) and most of the stock has been absorbed but is not completely dry.

3 Stir in 2 tablespoons of the parsley and season with pepper. Transfer the jambalaya to a warmed serving dish, garnish with the remaining parsley, and serve with crisp salad leaves, if using.

egg-fried rice with chicken

ingredients

SERVES 4

225 g/8 oz jasmine rice

3 skinless, boneless chicken
   breasts, cut into cubes

400 ml/14 fl oz canned
   coconut milk

50 g/1³/₄ oz block creamed
   coconut, chopped

2–3 coriander roots, chopped

thinly pared rind of 1 lemon

1 fresh green chilli, deseeded
   and chopped

3 fresh Thai basil leaves

1 tbsp fish sauce

1 tbsp oil

3 eggs, beaten

fresh chives and sprigs fresh
   coriander, to garnish

method

1 Cook the rice in boiling water for
12–15 minutes, drain well, then cool and
chill overnight.

2 Put the chicken into a saucepan and cover
with the coconut milk. Add the creamed
coconut, coriander roots, lemon rind and chilli
and bring to the boil. Simmer for 8–10 minutes,
until the chicken is tender. Remove from the
heat. Stir in the basil and fish sauce.

3 Meanwhile, heat the oil in a wok and stir-fry
the rice for 2–3 minutes. Pour in the eggs and
stir until they have cooked and mixed with the
rice. Line 4 small ovenproof bowls or ramekins
with clingfilm and pack with the rice. Turn out
carefully onto serving plates and remove the
clingfilm. Garnish with long chives and sprigs
of coriander. Serve with the chicken.

chicken with vegetables & coriander rice

ingredients

SERVES 4

2 tbsp vegetable or peanut oil

1 red onion, chopped

2 garlic cloves, chopped

2.5-cm/1-inch piece root
　　ginger, peeled and
　　chopped

2 skinless, boneless chicken
　　breasts, cut into strips

115 g/4 oz white mushrooms

400 g/14 oz canned coconut
　　milk

55 g/2 oz sugar snap peas,
　　trimmed and halved
　　lengthways

2 tbsp soy sauce

1 tbsp fish sauce

rice

1 tbsp vegetable or peanut oil

1 red onion, sliced

350 g/12 oz rice, cooked and
　　cooled

225 g/8 oz pak choi, torn into
　　large pieces

handful of fresh coriander,
　　chopped

2 tbsp Thai soy sauce

method

1 Heat the oil in a wok or large frying pan and sauté the onion, garlic and ginger together for 1–2 minutes.

2 Add the chicken and mushrooms and cook over high heat until browned. Add the coconut milk, sugar snap peas and sauces and bring to the boil. Simmer gently for 4–5 minutes until tender.

3 Heat the oil for the rice in a separate wok or large frying pan and cook the onion until softened, but not browned. Add the cooked rice, pak choi and fresh coriander and heat gently until the leaves have wilted and the rice is hot. Sprinkle over the soy sauce and serve immediately with the chicken.

meat

Meat is the mainstay of many family menus, but it is incredibly easy to get stuck in a rut of eating the same sort of chops, steak, sausages and mince simply because these are all straightforward to prepare and can be cooked quickly. Of course there's nothing wrong with that, but you may be surprised to find out how with a little know-how, and a handful of additional ingredients, you can easily transform these simple cuts and meat products into truly special meals in minutes.

All these recipes have been inspired by everyday dishes from across the world. Even in countries where it was once traditional to lavish hours on preparing the day's main meal, twenty-first century cooks have busy lives and so have developed straightforward, speedy dishes that still retain all the character of their local cuisine. So it's really easy to extend your repertoire and ring the changes at the family dinner table with Italian pasta, Thai stir-fry, Greek kebabs or Spanish sausage casserole, for example.

There's a wealth of recipes for beef, lamb and pork, as well as delicious dishes based on bacon and sausages. You're sure to find an easy-to-cook dish that suits your taste and budget and there are also intriguing international versions of familiar favourites. As many of them include pasta, noodles, rice or potatoes and vegetables, they constitute a complete main

course and you won't have to spend time and energy preparing accompaniments. Lots of others require nothing more complicated than a simple salad and some fresh bread to turn them into a veritable feast.

spaghetti with meatballs

ingredients

SERVES 6

1 potato, diced

salt and pepper

400 g/14 oz steak mince

1 onion, finely chopped

1 egg

4 tbsp chopped fresh flat-leaf
    parsley

plain flour, for dusting

5 tbsp virgin olive oil

400 ml/14 fl oz passata

2 tbsp tomato purée

400 g/14 oz dried spaghetti

6 fresh basil leaves, shredded

freshly grated Parmesan
    cheese, to garnish

method

1 Place the potato in a small saucepan, add cold water to cover and a pinch of salt, and bring to the boil. Cook for 10–15 minutes, until tender, then drain. Either mash thoroughly with a potato masher or fork or pass through a potato ricer.

2 Combine the potato, steak, onion, egg and parsley in a bowl and season to taste with salt and pepper. Spread out the flour on a plate. With dampened hands, shape the meat mixture into walnut-size balls and roll in the flour. Shake off any excess.

3 Heat the oil in a heavy-based frying pan, add the meatballs and cook over a medium heat, stirring and turning frequently, for 8–10 minutes, until golden all over.

4 Add the passata and tomato purée and cook for a further 10 minutes, until the sauce is reduced and thickened.

5 Meanwhile, bring a large saucepan of lightly salted water to the boil. Add the pasta, bring back to the boil and cook for 8–10 minutes, until tender but still firm to the bite.

6 Drain well and add to the meatball sauce, tossing well to coat. Transfer to a warmed serving dish, garnish with the basil leaves and Parmesan and serve immediately.

tagliatelle with a rich meat sauce

ingredients

SERVES 4

4 tbsp olive oil, plus extra
for drizzling

85 g/3 oz pancetta or rindless
lean bacon, diced

1 onion, chopped

1 garlic clove, finely chopped

1 carrot, chopped

1 celery stick, chopped

225 g/8 oz steak mince

225 g/8 oz chicken livers,
chopped

2 tbsp passata

125 ml/4 fl oz dry white wine

225 ml/8 fl oz beef stock
or water

1 tbsp chopped fresh oregano

1 bay leaf

salt and pepper

450 g/1 lb dried tagliatelle

freshly grated Parmesan
cheese, to serve

method

1 Heat the olive oil in a large heavy-based saucepan. Add the pancetta or bacon and cook over a medium heat, stirring occasionally, for 3–5 minutes, until it is just turning brown. Add the onion, garlic, carrot and celery and cook, stirring occasionally, for a further 5 minutes.

2 Add the steak and cook over a high heat, breaking up the meat with a wooden spoon, for 5 minutes, until browned. Stir in the chicken livers and cook, stirring occasionally, for 2–3 minutes. Add the passata, wine, stock, oregano and bay leaf, and season to taste with salt and pepper. Bring to the boil, reduce the heat, cover and simmer for 30–35 minutes.

3 When the sauce is almost cooked, bring a large saucepan of lightly salted water to the boil. Add the pasta, bring back to the boil and cook for 8–10 minutes, until tender but still firm to the bite. Drain, transfer to a warmed serving dish, drizzle with a little olive oil and toss well.

4 Remove and discard the bay leaf from the sauce, then pour the sauce over the pasta, toss again and serve immediately with the grated Parmesan.

grilled steak with tomatoes & garlic

ingredients

SERVES 4

3 tbsp olive oil, plus extra
    for brushing

700 g/1 lb 9 oz tomatoes,
    peeled and chopped

1 red pepper, deseeded
    and chopped

1 onion, chopped

2 garlic cloves, finely chopped

1 tbsp chopped fresh flat-leaf
    parsley

1 tsp dried oregano

1 tsp sugar

salt and pepper

4 x 175-g/6-oz entrecôte or
    rump steaks

method

1 Place the oil, tomatoes, red pepper, onion, garlic, parsley, oregano and sugar in a heavy-based saucepan and season to taste with salt and pepper. Bring to the boil, reduce the heat and simmer for 15 minutes.

2 Meanwhile, trim any fat around the outsides of the steaks. Season each generously with pepper (but no salt) and brush with olive oil. Cook under a preheated grill according to taste: 2–3 minutes each side for rare; 3–4 minutes each side for medium and 4–5 minutes on each side for well done.

3 Transfer the steaks to warmed individual plates and spoon the sauce over them. Serve immediately.

beef chop suey

ingredients

SERVES 4

450 g/1 lb ribeye or sirloin
    steak, finely sliced
1 head of broccoli, cut into
    small florets
2 tbsp vegetable or peanut oil
1 onion, finely sliced
2 celery sticks, finely sliced
    diagonally
225 g/8 oz mangetout, sliced
    in half lengthways
55 g/2 oz fresh or canned
    bamboo shoots, rinsed and
    julienned (if using fresh
    shoots, boil in water first for
    30 minutes)
8 water chestnuts, finely sliced
225 g/8 oz finely sliced
    mushrooms
1 tbsp oyster sauce
1 tsp salt

marinade
1 tbsp Shaoxing rice wine
pinch of white pepper
pinch of salt
1 tbsp light soy sauce
1/2 tsp sesame oil

method

1 Combine all the marinade ingredients in a bowl and marinate the beef for at least 20 minutes. Blanch the broccoli florets in a large saucepan of boiling water for 30 seconds. Drain and set aside.

2 In a preheated wok or deep saucepan, heat 1 tablespoon of the oil and stir-fry the beef until the colour has changed. Remove and set aside.

3 In the clean wok or deep saucepan, heat the remaining oil and stir-fry the onion for 1 minute. Add the celery and broccoli and cook for 2 minutes. Add the mangetout, bamboo shoots, chestnuts and mushrooms and cook for 1 minute. Add the beef, then season with the oyster sauce and salt and serve immediately.

hot sesame beef

ingredients

SERVES 4

500 g/1 lb 2 oz beef fillet, cut
    into thin strips

1¹/₂ tbsp sesame seeds

125 ml/4 fl oz beef stock

2 tbsp soy sauce

2 tbsp grated fresh ginger

2 garlic cloves, finely chopped

1 tsp cornflour

¹/₂ tsp chilli flakes

3 tbsp sesame oil

1 large head of broccoli, cut
    into florets

1 orange pepper, thinly sliced

1 red chilli, seeded and finely
    sliced

1 tbsp chilli oil, to taste

1 tbsp chopped fresh
    coriander, to garnish

method

1 Mix the beef strips with 1 tablespoon of the sesame seeds in a small bowl. In a separate bowl, whisk together the beef stock, soy sauce, ginger, garlic, cornflour and chilli flakes.

2 Heat 1 tablespoon of the sesame oil in a large frying pan or wok. Stir-fry the beef strips for 2–3 minutes. Remove and set aside.

3 Discard any oil left in the pan, then wipe with kitchen paper to remove any stray sesame seeds. Heat the remaining oil, add the broccoli, orange pepper, chilli and chilli oil, if using, and stir-fry for 2–3 minutes. Stir in the beef stock mixture, cover and simmer for 2 minutes.

4 Return the beef to the frying pan and simmer until the juices thicken, stirring occasionally. Cook for another 1–2 minutes.

5 Sprinkle with the remaining sesame seeds. Serve garnished with chopped coriander.

rice sticks with beef in black bean sauce

ingredients

SERVES 4

225 g/8 oz rump steak,
    finely sliced
225 g/8 oz rice sticks
2–3 tbsp vegetable or
    peanut oil
1 small onion, finely sliced
1 green pepper, finely sliced
1 red pepper, finely sliced
2 tbsp black bean sauce
2–3 tbsp light soy sauce

marinade
1 tbsp dark soy sauce
1 tsp Shaoxing rice wine
$1/2$ tsp sugar
$1/2$ tsp white pepper

method

1 Combine all the marinade ingredients in a bowl, add the beef and marinate for at least 20 minutes.

2 Cook the rice sticks according to the directions on the packet. When cooked, drain and set aside.

3 In a preheated wok or deep saucepan, heat the oil and stir-fry the beef for 1 minute, or until the meat has changed colour. Drain the meat and set aside.

4 Pour off any excess oil from the wok and stir-fry the onion and peppers for 1 minute. Add the black bean sauce and stir well, then pour in the light soy sauce. Toss the rice sticks in the vegetables and when fully incorporated, add the beef and stir until warmed through. Serve immediately.

beef stir-fry

ingredients

SERVES 4

2 tbsp vegetable or peanut oil

2 medium red onions,
     sliced thinly

2 garlic cloves, chopped

2.5-cm/1-inch piece fresh root
     ginger, cut into thin sticks

2 x 115 g/4-oz beef fillets,
     sliced thinly

1 green pepper, deseeded and
     sliced

150 g/5½ oz canned bamboo
     shoots

115 g/4 oz beansprouts

2 tbsp magic paste

1 tbsp Thai red curry paste

handful of fresh coriander,
     chopped

a few sprigs Thai basil

boiled rice, to serve

method

1 Heat the oil in a wok or large frying pan and stir-fry the onions, garlic and ginger for 1 minute. Add the beef strips and stir-fry over high heat until browned all over. Add the vegetables and the two pastes and cook for 2–3 minutes until blended and cooked.

2 Stir in the coriander and basil and serve immediately with boiled rice.

beef with fresh noodles

ingredients

SERVES 4

6 dried black cloud Chinese
    mushrooms
2 tbsp vegetable or peanut oil
2 x 225-g/8-oz sirloin steaks,
    sliced thickly
1 onion, cut into thin wedges
2 garlic cloves, chopped
1 green pepper, deseeded and
    chopped
3 celery stalks, sliced
2 tbsp Thai green curry paste
300 ml/10 fl oz beef stock
4 tbsp black bean sauce
225 g/8 oz fresh egg noodles
4 tbsp chopped fresh parsley

method

1 Put the mushrooms in a bowl, cover with boiling water and set aside to soak for 30 minutes. Drain and break up any larger pieces.

2 Heat the oil in a wok and stir-fry the steak over high heat until browned. Add the mushrooms, onion, garlic, pepper and celery and stir-fry for 3–4 minutes. Add the curry paste, beef stock and black bean sauce and stir-fry for 2–3 minutes.

3 Meanwhile, cook the noodles in boiling water for 3–4 minutes, drain well, and stir into the wok. Sprinkle the parsley over and stir. Serve immediately.

beef chow mein

ingredients

SERVES 4

280 g/10 oz sirloin steak, cut
　　into slivers

225 g/8 oz dried egg noodles

2 tbsp vegetable or peanut oil

1 onion, finely sliced

1 green pepper, finely sliced

140 g/5 oz beansprouts,
　　trimmed

1 tsp salt

pinch of sugar

2 tsp Shaoxing rice wine

2 tbsp light soy sauce

1 tbsp dark soy sauce

1 tbsp finely shredded spring
　　onion

m a r i n a d e

1 tsp light soy sauce

dash of sesame oil

$1/2$ tsp Shaoxing rice wine

pinch of white pepper

method

1 Combine all the marinade ingredients in a bowl and marinate the beef for at least 20 minutes.

2 Cook the noodles according to the directions on the packet. When cooked, rinse under cold water and set aside.

3 In a preheated wok, heat the oil and stir-fry the beef for about 1 minute, or until the meat has changed colour, then add the onion and cook for 1 minute, followed by the pepper and beansprouts. Evaporate off any water from the vegetables. Add the salt, sugar, Shaoxing and soy sauces. Stir in the noodles and toss for 1 minute. Finally, stir in the spring onion and serve.

stir-fried beef with beansprouts

ingredients

SERVES 4

1 bunch of spring onions

2 tbsp corn oil

1 garlic clove, crushed

1 tsp finely chopped fresh root
    ginger

500 g/1 lb 2 oz lean beef fillet,
    cut into thin strips

1 large red pepper, deseeded
    and sliced

1 small fresh red chilli,
    deseeded and chopped

225 g/8 oz fresh beansprouts

1 small lemon grass stem,
    finely chopped

2 tbsp smooth peanut butter

4 tbsp coconut milk

1 tbsp rice vinegar or white
    wine vinegar

1 tbsp soy sauce

1 tsp brown sugar

250 g/9 oz medium egg
    noodles

salt and pepper

method

1 Thinly slice the spring onions, reserving some slices to use as a garnish.

2 Heat the oil in a frying pan or preheated wok over high heat. Add the spring onions, garlic and ginger and stir-fry for 2–3 minutes to soften. Add the beef and continue stir-frying for 4–5 minutes, or until evenly browned.

3 Add the pepper and stir-fry for a further 3–4 minutes. Add the chilli and beansprouts and stir-fry for 2 minutes. Mix the lemon grass, peanut butter, coconut milk, vinegar, soy sauce and sugar together in a bowl, then stir into the pan.

4 Meanwhile, cook the egg noodles in boiling salted water for 4 minutes, or according to the packet directions. Drain and stir into the pan, tossing to mix evenly.

5 Season to taste with salt and pepper. Sprinkle with the reserved spring onions and serve hot.

spicy beef with potato

ingredients

SERVES 4

450 g/1 lb beef fillet
2 tbsp Thai soy sauce
2 tbsp fish sauce
2 tbsp vegetable or peanut oil
3–4 coriander roots, chopped
1 tbsp crushed black
    peppercorns
2 garlic cloves, chopped
1 tbsp jaggery or soft light
    brown sugar
350 g/12 oz potatoes, diced
150 ml/5 fl oz water
bunch of spring onions,
    chopped
225 g/8 oz baby spinach
    leaves
cooked rice or noodles,
    to serve

method

1 Cut the beef into thick slices and place in a shallow dish. Put the soy sauce, fish sauce, 1 tablespoon of the oil, the coriander roots, peppercorns, garlic and sugar in a food processor and process to a thick paste.

2 Scrape the paste into the dish and toss the beef to coat. Cover with clingfilm and set aside to marinate in the refrigerator for at least 3 hours, preferably overnight.

3 Heat the remaining oil in a wok. Lift the beef out of the marinade, reserving the marinade, and cook for 3–4 minutes on each side, until browned. Add the reserved marinade and the potatoes with the measured water and gradually bring to the boil. Simmer for 6–8 minutes, or until the potatoes are tender.

4 Add the spring onions and spinach. Cook gently until the greens have wilted. Serve immediately with rice or noodles.

mussaman curry

ingredients

SERVES 4

1 tbsp vegetable or peanut oil

450 g/1 lb beef top round, cut into cubes

2 tbsp Mussaman curry paste

2 large onions, cut into wedges

2 large potatoes, cut into chunks

400 ml/14 fl oz coconut milk

150 ml/5 fl oz water

2 cardamom pods

2 tbsp tamarind paste

2 tsp jaggery or soft light brown sugar

75 g/2¾ oz unsalted peanuts, toasted or dry-fried

1 fresh red chilli, sliced thinly

boiled rice, to serve

method

1 Heat the oil in a wok and cook the meat, in batches, until browned all over. Remove with a slotted spoon and set aside.

2 Add the curry paste to the wok and stir-fry for 1–2 minutes. Add the onions and potatoes and stir–fry for 4–5 minutes, until golden brown. Remove with a slotted spoon and set aside.

3 Pour the coconut milk into the wok with the measured water and bring to the boil. Reduce the heat and simmer for 8–10 minutes.

4 Return the meat and cooked vegetables to the wok.

5 Add the cardamom, tamarind paste and sugar and simmer for 15–20 minutes, until the meat is tender. Stir in the peanuts and chilli and serve with rice.

hot beef & coconut curry

ingredients

SERVES 4

400 ml/14 fl oz coconut milk

2 tbsp Thai red curry paste

2 garlic cloves, crushed

500 g/1 lb 2 oz braising steak

2 fresh kaffir lime leaves,
    shredded

3 tbsp lime juice

2 tbsp Thai fish sauce

1 large fresh red chilli,
    deseeded and sliced

1/2 tsp ground turmeric

salt and pepper

2 tbsp chopped fresh basil
    leaves

2 tbsp chopped coriander
    leaves

shredded coconut, to garnish

freshly cooked rice, to serve

method

1 Place the coconut milk in a large saucepan and bring to the boil. Reduce the heat and simmer gently for 10 minutes, or until it has thickened. Stir in the curry paste and garlic and simmer for a further 5 minutes.

2 Cut the beef into 2-cm/3/4-inch chunks. Add to the pan and bring to the boil, stirring constantly. Reduce the heat and add the kaffir lime leaves, lime juice, fish sauce, sliced chilli, turmeric and 1/2 teaspoon of salt.

3 Cover the pan and continue simmering for 20–25 minutes, or until the meat is tender, adding a little water if the sauce looks too dry.

4 Stir in the basil and coriander and season to taste with salt and pepper. Sprinkle with shredded coconut and serve with freshly cooked rice.

egg-fried rice with seven-spice beef

ingredients

SERVES 4

225 g/8 oz long-grain
  white rice
600 ml/1 pint water
350 g/12 oz beef fillet
2 tbsp dark soy sauce
2 tbsp tomato ketchup
1 tbsp seven-spice seasoning
2 tbsp peanut oil
1 onion, diced
3 small carrots, diced
100 g/3½ oz frozen peas
2 eggs, beaten
2 tbsp cold water

method

1 Rinse the rice under cold running water, then drain thoroughly. Place the rice in a saucepan with the water, bring to the boil, cover and simmer for 12 minutes. Turn the cooked rice out onto a baking sheet and set aside to cool.

2 Using a sharp knife, thinly slice the beef fillet and place in a large, shallow dish. Mix the soy sauce, tomato ketchup and seven-spice seasoning. Spoon over the beef and toss well to coat.

3 Heat the peanut oil in a preheated wok. Add the beef and stir-fry for 3–4 minutes. Add the onion, carrots and peas and stir-fry for a further 2–3 minutes. Add the cooked rice to the wok and mix together.

4 Beat the eggs with 2 tablespoons of cold water. Drizzle the egg mixture over the rice and stir-fry for 3–4 minutes or until the rice is heated through and the egg has set. Transfer the rice and beef to a warm serving bowl and serve immediately.

greek-style beef kebabs

ingredients

SERVES 4

1 small onion, finely chopped

1 tbsp chopped fresh
   coriander

large pinch of paprika

1/4 tsp ground allspice

1/4 tsp ground coriander

1/4 tsp brown sugar

450 g/1 lb beef mince

salt and pepper

vegetable oil, for brushing

fresh coriander leaves,
   to garnish

freshly cooked bulgar wheat
   or rice, and mixed salad,
   to serve

method

1 If you are using wooden skewers, soak them in cold water for 30 minutes before use.

2 Put the onion, fresh coriander, spices, sugar and beef into a large bowl and mix until well combined. Season with salt and pepper.

3 On a clean work surface, use your hands to shape the mixture into sausages around skewers. Brush them lightly with vegetable oil.

4 Grill the kebabs over hot coals, turning them frequently, for 15–20 minutes, or until cooked right through. Arrange the kebabs on a platter of freshly cooked bulgar wheat and garnish with fresh coriander leaves. Serve with a mixed salad.

beef skewers with orange & garlic

ingredients

SERVES 6–8

3 tbsp white wine

2 tbsp olive oil

3 garlic cloves, finely chopped

juice of 1 orange

450 g/1 lb rump steak, cubed

salt and pepper

450 g/1 lb baby onions, halved

2 orange peppers, deseeded
    and cut into squares

225 g/8 oz cherry tomatoes,
    halved

method

1 Mix the wine, olive oil, garlic and orange juice together in a shallow, non-metallic dish. Add the cubes of steak, season to taste with salt and pepper and toss to coat. Cover with clingfilm and marinate in the refrigerator for 2–8 hours.

2 Preheat the grill to high. Drain the steak, reserving the marinade. Thread the steak, onions, peppers and tomatoes alternately onto several small skewers.

3 Cook the skewers under the hot grill, turning and brushing frequently with the marinade, for 10 minutes or until cooked through. Transfer to warmed serving plates and serve immediately.

red lamb curry

ingredients

SERVES 4

2 tbsp vegetable oil

1 large onion, sliced

2 garlic cloves, crushed

500 g/1 lb 2 oz lean boneless
   leg of lamb, cut into 3-cm/
   1¼-inch cubes

2 tbsp Thai red curry paste

150 ml/5 fl oz coconut milk

1 tbsp brown sugar

1 large red pepper, deseeded
   and thickly sliced

150 ml/5 fl oz lamb or beef
   stock

1 tbsp Thai fish sauce

2 tbsp lime juice

225 g/8 oz canned water
   chestnuts, drained

2 tbsp chopped coriander

2 tbsp chopped fresh basil

salt and pepper

fresh basil leaves, to garnish

freshly cooked jasmine rice,
   to serve

method

1 Heat the oil in a large frying pan or preheated wok over high heat. Add the onion and garlic and stir-fry for 2–3 minutes to soften. Add the meat and stir-fry the mixture quickly until lightly browned.

2 Stir in the curry paste and cook for a few seconds, then add the coconut milk and sugar and bring to the boil. Reduce the heat and simmer for 15 minutes, stirring occasionally.

3 Stir in the pepper, stock, fish sauce and lime juice, then cover and simmer for a further 15 minutes, or until the meat is tender.

4 Add the water chestnuts, coriander and basil and season to taste with salt and pepper. Transfer to serving plates, then garnish with basil leaves and serve with jasmine rice.

lamb with lime leaves

ingredients

SERVES 4

2 fresh red Thai chillies

2 tbsp peanut oil

2 garlic cloves, crushed

4 shallots, chopped

2 lemon grass stems, sliced

6 fresh kaffir lime leaves

1 tbsp tamarind paste

2 tbsp palm sugar

450 g/1 lb lean boneless lamb
   (leg or loin fillet)

300 ml/10 fl oz coconut milk

175 g/6 oz cherry tomatoes,
   halved

1 tbsp chopped coriander

freshly cooked Thai fragrant
   rice, to serve

method

1 Using a sharp knife, deseed and very finely chop the chillies. Reserve until required.

2 Heat the oil in a large, preheated wok. Add the garlic, shallots, lemon grass, lime leaves, tamarind paste, sugar and chillies to the wok and stir-fry for 2 minutes.

3 Using a sharp knife, cut the lamb into thin strips or cubes.

4 Add the lamb to the wok and stir-fry for 5 minutes, tossing well so that the lamb is evenly coated in the spice mixture.

5 Pour the coconut milk into the wok and bring to the boil. Reduce the heat and simmer for 20 minutes.

6 Add the cherry tomatoes and chopped coriander to the wok and simmer for 5 minutes. Transfer to serving plates and serve hot with fragrant rice.

stir-fried lamb with mint

ingredients

SERVES 4

2 tbsp vegetable oil

2 garlic cloves, finely sliced

2 fresh red chillies, deseeded
    and cut into thin strips

1 onion, thinly sliced

$1^1/_2$ tbsp Madras curry paste

500 g/1 lb 2 oz lamb fillet,
    cut into thin strips

225 g/8 oz canned baby corn
    cobs, drained

4 spring onions, finely
    chopped

55 g/2 oz fresh mint leaves,
    coarsely shredded

1 tbsp Thai fish sauce

freshly cooked rice, to serve

method

1 Heat half the oil in a preheated wok or large frying pan. Add the garlic and chillies and cook until soft. Remove and reserve. Add the onion and cook for 5 minutes, or until soft. Remove and reserve.

2 Heat the remaining oil in the wok. Add the curry paste and cook for 1 minute. Add the lamb, in batches if necessary, and cook for 5–8 minutes, or until cooked through and tender.

3 Return the onion to the wok with the baby corn cobs, spring onions, mint and fish sauce. Cook until heated through. Sprinkle the garlic and chillies over and serve with rice.

lamb skewers with lemon

ingredients

SERVES 8

2 garlic cloves, finely chopped

1 Spanish onion,
    finely chopped

2 tsp finely grated lemon rind

2 tbsp lemon juice

1 tsp fresh thyme leaves

1 tsp ground coriander

1 tsp ground cumin

2 tbsp red wine vinegar

125 ml/4 fl oz olive oil

1 kg/2 lb 4 oz lamb fillet, cut
    into 2-cm/³/₄-inch pieces

orange or lemon slices,
    to garnish

method

1 Mix the garlic, onion, lemon rind, lemon juice, thyme, coriander, cumin, vinegar and olive oil together in a large, shallow, non-metallic dish, whisking well until combined.

2 Thread the pieces of lamb onto 16 wooden skewers and add to the dish, turning well to coat. Cover with clingfilm and marinate in the refrigerator for 2–8 hours, turning occasionally.

3 Preheat the grill to medium. Drain the skewers, reserving the marinade. Cook under the hot grill, turning frequently and brushing with the marinade, for 10 minutes or until tender and cooked to your liking. Serve immediately, garnished with orange slices.

marinated lamb & vegetable kebabs

ingredients

SERVES 4

juice of 2 large lemons
100 ml/3¹/₂ fl oz olive oil, plus
  extra for oiling
1 garlic clove, crushed
1 tbsp chopped fresh oregano
  or mint
salt and pepper
700 g/1 lb 9 oz boned leg or
  fillet of lamb, trimmed and
  cut into 4-cm/1¹/₂-inch
  cubes
2 green peppers
2 courgettes
12 baby onions, peeled and
  left whole
8 large bay leaves
lemon wedges, to garnish
rice, to serve

cucumber &
yogurt dip
1 small cucumber
300 ml/10 fl oz Greek-style
  yogurt
1 large garlic clove, crushed
1 tbsp chopped fresh mint
  or dill
salt and pepper

method

1 To make the cucumber and yogurt dip, peel then coarsely grate the cucumber. Put in a sieve and squeeze out as much of the water as possible. Put the cucumber into a bowl. Add the yogurt, garlic and chopped mint, season with pepper and mix thoroughly. Chill in the refrigerator for 2 hours. Sprinkle with salt just before serving.

2 Put the lemon juice, oil, garlic, oregano, salt and pepper in a bowl and whisk together. Add the lamb to the marinade.

3 Toss the lamb in the marinade, cover and refrigerate overnight or for at least 8 hours. Stir occasionally to coat the lamb.

4 When ready to serve, core and deseed the peppers, and cut into 4-cm/1¹/₂-inch pieces. Cut the courgettes into 2.5-cm/1-inch pieces. Thread the lamb, peppers, courgettes, onions and bay leaves onto 8 flat, oiled metal kebab skewers, alternating and dividing the ingredients as evenly as possible. Place on an oiled grill pan.

5 Cook the kebabs under a preheated grill for 10–15 minutes, turning frequently and basting with any remaining marinade. Serve hot, garnished with lemon wedges, with rice and the cucumber and yogurt dip.

grecian meatballs

ingredients

SERVES 4

450 g/1 lb lean beef or lamb,
    finely minced

1 medium onion

1 garlic clove, crushed

25 g/1 oz fresh white or brown
    breadcrumbs

1 tbsp chopped fresh mint

1 tbsp chopped fresh parsley

salt and pepper

1 egg, beaten

olive oil, for brushing

rice or warm pitta bread,
    to serve

method

1 Put the beef mince in a bowl. Grate in the onion, then add the garlic, breadcrumbs, mint and parsley. Season well with salt and pepper. Mix the ingredients well then add the beaten egg and mix to bind the mixture together.

2 With damp hands, form the mixture into 16 small balls and thread onto 4 flat metal skewers. Lightly oil a grill pan and brush the meatballs with oil.

3 Preheat the grill and cook the meatballs under a medium heat for 10 minutes, turning frequently and brushing with more oil if necessary, until browned. Serve the meatballs with rice or tucked into warm pitta bread.

moussaka

ingredients

SERVES 4

2 aubergines, thinly sliced

450 g/1 lb fresh lean beef or
   lamb mince

2 onions, thinly sliced

1 tsp finely chopped garlic

400 g/14 oz canned tomatoes

2 tbsp chopped fresh parsley

salt and pepper

2 eggs

300 ml/10 fl oz Greek-style
   yogurt

1 tbsp freshly grated
   Parmesan cheese

method

1 Dry-fry the aubergine slices, in batches, in a non-stick frying pan on both sides until browned. Remove from the pan.

2 Add the beef to the frying pan and cook for 5 minutes, stirring, until browned. Stir in the onions and garlic and cook for a further 5 minutes or until browned. Add the tomatoes, parsley, salt and pepper, then bring to the boil and simmer for 20 minutes or until the meat is tender.

3 Arrange half the aubergine slices in a layer in an ovenproof dish. Add the meat mixture, then the remaining aubergine slices.

4 Beat the eggs in a bowl, then beat in the yogurt and add salt and pepper to taste. Pour the mixture over the aubergines and sprinkle the grated cheese on top.

5 Bake the moussaka in a preheated oven, 180°C/350°F/Gas Mark 4, for 45 minutes or until golden brown. Serve straight from the dish.

lamb with balsamic & rosemary marinade

ingredients

SERVES 4

6 racks of lamb, each with
   3 chops
fresh rosemary sprigs,
   to garnish

m a r i n a d e

3 tbsp chopped fresh
   rosemary
1 small onion, finely chopped
3 tbsp olive oil
1 tbsp balsamic vinegar
1 tbsp lemon juice
salt and pepper

method

1 Put the lamb in a large, shallow dish and sprinkle with the chopped rosemary and onion. Whisk together the olive oil, balsamic vinegar and lemon juice and season with salt and pepper.

2 Pour the balsamic mixture over the lamb, turning well to coat. Cover with clingfilm and set aside in a cool place to marinate for 1–2 hours.

3 Drain the lamb, reserving the marinade. Barbecue the racks over hot coals, brushing frequently with the reserved marinade, for 8–10 minutes on each side. Serve garnished with rosemary sprigs.

lamb with courgettes & tomatoes

ingredients

SERVES 4

4–8 lamb chops
salt and pepper
2 tbsp olive oil
1 onion, finely chopped
1 garlic clove, finely chopped
4 tbsp ouzo (optional)
400 g/14 oz canned tomatoes
   in juice
pinch of sugar
250 g/9 oz courgettes, sliced
2 tbsp chopped fresh thyme

method

1 Season the lamb chops with pepper. Heat the oil in a large, flameproof casserole, add the onion and garlic and fry for 5 minutes or until softened. Add the lamb chops and fry until browned on both sides.

2 Stir in the ouzo, if using, then add the tomatoes with their juice, sugar, courgettes and thyme. Season with salt.

3 Bring to the boil and then simmer for 30–45 minutes, stirring occasionally and turning the chops once during cooking, until the lamb and courgettes are tender. If necessary, add a little water during cooking.

4 Serve hot.

lamb stew with chickpeas

ingredients

SERVES 4–6

olive oil

225 g/8 oz chorizo sausage, cut into 5-mm/1/4-inch thick slices, casings removed

2 large onions, chopped

6 large garlic cloves, crushed

900 g/2 lb boned leg of lamb, cut into 5-cm/2-inch chunks

250 ml/9 fl oz lamb stock or water

125 ml/4 fl oz red wine, such as Rioja or Tempranillo

2 tbsp sherry vinegar

800 g/1 lb 12 oz canned chopped tomatoes

salt and pepper

4 sprigs fresh thyme

2 bay leaves

1/2 tsp sweet Spanish paprika

800 g/1 lb 12 oz canned chickpeas, rinsed and drained

sprigs fresh thyme, to garnish

method

1 Heat 4 tablespoons of oil in a large, heavy-based casserole over medium–high heat. Reduce the heat, add the chorizo and cook for 1 minute; set aside. Add the onions to the casserole and cook for 2 minutes, then add the garlic and continue cooking for 3 minutes or until the onions are soft but not brown. Remove from the casserole and set aside.

2 Heat a further 2 tablespoons of oil in the casserole. Add the lamb chunks in a single layer without overcrowding the casserole and cook until browned on each side; work in batches, if necessary.

3 Return the onion mixture to the casserole with all the lamb. Stir in the stock, wine, vinegar, tomatoes with their juices, and salt and pepper to taste. Bring to the boil, scraping any glazed bits from the bottom of the casserole. Reduce the heat and stir in the thyme, bay leaves and paprika.

4 Transfer to a preheated oven, 160°C/325°F/Gas Mark 3, and cook, covered, for 40–45 minutes until the lamb is tender. Stir in the chickpeas and return to the oven, uncovered, for 10 minutes or until they are heated through and the juices are reduced.

5 Taste and adjust the seasoning. Garnish with thyme and serve.

xinjiang rice pot with lamb

ingredients

SERVES 6–8

2 tbsp vegetable or peanut oil

300 g/10^1/$_2$ oz lamb or
    mutton, cut into bite-sized
    cubes

2 carrots, roughly chopped

2 onions, roughly chopped

1 tsp salt

1 tsp ground ginger

1 tsp Szechuan peppercorns,
    lightly roasted and lightly
    crushed

450 g/1 lb short- or medium-
    grain rice

850 ml/1^1/$_2$ pints water

method

1 In a large casserole, heat the oil and stir-fry the meat for 1–2 minutes, or until the pieces are sealed on all sides. Add the carrot and onion and stir-fry until the vegetables are beginning to soften. Add the salt, ginger and peppercorns and mix well.

2 Finally, add the rice and water and bring to the boil. Cover the pan and cook over a low heat for 30 minutes, or until the rice has absorbed all the water. Serve alone or as part of a meal.

xinjiang lamb casserole

ingredients

SERVES 5–6

1–2 tbsp vegetable or
   peanut oil

400 g/14 oz lamb or mutton,
   cut into bite-sized cubes

1 onion, roughly chopped

1 green pepper, roughly
   chopped

1 carrot, roughly chopped

1 turnip, roughly chopped

2 tomatoes, roughly chopped

2.5-cm/1-inch piece of fresh
   ginger, finely sliced

300 ml/10 fl oz water

1 tsp salt

method

1 In a preheated wok or deep saucepan, heat the oil and stir-fry the lamb for 1–2 minutes, or until the meat is sealed on all sides.

2 Transfer the meat to a large casserole and add all the other ingredients. Bring to the boil, then cover and simmer over a low heat for 35 minutes.

hot pepper lamb in red wine risotto

ingredients

SERVES 4

4 tbsp seasoned plain flour

8 pieces neck of lamb
   or lamb chops

4 tbsp olive oil

1 green pepper, deseeded and
   thinly sliced

1–2 fresh green chillies,
   deseeded and thinly sliced

2 small onions, 1 thinly sliced
   and 1 finely chopped

2 garlic cloves, thinly sliced

2 tbsp torn fresh basil

125 ml/4 fl oz red wine

4 tbsp red wine vinegar

8 cherry tomatoes

125 ml/4 fl oz water

3 tbsp butter

280 g/10 oz risotto rice

1.2 litres/2 pints simmering
   chicken stock

85 g/3 oz freshly grated
   Parmesan or Grana
   Padano cheese

salt and pepper

method

1 Coat the lamb in the seasoned flour, shaking off any excess. Heat 3 tablespoons of the oil in a large ovenproof casserole over high heat. Add the lamb and cook until browned all over. Remove from the casserole and set aside.

2 Toss the pepper, chillies, sliced onion, garlic and basil in the oil left in the casserole until lightly browned. Add the wine and vinegar, bring to the boil and cook for 3–4 minutes to reduce the liquid to 2 tablespoons. Add the tomatoes and the water, stir, and bring to the boil. Return the meat, cover, and cook over low heat for 30 minutes or until the meat is tender, turning occasionally.

3 To make the risotto, melt 2 tablespoons of the butter with the remaining oil in a saucepan over medium heat. Add the chopped onion and cook, stirring, until soft and starting to turn golden. Reduce the heat, add the rice, and mix to coat in oil and butter. Cook, stirring, for 2–3 minutes or until translucent. Add the hot stock, a ladleful at a time, stirring constantly, until all the liquid is absorbed and the rice is creamy. Season to taste.

4 Remove the risotto from the heat and stir in the remaining butter and the Parmesan. Serve topped with peppers, tomatoes and lamb.

linguine with lamb & yellow pepper sauce

ingredients

SERVES 4

4 tbsp olive oil

280 g/10 oz boneless lamb, cubed

1 garlic clove, finely chopped

1 bay leaf

125 ml/4 fl oz dry white wine

salt and pepper

2 large yellow peppers, deseeded and diced

4 tomatoes, peeled and chopped

250 g/9 oz dried linguine

method

1 Heat half the olive oil in a large, heavy-based frying pan. Add the lamb and cook over medium heat, stirring frequently, until browned on all sides. Add the garlic and cook for a further minute. Add the bay leaf, pour in the wine and season with salt and pepper. Bring to the boil and cook for 5 minutes, or until reduced.

2 Stir in the remaining oil, peppers and tomatoes. Reduce the heat, cover and simmer, stirring occasionally, for 45 minutes.

3 Meanwhile, bring a large, heavy-based saucepan of lightly salted water to the boil. Add the pasta, return to the boil and cook for 8–10 minutes, or until tender but still firm to the bite. Drain and transfer to a warmed serving dish. Remove and discard the bay leaf from the lamb sauce and spoon the sauce onto the pasta. Toss well and serve at once.

pan-fried pork with mozzarella

ingredients

SERVES 4

450 g/1 lb loin of pork

2–3 garlic cloves, finely
  chopped

175 g/6 oz buffalo mozzarella,
  drained

salt and pepper

12 slices prosciutto

12 fresh sage leaves

55 g/2 oz unsalted butter

flat-leaf parley sprigs and
  lemon slices, to garnish

mostarda di Verona, to serve

method

1 Trim any excess fat from the meat, then slice it crossways into 12 pieces, each about 2.5 cm/ 1 inch thick. Beat each slice with the flat end of a meat mallet or the side of a rolling pin until thoroughly flattened. Rub each piece all over with garlic, transfer to a plate and cover with clingfilm. Set aside in a cool place for 30 minutes–1 hour.

2 Cut the mozzarella into 12 slices. Season the pork to taste with salt and pepper, then place a slice of cheese on top of each slice of pork. Top with a slice of prosciutto, letting it fall in folds. Place a sage leaf on each portion and secure with a cocktail stick.

3 Melt the butter in a large heavy-based frying pan. Add the pork, in batches if necessary, and cook for 2–3 minutes on each side, until the meat is tender and the cheese has melted. Remove with a slotted spoon and keep warm while you cook the remaining pork.

4 Remove and discard the cocktail sticks. Transfer the pork to 4 warmed individual plates, garnish with parsley sprigs and lemon slices, and serve immediately with mostarda di Verona.

pork fillets with fennel

ingredients

SERVES 4

450 g/1 lb pork fillet

2–3 tbsp virgin olive oil

2 tbsp sambuca

1 large fennel bulb, sliced,
    fronds reserved

85 g/3 oz Gorgonzola cheese,
    crumbled

2 tbsp single cream

1 tbsp chopped fresh sage

1 tbsp chopped fresh thyme

salt and pepper

method

1 Trim any fat from the pork and cut into 5-mm/¼-inch-thick slices. Place the slices between 2 sheets of clingfilm and beat with the flat end of a meat mallet or with a rolling pin to flatten slightly.

2 Heat 2 tablespoons of the oil in a heavy-based frying pan and add the pork, in batches. Cook over a medium heat for 2–3 minutes on each side, until tender. Remove from the pan and keep warm. Cook the remaining batches, adding more oil if necessary.

3 Stir the sambuca into the frying pan, increase the heat and cook, stirring constantly and scraping up the glazed bits from the bottom. Add the fennel and cook, stirring and turning frequently, for 3 minutes. Remove from the pan and keep warm.

4 Reduce the heat, add the Gorgonzola and cream and cook, stirring constantly, until smooth. Remove the pan from the heat, stir in the sage and thyme and season to taste with salt and pepper.

5 Divide the pork and fennel between 4 warmed individual serving plates and pour over the sauce. Garnish with the reserved fennel fronds and serve immediately.

spaghetti alla carbonara

ingredients

SERVES 4

450 g/1 lb dried spaghetti

1 tbsp olive oil

225 g/8 oz rindless pancetta
  or lean bacon, chopped

4 eggs

5 tbsp single cream

salt and pepper

4 tbsp freshly grated
  Parmesan cheese

method

1 Bring a large heavy-based saucepan of lightly salted water to the boil. Add the pasta, return to the boil and cook for 8–10 minutes, or until tender but still firm to the bite.

2 Meanwhile, heat the olive oil in a heavy-based frying pan. Add the chopped pancetta and cook over a medium heat, stirring frequently, for 8–10 minutes.

3 Beat the eggs with the cream in a small bowl and season to taste with salt and pepper. Drain the pasta and return it to the pan. Tip in the contents of the frying pan, then add the egg mixture and half the Parmesan cheese. Stir well, then transfer to a warmed serving dish. Serve immediately, sprinkled with the remaining Parmesan cheese.

linguine with bacon & olives

ingredients

SERVES 4

3 tbsp olive oil

2 onions, thinly sliced

2 garlic cloves, finely chopped

175 g/6 oz rindless lean
    bacon, diced

225 g/8 oz mushrooms, sliced

5 canned anchovy fillets,
    drained

6 black olives, stoned and
    halved

salt and pepper

450 g/1 lb dried linguine

25 g/1 oz freshly grated
    Parmesan cheese

method

1 Heat the olive oil in a large frying pan. Add the onions, garlic and bacon and cook over low heat, stirring occasionally, until the onions are softened. Stir in the mushrooms, anchovies and olives, then season with salt, if necessary, and pepper. Simmer for 5 minutes.

2 Meanwhile, bring a large heavy-based saucepan of lightly salted water to the boil. Add the pasta, return to the boil and cook for 8–10 minutes, or until tender but still firm to the bite.

3 Drain the pasta and transfer to a warmed serving dish. Spoon the sauce on top, toss lightly and sprinkle with the Parmesan cheese. Serve immediately.

chilli pork with tagliatelle

ingredients

SERVES 4

450 g/1 lb dried tagliatelle

3 tbsp peanut oil

350 g/12 oz pork fillet,
    cut into thin strips

1 garlic clove, finely chopped

1 bunch of spring onions,
    sliced

2.5-cm/1-inch piece fresh root
    ginger, grated

2 fresh Thai chillies, deseeded
    and finely chopped

1 red pepper, deseeded and
    cut into thin sticks

1 yellow pepper, deseeded
    and cut into thin sticks

3 courgettes cut into thin
    sticks

2 tbsp finely chopped peanuts

1 tsp ground cinnamon

1 tbsp oyster sauce

55 g/2 oz creamed coconut,
    grated

salt and pepper

2 tbsp chopped fresh
    coriander, to garnish

method

1 Bring a large, heavy-based saucepan of lightly salted water to the boil. Add the pasta, return to the boil and cook for 8–10 minutes, or until tender but still firm to the bite.

2 Meanwhile, heat the peanut oil in a preheated wok or large, heavy-based frying pan. Add the pork and stir-fry for 5 minutes. Add the garlic, spring onions, ginger and Thai chillies and stir-fry for 2 minutes.

3 Add the red and yellow peppers and the courgettes and stir-fry for 1 minute. Add the peanuts, cinnamon, oyster sauce and creamed coconut and stir-fry for a further 1 minute. Season with salt and pepper. Drain the pasta and transfer to a serving dish. Top with the chilli pork, sprinkle with the chopped coriander and serve.

macaroni with sausage, pepperoncini & olives

ingredients

SERVES 4

1 tbsp olive oil

1 large onion, chopped finely

2 garlic cloves, crushed

450 g/1 lb pork sausage, peeled and chopped coarsely

3 canned pepperoncini, or other hot red peppers, drained and sliced

400 g/14 oz canned chopped tomatoes

2 tsp dried oregano

125 ml/4 fl oz chicken stock or red wine

salt and pepper

450 g/1 lb dried macaroni

12–15 black olives, stoned and cut into quarters

75 g/2³/₄ oz freshly grated cheese, such as Cheddar or Gruyère

method

1 Heat the oil in a large frying pan over medium heat. Add the onion and fry for 5 minutes until soft. Add the garlic and fry for a few seconds until just beginning to colour. Add the sausage and fry until evenly browned.

2 Stir in the pepperoncini, tomatoes, oregano and stock. Season with salt and pepper. Bring to the boil, then simmer over medium heat for 10 minutes, stirring occasionally.

3 Cook the macaroni in plenty of boiling salted water until tender but still firm to the bite. Drain and transfer to a warmed serving dish.

4 Add the olives and half the cheese to the sauce, then stir until the cheese has melted. Pour the sauce over the pasta. Toss well to mix. Sprinkle with the remaining cheese and serve at once.

rigatoni with ham, tomato & chilli sauce

ingredients

SERVES 4

1 tbsp olive oil

2 tbsp butter

1 onion, chopped finely

150 g/5½ oz ham, diced

2 garlic cloves, chopped
    very finely

1 fresh red chilli, deseeded
    and chopped finely

800 g/1 lb 12 oz canned
    chopped tomatoes

salt and pepper

450 g/1 lb rigatoni or penne

2 tbsp chopped fresh flat-leaf
    parsley

6 tbsp freshly grated
    Parmesan cheese

method

1 Put the olive oil and 1 tablespoon of the butter in a large saucepan over medium–low heat. Add the onion and fry for 10 minutes until soft and golden. Add the ham and fry for 5 minutes until lightly browned. Stir in the garlic, chilli and tomatoes. Season with a little salt and pepper. Bring to the boil, then simmer over medium–low heat for 30–40 minutes until thickened.

2 Cook the pasta in plenty of boiling salted water until tender but still firm to the bite. Drain and transfer to a warmed serving dish.

3 Pour the sauce over the pasta. Add the parsley, Parmesan cheese and the remaining butter. Toss well to mix and serve immediately.

pork lo mein

ingredients

SERVES 4–6

175 g/6 oz boneless lean pork, shredded

225 g/8 oz egg noodles

1 1/2 tbsp vegetable or peanut oil

2 tsp finely chopped garlic

1 tsp finely chopped fresh ginger

1 carrot, julienned

225 g/8 oz finely sliced mushrooms

1 green pepper, thinly sliced

1 tsp salt

125 ml/4 fl oz hot chicken stock

200 g/7 oz beansprouts, trimmed

2 tbsp finely chopped spring onions

marinade

1 tsp light soy sauce

dash of sesame oil

pinch of white pepper

method

1 Combine all the marinade ingredients in a bowl, add the pork and marinate for at least 20 minutes.

2 Cook the noodles according to the packet instructions. When cooked, drain and set aside.

3 In a preheated wok or deep saucepan, heat 1 teaspoon of the oil and stir-fry the pork until it has changed colour. Remove and set aside.

4 In the clean wok or saucepan, heat the remaining oil and stir-fry the garlic and ginger until fragrant. Add the carrot and cook for 1 minute, then add the mushrooms and cook for a further 1 minute. Toss in the pepper and cook for 1 minute more. Add the pork, salt and stock and heat through. Finally, toss in the noodles, followed by the beansprouts, and stir well. Sprinkle with the spring onions and serve.

red curry pork with peppers

ingredients

SERVES 4

2 tbsp vegetable or peanut oil

1 onion, coarsely chopped

2 garlic cloves, chopped

450 g/1 lb pork fillet, sliced
   thickly

1 red pepper, deseeded and
   cut into squares

175 g/6 oz mushrooms,
   quartered

2 tbsp Thai red curry paste

115 g/4 oz creamed coconut,
   chopped

300 ml/10 fl oz pork or
   vegetable stock

2 tbsp Thai soy sauce

4 tomatoes, peeled, deseeded
   and chopped

handful of fresh coriander,
   chopped

boiled noodles or rice,
   to serve

method

1 Heat the oil in a wok or large frying pan and sauté the onion and garlic for 1–2 minutes, until they are softened but not browned.

2 Add the pork slices and stir-fry for 2–3 minutes until browned all over. Add the pepper, mushrooms and curry paste.

3 Dissolve the coconut in the hot stock and add to the wok with the soy sauce. Bring to the boil and simmer for 4–5 minutes until the liquid has reduced and thickened.

4 Add the tomatoes and coriander and cook for 1–2 minutes before serving with noodles or rice.

pad thai

ingredients

SERVES 4

225 g/8 oz thick rice-stick
    noodles
2 tbsp vegetable or peanut oil
2 garlic cloves, chopped
2 fresh red chillies, deseeded
    and chopped
175 g/6 oz pork fillet, sliced
    thinly
115 g/4 oz uncooked prawns,
    peeled and chopped
8 fresh Chinese chives,
    chopped
2 tbsp fish sauce
juice of 1 lime
2 tsp jaggery or soft light
    brown sugar
2 eggs, beaten
115 g/4 oz beansprouts
4 tbsp chopped fresh
    coriander
115 g/4 oz unsalted peanuts,,
    chopped, plus extra
    to serve
crispy fried onions, to serve

method

1 Soak the noodles in warm water for 10 minutes, drain well and set aside.

2 Heat the oil in a wok and stir-fry the garlic, chillies and pork for 2–3 minutes. Add the prawns and stir-fry for a further 2–3 minutes.

3 Add the chives and noodles, then cover and cook for 1–2 minutes. Add the fish sauce, lime juice, sugar and eggs. Cook, stirring and tossing constantly to mix in the eggs.

4 Stir in the beansprouts, coriander and peanuts and serve with small dishes of crispy fried onions and extra chopped peanuts.

spicy fried minced pork

ingredients

SERVES 4

2 tbsp corn oil

2 garlic cloves, finely chopped

3 shallots, finely chopped

2.5-cm/1-inch piece fresh root
   ginger, finely chopped

500 g/1 lb 2 oz minced lean
   pork

2 tbsp Thai fish sauce

1 tbsp dark soy sauce

1 tbsp Thai red curry paste

4 dried kaffir lime leaves,
   crumbled

4 plum tomatoes, chopped

3 tbsp chopped coriander

salt and pepper

freshly cooked fine egg
   noodles, to serve

coriander sprigs and spring
   onion tassels, to garnish

method

1 Heat the oil in a large frying pan or preheated wok over medium heat. Add the garlic, shallots and ginger and stir-fry for 2 minutes. Stir in the pork and continue stir-frying until golden brown.

2 Stir in the fish sauce, soy sauce, curry paste and lime leaves and stir-fry for a further 1–2 minutes over high heat.

3 Add the chopped tomatoes and cook for a further 5–6 minutes, stirring occasionally. Stir in the chopped coriander and season to taste with salt and pepper.

4 Serve hot, spooned onto freshly cooked fine egg noodles, garnished with coriander sprigs and spring onion tassels.

stir-fried pork with vegetables

ingredients

SERVES 4

8 tbsp vegetable or peanut oil

115 g/4 oz rice vermicelli
noodles

4 belly pork strips, sliced
thickly

1 red onion, sliced

2 garlic cloves, chopped

2.5-cm/1-inch piece fresh root
ginger, sliced thinly

1 large fresh red chilli,
deseeded and chopped

115 g/4 oz baby corn, halved
lengthways

1 red pepper, deseeded and
sliced

175 g/6 oz head of broccoli,
cut into florets

150-g/5^1/$_2$-oz jar black bean
sauce

115 g/4 oz beansprouts

method

1 Heat the oil in a wok and cook the rice noodles, in batches, for 15–20 seconds, until they puff up. Remove with a slotted spoon, drain on kitchen paper and set aside.

2 Pour off all but 2 tablespoons of the oil and stir-fry the pork, onion, garlic, ginger and chilli for 4–5 minutes, or until the meat has browned.

3 Add the corn, red pepper and broccoli and stir-fry for 3–4 minutes, until the vegetables are just tender. Stir in the black bean sauce and beansprouts, then cook for a further 2–3 minutes. Serve immediately, topped with the crispy noodles.

pork with mixed green beans

ingredients

SERVES 4

2 tbsp vegetable or peanut oil

2 shallots, chopped

225 g/8 oz pork fillet, sliced thinly

2.5-cm/1-inch piece fresh galangal, sliced thinly

2 garlic cloves, chopped

300 ml/10 fl oz chicken stock

4 tbsp chilli sauce

4 tbsp crunchy peanut butter

115 g/4 oz fine green beans

115 g/4 oz frozen broad beans

115 g/4 oz string beans, sliced

crispy noodles, to serve

method

1 Heat the oil in a wok and stir-fry the shallots, pork, galangal and garlic until lightly browned.

2 Add the chicken stock, chilli sauce and peanut butter and stir until the peanut butter has melted. Add all the beans and simmer for 3–4 minutes. Serve hot with crispy noodles.

spicy szechuan pork

ingredients

SERVES 4

280 g/10 oz pork belly,
  thinly sliced

1 tbsp vegetable or peanut oil

1 tbsp chilli bean sauce

1 tbsp fermented black beans,
  rinsed and lightly mashed

1 tsp sweet red bean paste
  (optional)

1 green pepper, finely sliced

1 red pepper, finely sliced

1 tsp sugar

1 tsp dark soy sauce

pinch of white pepper

method

1 Bring a saucepan of water to the boil and place the pork slices in the pan, then cover and simmer for about 20 minutes, skimming occasionally. Let the pork cool and rest before slicing thinly.

2 In a preheated wok or deep saucepan, heat the oil and stir-fry the pork slices until they begin to shrink. Stir in the chilli bean sauce, then add the black beans and the red bean paste, if using. Finally, toss in the peppers and the remaining ingredients and stir-fry for a couple of minutes.

szechuan-style pork with peppers

ingredients

SERVES 4

500 g/1 lb 2 oz pork fillet, cubed

2 tbsp cornflour

3 tbsp soy sauce

1 tbsp white wine vinegar

250 ml/9 fl oz water

2 tbsp peanut oil

2 leeks, thinly sliced

1 red pepper, cut into thin strips

1 courgette, cut into thin strips

1 carrot, cut into thin strips

pinch of salt

freshly cooked white and wild rice, to serve

marinade

1 tbsp soy sauce

pinch of chilli flakes

method

1 To make the marinade, mix the soy sauce and chilli flakes in a bowl. Add the pork cubes and toss to coat. Cover with clingfilm and set aside for 30 minutes.

2 Combine the cornflour, soy sauce and white wine vinegar in a small bowl. Stir in the water gradually, then set aside.

3 Heat 1 tablespoon of the oil in a wok or frying pan. Add the pork and marinade mixture and stir-fry for 2–3 minutes. Remove the pork from the frying pan with a slotted spoon and set aside.

4 Heat the remaining oil in the frying pan, add the leeks and red pepper and stir-fry for 2 minutes. Then add the courgette, carrot and salt and stir-fry for a further 2 minutes.

5 Stir in the pork and the cornflour mixture and bring to the boil, stirring constantly until the sauce thickens. Remove from the heat and serve immediately with freshly cooked white and wild rice.

five-spice crispy pork with egg-fried rice

ingredients

SERVES 4

275 g/9¾ oz long-grain white rice

600 ml/1 pint cold water

salt and pepper

350 g/12 oz pork fillet

2 tsp Chinese five-spice powder

4 tbsp cornflour

3 extra-large eggs

2 tbsp demerara sugar

2 tbsp corn oil

1 onion, chopped

2 garlic cloves, crushed

1 large carrot, diced

1 red pepper, deseeded and diced

100 g/3½ oz peas

1 tbsp butter

method

1 Rinse the rice in a sieve under cold running water. Place in a large saucepan, then add the cold water and a pinch of salt. Bring to the boil, cover, then reduce the heat and simmer for about 9 minutes or until all of the liquid has been absorbed and the rice is tender.

2 Meanwhile, slice the pork into very thin, even-sized pieces, using a sharp knife or meat cleaver. Set aside.

3 Stir together the Chinese five-spice powder, cornflour, 1 egg and the sugar. Toss the pork in the mixture until coated.

4 Heat the oil in a preheated wok or frying pan. Add the pork and cook over high heat until the pork is cooked through and crispy. Remove the pork from the wok or frying pan with a slotted spoon and keep warm.

5 Add the onion, garlic, carrot, pepper and peas to the wok or frying pan and stir-fry for 5 minutes. Return the pork to the wok, together with the cooked rice, and stir-fry for 5 minutes.

6 Heat the butter in a frying pan. Beat the remaining eggs, add to the frying pan, and cook until set. Turn out onto a clean board and slice thinly. Toss the strips of egg into the rice mixture and serve immediately.

hoisin pork with garlic noodles

ingredients

SERVES 4

250 g/9 oz dried thick Chinese
egg noodles, or Chinese
wholemeal egg noodles

450 g/1 lb pork fillet,
thinly sliced

1 tsp sugar

1 tbsp peanut or corn oil

4 tbsp rice vinegar

4 tbsp white wine vinegar

4 tbsp bottled hoisin sauce

2 spring onions, sliced on
the diagonal

about 2 tbsp garlic-flavoured
corn oil

2 large garlic cloves, thinly
sliced

chopped fresh coriander,
to garnish

method

1 Start by boiling the noodles for 3 minutes, until soft. Alternatively, cook according to the packet instructions. Drain well, rinse under cold water to stop the cooking and drain again, then set aside.

2 Meanwhile, sprinkle the pork slices with the sugar and use your hands to toss together. Heat a wok over high heat. Add the oil and heat until it shimmers. Add the pork and stir-fry for about 3 minutes, until the pork is cooked through and is no longer pink. Use a slotted spoon to remove the pork from the wok and keep warm. Add both vinegars to the wok and boil until they are reduced to about 5 tablespoons. Pour in the hoisin sauce with the spring onions and let it bubble until reduced by half. Add to the pork and stir together.

3 Quickly wipe out the wok and reheat. Add the garlic-flavoured oil and heat until it shimmers. Add the garlic slices and stir round for about 30 seconds, until they are golden and crisp, then use a slotted spoon to scoop them out of the wok and set aside.

4 Add the noodles to the wok and stir them round to warm them through. Divide the noodles between 4 plates, top with the pork and onion mixture and sprinkle over the garlic slices and coriander.

sour & spicy pork

ingredients

SERVES 4

55 g/2 oz dried Chinese cloud
  ear mushrooms

100 g/3½ oz baby corn,
  halved lengthways

2 tbsp honey

1 tbsp tamarind paste

4 tbsp boiling water

2 tbsp dark soy sauce

1 tbsp rice vinegar

2 tbsp peanut or corn oil

1 large garlic clove, very finely
  chopped

1-cm/½-inch piece fresh root
  ginger, peeled and very
  finely chopped

½ tsp dried red pepper flakes,
  or to taste

350 g/12 oz pork fillet,
  thinly sliced

4 spring onions, thickly sliced
  on the diagonal

1 green pepper, cored,
  deseeded and sliced

250 g/9 oz fresh Hokkien
  noodles

chopped fresh coriander,
  to garnish

method

1 Soak the mushrooms in enough boiling water to cover for 20 minutes, or until they are tender. Drain them well, then cut off and discard any thick stems, and slice the cups if they are large. Meanwhile, bring a large saucepan of lightly salted water to the boil, add the baby corn and blanch for 3 minutes. Drain the corn and run it under cold running water to stop the cooking, then set aside. Put the honey and tamarind paste in a small bowl and stir in the water, stirring until the paste dissolves. Stir in the soy sauce and rice vinegar and set aside.

2 Heat a wok over high heat. Add 1 tablespoon of the oil and heat until it shimmers. Add the garlic, root ginger and red pepper flakes and stir-fry for about 30 seconds. Add the pork and continue stir-frying for 2 minutes.

3 Add the remaining oil to the wok and heat. Add the spring onions, pepper, mushrooms and baby corn, along with the tamarind mixture, and stir-fry for a further 2–3 minutes, until the pork is cooked through and the vegetables are tender, but still firm to the bite. Add the noodles and use 2 forks to mix all the ingredients together. When the noodles and sauce are hot, sprinkle with coriander.

paella with pork & chorizo

ingredients

SERVES 4–6

1.2 litres/2 pints simmering fish stock

12 large raw prawns, in their shells

$1/2$ tsp saffron threads

2 tbsp hot water

100 g/$3^1/2$ oz skinless, boneless chicken breast, cut into 1-cm/$1/2$-inch pieces

100 g/$3^1/2$ oz pork fillet, cut into 1-cm/$1/2$-inch pieces

salt and pepper

3 tbsp olive oil

100 g/$3^1/2$ oz Spanish chorizo sausage, casing removed, cut into 1-cm/$1/2$-inch slices

1 large red onion, chopped

2 garlic cloves, crushed

$1/2$ tsp cayenne pepper

$1/2$ tsp paprika

1 red pepper, deseeded and sliced

1 green pepper, deseeded and sliced

12 cherry tomatoes, halved

375 g/13 oz paella rice

1 tbsp chopped fresh parsley

2 tsp chopped fresh tarragon

method

1 Add the prawns to the simmering stock and cook for 2 minutes, then transfer to a bowl and set aside. Put the saffron threads and water in a small bowl and infuse for a few minutes.

2 Season the chicken and pork with salt and pepper. Heat the oil in a paella pan and cook the chicken, pork and chorizo over medium heat, stirring, until golden. Add the onion and cook, stirring, until softened. Add the garlic, cayenne pepper, paprika and saffron and its soaking liquid and cook, stirring constantly, for 1 minute. Add the peppers and tomatoes and cook, stirring, for a further 2 minutes.

3 Add the rice and herbs and cook, stirring constantly, for 1 minute. Pour in most of the hot stock, bring to the boil, then simmer, uncovered, for 10 minutes. Do not stir during cooking, but shake the pan once or twice and when adding ingredients. Season, then cook for a further 10 minutes, or until the rice is almost cooked, adding a little more hot stock if necessary. Add the prawns and cook for a further 2 minutes.

4 When all the liquid has been absorbed and you detect a faint toasty aroma coming from the rice, remove from the heat. Cover with foil and stand for 5 minutes. Serve.

sausages with lentils

ingredients

SERVES 4–6

2 tbsp olive oil

12 merguez sausages

2 onions, chopped finely

2 red peppers, cored, deseeded and chopped

1 orange or yellow pepper, cored, deseeded and chopped

280 g/10 oz small green lentils, rinsed

1 tsp dried thyme or marjoram

450 ml/16 fl oz vegetable stock

salt and pepper

4 tbsp chopped fresh parsley

red wine vinegar, to serve

method

1 Heat the oil in a large, preferably non-stick, lidded frying pan over medium–high heat. Add the sausages and cook, stirring frequently, for about 10 minutes until they are brown all over and cooked through; remove from the pan and set aside.

2 Pour off all but 2 tablespoons of oil from the frying pan. Add the onions and peppers and cook for about 5 minutes until soft, but not brown. Add the lentils and thyme or marjoram and stir until coated with oil.

3 Stir in the stock and bring to the boil. Reduce the heat, cover, and simmer for about 30 minutes until the lentils are tender and the liquid is absorbed; if the lentils are tender but too much liquid remains, uncover the frying pan and simmer until it evaporates. Season to taste with salt and pepper.

4 Return the sausages to the frying pan and reheat. Stir in the parsley. Serve the sausages with lentils on the side, then splash a little red wine vinegar over each portion.

sausage & rosemary risotto

ingredients

SERVES 4–6

2 long fresh rosemary sprigs,
   plus extra to garnish

2 tbsp olive oil

55 g/2 oz butter

1 large onion, finely chopped

1 celery stick, finely chopped

2 garlic cloves, finely chopped

1/2 tsp dried thyme leaves

450 g/1 lb pork sausage,
   such as luganega or
   cumberland, cut into
   1-cm/1/2-inch pieces

350 g/12 oz risotto rice

125 ml/4 fl oz fruity red wine

1.3 litres/21/4 pints simmering
   chicken stock

salt and pepper

85 g/3 oz freshly grated
   Parmesan cheese

method

1 Strip the long thin leaves from the rosemary sprigs and chop finely, then set aside.

2 Heat the oil and half the butter in a deep saucepan over a medium heat. Add the onion and celery and cook, stirring occasionally, for 2 minutes. Stir in the garlic, thyme, sausage and rosemary. Cook, stirring frequently, for 5 minutes, or until the sausage starts to brown. Transfer the sausage to a plate.

3 Reduce the heat and stir in the rice. Cook, stirring constantly, for 2–3 minutes, or until the grains are translucent.

4 Add the wine and cook, stirring, for 1 minute until reduced. Gradually add the hot stock, a ladleful at a time. Stir constantly and add more liquid as the rice absorbs each addition. Increase the heat to medium so that the liquid bubbles. Cook for 20 minutes, or until all the liquid is absorbed and the rice is creamy.

5 Toward the end of cooking, return the sausage pieces to the risotto and heat through. Season to taste. Remove from the heat and add the remaining butter. Mix well, then stir in the Parmesan until it melts. Spoon the risotto onto warmed plates, garnish with rosemary sprigs and serve.

pork hash

ingredients

SERVES 4

400 g/14 oz canned chopped
    tomatoes
600–700 ml/1–1¼ pints
    beef stock
1 tbsp corn oil
450 g/1 lb fresh minced pork
1 large onion, chopped
1 red pepper, deseeded and
    chopped
400 g/14 oz long-grain rice
1 tbsp chilli powder
450 g/1 lb fresh or frozen
    green beans
salt and pepper

method

1 Drain the tomatoes, reserving their juices, and reserve. Make the juices up to 850 ml/ 1½ pints with the stock and reserve.

2 Heat the oil in a large, flameproof casserole dish. Add the pork, onion and red pepper and cook over medium heat, stirring frequently, for 8–10 minutes or until the onion is softened and the meat is broken up and golden brown. Add the rice and cook, stirring constantly, for 2 minutes.

3 Add the tomatoes, stock mixture, chilli powder and beans to the casserole dish and season to taste with salt and pepper. Bring to the boil, then cover and transfer to a preheated oven, 180°C/350°F/Gas Mark 4, to bake for 40 minutes. Serve immediately.

fish & seafood

The ideal choice for busy people who care about food but have little time to cook, fish and seafood really benefit from quick cooking and simple recipes that don't disguise their natural flavours. What's more, they taste delicious and are low in fat and highly nutritious.

Fish that have a meaty texture, like salmon, swordfish and tuna, are perfect for pan-frying, grilling and griddling – fillets and steaks take only about 5 minutes and if you like your tuna rare, the cooking time is even less. Gentle poaching is the perfect technique for more delicate fish fillets, while whole fish is superb when roasted. Fish stews will take less time to prepare and cook than those made with meat and are spectacular enough to impress the most discerning guests. Easiest of all is to bake fish in the oven in a foil or greaseproof paper parcel.

Seafood is the ultimate fast food – most types must be cooked very rapidly or they become tough. Cooked prawns need only be heated through and raw ones cook in a matter of minutes, depending on their size. Shellfish, such as clams and mussels, just need a good scrub and brief steaming. Scallops can be tricky and time-consuming to remove from their shells but they are available ready shelled or you can ask your fishmonger to do it for you. Similarly, ready-prepared squid is widely available.

Fish combines well with an extensive range of other ingredients, whether the Mediterranean flavours of garlic, onion and tomatoes or the Asian tang of ginger, chillies and lime. Seafood is equally versatile being just as delicious in curries, risottos, cream sauces and even omelettes.

roast salmon with lemon & herbs

ingredients

SERVES 4

6 tbsp extra virgin olive oil

1 onion, sliced

1 leek, sliced

juice of ½ lemon

2 tbsp chopped fresh parsley

2 tbsp chopped fresh dill

salt and pepper

500 g/1 lb 2 oz salmon fillets

freshly cooked baby spinach
    leaves, to serve

lemon slices, to garnish

method

1 Heat 1 tablespoon of the oil in a frying pan over a medium heat. Add the onion and leek and cook, stirring occasionally, for 4 minutes, or until slightly softened.

2 Meanwhile, place the remaining oil in a small bowl with the lemon juice and herbs and season with salt and pepper. Stir together well. Rinse the fish under cold running water, then pat dry with kitchen paper. Arrange the fish in a shallow ovenproof dish.

3 Remove the frying pan from the heat and spread the onion and leek over the fish. Pour the oil mixture over the top, making sure that everything is well coated. Roast in the centre of a preheated oven, 200°C/400°F/Gas Mark 6, for 10 minutes, or until the fish is cooked through.

4 Arrange the cooked spinach on serving plates. Remove the fish and vegetables and serve next to the spinach, with the vegetables arranged on top of the fish. Garnish with lemon slices and serve immediately.

pan-fried spiced salmon

ingredients

SERVES 4

2.5-cm/1-inch piece fresh root
  ginger, grated

1 tsp coriander seeds,
  crushed

1/4 tsp chilli powder

1 tbsp lime juice

1 tsp sesame oil

4 salmon fillet pieces with
  skin, about 150 g/5 1/2 oz
  each

2 tbsp vegetable oil

stir-fried vegetables and freshly
  cooked rice, to serve

coriander leaves, to garnish

method

1 Mix the ginger, crushed coriander, chilli powder, lime juice and sesame oil together in a bowl.

2 Place the salmon on a wide, non-metallic plate or dish and spoon the mixture over the flesh side of the fillets, spreading it to coat each piece of salmon evenly.

3 Cover the dish with clingfilm and chill in the refrigerator for 30 minutes.

4 Heat a wide, heavy-based frying pan or ridged griddle pan with the vegetable oil over high heat. Place the salmon in the hot pan, skin-side down, and cook for 4–5 minutes, without turning, until the salmon is crusty underneath and the flesh flakes easily.

5 Serve the salmon immediately, with stir-fried vegetables and freshly cooked rice garnished with coriander leaves.

salmon steaks with green sauce

ingredients

SERVES 4

green sauce

70 g/2¹/₂ oz sprigs fresh flat-
leaf parsley

8 large fresh basil leaves

2 sprigs fresh oregano, or
¹/₂ tsp dried

3–4 anchovy fillets in oil,
drained and chopped

2 tsp capers in brine, rinsed

1 shallot, chopped

1 large garlic clove

2–3 tsp lemon juice, to taste

125 ml/4 fl oz extra virgin
olive oil

4 skinned salmon fillets, each
about 150 g/5¹/₂ oz

2 tbsp olive oil

salt and pepper

method

1 To make the green sauce, put the parsley, basil, oregano, anchovies, capers, shallot, garlic and lemon juice in a food processor or blender and process until chopped. With the motor running, slowly add the oil through the feed tube. Taste and adjust the seasoning, if necessary, remembering that the anchovies and capers can be salty. Transfer the sauce to a serving bowl, cover with clingfilm and chill until required.

2 When ready to serve, brush the salmon fillets on both sides with the olive oil and season with salt and pepper to taste. Heat a large frying pan until you can feel the heat rising from the surface. Add the salmon steaks and cook for 3 minutes. Flip the steaks over and continue cooking for 2–3 minutes until they feel springy and the flesh flakes easily.

3 Serve the hot salmon steaks with a little of the chilled sauce spooned over.

salmon with red curry in banana leaves

ingredients

SERVES 4

4 salmon steaks, about
    175 g/6 oz each
2 banana leaves, halved
1 garlic clove, crushed
1 tsp grated fresh root ginger
1 tbsp Thai red curry paste
1 tsp brown sugar
1 tbsp Thai fish sauce
2 tbsp lime juice

to garnish
lime wedges
whole fresh red chillies
finely chopped fresh red chilli

method

1 Place a salmon steak in the centre of each half banana leaf. Mix the garlic, ginger, curry paste, sugar and fish sauce together, then spread over the surface of the fish. Sprinkle with lime juice.

2 Carefully wrap the banana leaves around the fish, tucking in the sides as you go to make neat, compact pockets.

3 Place the pockets seam-side down on a baking sheet. Bake in a preheated oven, 220°C/425°F/ Gas Mark 7, for 15–20 minutes, or until the fish is cooked and the banana leaves are beginning to brown.

4 Serve garnished with lime wedges, whole chillies and finely chopped chilli.

linguine with smoked salmon & rocket

ingredients

SERVES 4

350 g/12 oz dried linguine

2 tbsp olive oil

1 garlic clove, finely chopped

115 g/4 oz smoked salmon,
    cut into thin strips

55 g/2 oz rocket

salt and pepper

4 lemon halves, to garnish

method

1 Bring a large, heavy-based saucepan of lightly salted water to the boil. Add the pasta, return to the boil and cook for 8–10 minutes, or until tender but still firm to the bite.

2 Just before the end of the cooking time, heat the olive oil in a heavy-based frying pan. Add the garlic and cook over low heat, stirring constantly, for 1 minute. Do not allow the garlic to brown or it will taste bitter. Add the salmon and rocket. Season with salt and pepper and cook, stirring constantly, for 1 minute. Remove the pan from the heat.

3 Drain the pasta and transfer to a warmed dish. Add the smoked salmon and rocket mixture, toss lightly and serve, garnished with lemon halves.

spiced tuna in sweet-&-sour sauce

ingredients

SERVES 4

4 fresh tuna steaks, about
500 g/1 lb 2 oz in total

1/4 tsp pepper

2 tbsp peanut oil

1 onion, diced

1 small red pepper, deseeded
and cut into short thin
sticks

1 garlic clove, crushed

1/2 cucumber, deseeded and
cut into short thin sticks

2 pineapple slices, diced

1 tsp finely chopped fresh root
ginger

1 tbsp brown sugar

1 tbsp cornflour

1 1/2 tbsp lime juice

1 tbsp Thai fish sauce

300 ml/10 fl oz fish stock

lime slices and cucumber
slices, to garnish

method

1 Sprinkle the tuna steaks with pepper on both sides. Heat a heavy-based frying pan or ridged griddle pan and brush with a little of the oil. Arrange the tuna steaks in the pan and cook for 8 minutes, turning them once.

2 Meanwhile, heat the remaining oil in a separate frying pan. Add the onion, pepper and garlic and cook gently for 3–4 minutes to soften.

3 Remove the pan from the heat and stir in the cucumber, pineapple, ginger and sugar.

4 Blend the cornflour with the lime juice and fish sauce, then stir into the stock and add to the pan. Stir over medium heat until boiling, then cook for 1–2 minutes, or until thickened and clear.

5 Spoon the sauce over the tuna and serve immediately, garnished with slices of lime and cucumber.

sicilian tuna

ingredients

SERVES 4

marinade

125 ml/4 fl oz extra virgin
   olive oil
4 garlic cloves, finely chopped
4 fresh red chillies, deseeded
   and finely chopped
juice and finely grated rind
   of 2 lemons
4 tbsp finely chopped fresh
   flat-leaf parsley
salt and pepper

4 x 150-g/5-oz tuna steaks
2 fennel bulbs, thickly sliced
   lengthways
2 red onions, sliced
2 tbsp virgin olive oil
rocket salad and crusty bread,
   to serve

method

1 First, make the marinade by whisking all the ingredients together in a bowl. Place the tuna steaks in a large shallow dish and spoon over 4 tablespoons of the marinade, turning to coat. Cover and set aside for 30 minutes. Set aside the remaining marinade.

2 Heat a ridged griddle pan. Put the fennel and onions in a bowl, add the oil and toss well to coat. Add to the griddle pan and cook for 5 minutes on each side, until just starting to colour. Transfer to 4 warmed serving plates, drizzle with the reserved marinade, and keep warm.

3 Add the tuna steaks to the griddle pan and cook, turning once, for 4–5 minutes, until firm to the touch but still moist inside. Transfer the tuna to the plates and serve immediately with the rocket salad and crusty bread.

grilled tuna & vegetable kebabs

ingredients

SERVES 4

4 tuna steaks, about 140 g/
    5 oz each

2 red onions

12 cherry tomatoes

1 red pepper, deseeded and
    diced into 2.5-cm/1-inch
    pieces

1 yellow pepper, deseeded
    and diced into 2.5-cm/
    1-inch pieces

1 courgette, sliced

1 tbsp chopped fresh oregano

4 tbsp olive oil

pepper

lime wedges, to garnish

method

1 Preheat the grill to high. Cut the tuna into 2.5-cm/1-inch dice. Peel the onions, leaving the root intact, and cut each onion lengthways into 6 wedges.

2 Divide the fish, onions, tomatoes, peppers and courgette evenly between 8 wooden skewers (presoaked to avoid burning) and arrange on the grill pan.

3 Mix the oregano and oil together in a small bowl. Season with pepper. Lightly brush the kebabs with the oil and cook under a grill preheated to high for 10–15 minutes or until evenly cooked, turning occasionally. If you cannot fit all the kebabs on the grill pan at once, cook them in batches, keeping the cooked kebabs warm while cooking the remainder. Alternatively, these kebabs can be cooked on a barbecue.

4 Garnish with lime wedges.

risotto with tuna & pine kernels

ingredients

SERVES 4

3 tbsp butter

4 tbsp olive oil

1 small onion, finely chopped

280 g/10 oz risotto rice

1.2 litres/2 pints simmering
fish or chicken stock

salt and pepper

225 g/8 oz tuna, canned
and drained, or grilled
fresh steaks

8–10 black olives, stoned and
sliced

1 small pimiento, thinly sliced

1 tsp finely chopped
fresh parsley

1 tsp finely chopped
fresh marjoram

2 tbsp white wine vinegar

55 g/2 oz pine kernels

1 garlic clove, chopped

225 g/8 oz fresh tomatoes,
peeled, deseeded and
diced

85 g/3 oz Parmesan or Grana
Padano cheese

method

1 Melt 2 tablespoons of the butter with 1 tablespoon of the oil in a deep saucepan over a medium heat. Add the onion and cook, stirring occasionally, until soft and starting to turn golden. Reduce the heat, add the rice and mix to coat in oil and butter. Cook, stirring constantly, until the grains are translucent. Add the hot stock, a ladleful at a time, stirring constantly, until all the liquid is absorbed and the rice is creamy. Season to taste.

2 While the risotto is cooking, flake the tuna into a bowl and mix in the olives, pimiento, parsley, marjoram and vinegar. Season with salt and pepper.

3 Heat the remaining oil in a small frying pan over a high heat. Add the pine kernels and garlic. Cook, stirring constantly, for 2 minutes, or until they just start to brown. Add the tomatoes and mix well. Continue cooking over a medium heat for 3–4 minutes or until they are thoroughly warm. Pour the tomato mixture over the tuna mixture and mix. Fold into the risotto 5 minutes before the end of the cooking time.

4 Remove the risotto from the heat when all the liquid has been absorbed and add the remaining butter. Mix well, then stir in the Parmesan until it melts. Serve immediately.

spaghetti with tuna & parsley

ingredients

SERVES 4

500 g/1 lb 2 oz dried spaghetti
25 g/1 oz butter
fresh flat-leaf parsley sprigs,
  to garnish
black olives, to serve (optional)

s a u c e

200 g/7 oz canned tuna,
  drained
55 g/2 oz canned anchovies,
  drained
250 ml/9 fl oz olive oil
55 g/2 oz coarsely chopped
  fresh flat-leaf parsley
150 ml/5 fl oz soured cream
  or yogurt
salt and pepper

method

1 Bring a large, heavy-based saucepan of lightly salted water to the boil. Add the spaghetti, return to the boil and cook for 8–10 minutes, or until tender but still firm to the bite. Drain the spaghetti in a colander and return to the pan. Add the butter, toss thoroughly to coat and keep warm until required.

2 Flake the tuna into smaller pieces using 2 forks. Place the tuna in a blender or food processor with the anchovies, olive oil and parsley and process until the sauce is smooth. Pour in the soured cream or yogurt and process for a few seconds to blend. Taste the sauce and season with salt and pepper, if necessary.

3 Warm 4 plates. Shake the pan of spaghetti over medium heat for a few minutes, or until it is thoroughly warmed through.

4 Pour the sauce over the spaghetti and toss quickly, using 2 forks. Garnish with parsley sprigs and serve immediately with a small dish of black olives, if liked.

linguine with anchovies, olives & capers

ingredients

SERVES 4

3 tbsp olive oil

2 garlic cloves, finely chopped

10 anchovy fillets, drained and
chopped

140 g/5 oz black olives, stoned
and chopped

1 tbsp capers, rinsed

450 g/1 lb plum tomatoes,
peeled, deseeded and
chopped

pinch of cayenne pepper

salt

400 g/14 oz dried linguine

2 tbsp chopped fresh flat-leaf
parsley, to garnish

method

1 Heat the olive oil in a heavy-based saucepan. Add the garlic and cook over a low heat, stirring frequently, for 2 minutes. Add the anchovies and mash them to a pulp with a fork. Add the olives, capers and tomatoes and season to taste with cayenne pepper. Cover and simmer for 25 minutes.

2 Meanwhile, bring a pan of lightly salted water to the boil. Add the pasta, bring back to the boil and cook for 8–10 minutes, until tender but still firm to the bite. Drain and transfer to a warmed serving dish.

3 Spoon the anchovy sauce into the dish and toss the pasta, using 2 large forks. Garnish with the parsley and serve immediately.

grilled sardines with lemon sauce

ingredients

SERVES 4

1 large lemon

85 g/3 oz unsalted butter

salt and pepper

20 fresh sardines, cleaned
   and heads removed

1 tbsp chopped fresh fennel
   leaves

method

1 Peel the lemon. Remove all the bitter pith and discard. Using a small, serrated knife, cut between the membranes and ease out the flesh segments, discarding any seeds. Chop finely and set aside.

2 Melt 25 g/1 oz of the butter in a small saucepan and season with salt and pepper. Brush the sardines all over with the melted butter and cook under a preheated grill or on a barbecue, turning once, for 5–6 minutes, until cooked through.

3 Meanwhile, melt the remaining butter, then remove the pan from the heat. Stir in the chopped lemon and fennel.

4 Transfer the sardines to a warmed platter, pour the sauce over them and serve immediately.

fresh sardines baked with lemon & oregano

ingredients

SERVES 4

2 lemons, plus extra lemon
wedges, to garnish
12 large fresh sardines,
cleaned
4 tbsp olive oil
4 tbsp chopped fresh oregano
salt and pepper

method

1 Slice one of the lemons and grate the rind and squeeze the juice from the second lemon.

2 Cut the heads off the sardines. Put the fish in a shallow, ovenproof dish large enough to hold them in a single layer. Put the lemon slices between the fish. Drizzle the lemon juice and oil over the fish. Sprinkle over the lemon rind and oregano and season with salt and pepper.

3 Bake in a preheated oven, 190°C/375°F/Gas Mark 5, for 20–30 minutes until the fish are tender. Serve garnished with lemon wedges.

swordfish with olives & capers

ingredients

SERVES 4

2 tbsp plain flour

salt and pepper

4 x 225-g/8-oz swordfish
    steaks

100 ml/3¹/₂ fl oz olive oil

2 garlic cloves, halved

1 onion, chopped

4 anchovy fillets, drained and
    chopped

4 tomatoes, peeled, deseeded
    and chopped

12 green olives, stoned and
    sliced

1 tbsp capers, rinsed

fresh rosemary leaves,
    to garnish

method

1 Spread out the flour on a plate and season with salt and pepper. Coat the fish in the seasoned flour, shaking off any excess.

2 Gently heat the olive oil in a large heavy-based frying pan. Add the garlic and cook over a low heat for 2–3 minutes, until just golden. Do not let it turn brown or burn. Remove the garlic and discard.

3 Add the fish to the pan and cook over a medium heat for about 4 minutes on each side, until cooked through and golden brown. Remove the fish from the pan and set aside.

4 Add the onion and anchovies to the pan and cook, mashing the anchovies with a wooden spoon until they have turned to a purée and the onion is golden. Add the tomatoes and cook over a low heat, stirring occasionally, for about 20 minutes, until the mixture has thickened.

5 Stir in the olives and capers and taste and adjust the seasoning. Return the steaks to the pan and heat through gently. Serve garnished with rosemary.

spanish swordfish stew

ingredients

SERVES 4

4 tbsp olive oil

3 shallots, chopped

2 garlic cloves, chopped

225 g/8 oz canned chopped
     tomatoes

1 tbsp tomato paste

650 g/1 lb 7 oz potatoes,
     sliced

250 ml/9 fl oz vegetable stock

2 tbsp lemon juice

1 red pepper, deseeded and
     chopped

1 orange pepper, deseeded
     and chopped

20 black olives, stoned
     and halved

1 kg/2 lb 4 oz swordfish steak,
     skinned and cut into bite-
     sized pieces

salt and pepper

fresh flat-leaf parsley sprigs
     and lemon slices, to
     garnish

method

1 Heat the oil in a saucepan over a low heat, add the shallots and cook, stirring frequently, for 4 minutes, or until softened. Add the garlic, tomatoes and tomato paste, cover and simmer gently for 20 minutes.

2 Meanwhile, put the potatoes in an ovenproof casserole with the stock and lemon juice. Bring to the boil, then reduce the heat and add the peppers. Cover and cook for 15 minutes.

3 Add the olives, swordfish and the tomato mixture to the potatoes. Season with salt and pepper. Stir well, then cover and simmer for 7–10 minutes, or until the swordfish is cooked to your taste.

4 Remove from the heat and garnish with parsley sprigs and lemon slices.

fusilli with monkfish & broccoli

ingredients

SERVES 4

115 g/4 oz head of broccoli, divided into florets
3 tbsp olive oil
350 g/12 oz monkfish fillet, skinned and cut into bite-size pieces
2 garlic cloves, crushed
salt and pepper
125 ml/4 fl oz dry white wine
225 ml/8 fl oz double cream
400 g/14 oz dried fusilli bucati
85 g/3 oz Gorgonzola cheese, diced

method

1 Divide the broccoli florets into tiny sprigs. Bring a saucepan of lightly salted water to the boil, add the broccoli and cook for 2 minutes. Drain and refresh under cold running water.

2 Heat the olive oil in a large, heavy-based frying pan. Add the monkfish and garlic and season with salt and pepper. Cook, stirring frequently, for 5 minutes, or until the fish is opaque. Pour in the white wine and cream and cook, stirring occasionally, for 5 minutes, or until the fish is cooked through and the sauce has thickened. Stir in the broccoli sprigs.

3 Meanwhile, bring a large, heavy-based saucepan of lightly salted water to the boil. Add the pasta, return to the boil and cook for 8–10 minutes, or until tender but still firm to the bite. Drain the pasta and tip it into the pan with the fish, add the cheese and toss lightly. Serve immediately.

basque-style cod

ingredients

SERVES 4

3 tbsp olive oil

4 cod fillets, about 175 g/6 oz
    each, all skin and bones
    removed, rinsed and
    patted dry

1 tbsp plain flour

salt and pepper

1 large onion, finely chopped

4 large tomatoes, peeled,
    deseeded and chopped

2 large garlic cloves, crushed

150 ml/5 fl oz dry white wine

1/2 tsp paprika, to taste

2 red peppers, chargrilled,
    peeled and deseeded, then
    cut into strips

2 green peppers, chargrilled,
    peeled and deseeded, then
    cut into strips

rind of 1 lemon, in broad strips

finely chopped fresh flat-leaf
    parsley, to garnish

method

1 Heat 1 tablespoon of the oil in a flameproof casserole over a medium–high heat. Very lightly dust one side of each cod fillet with the flour, seasoned with salt and pepper.

2 Pan-fry, floured-side down, for 2 minutes, or until just golden. Set aside. Wipe out the casserole, then heat the remaining oil over a medium–high heat. Add the onion and sauté for 5 minutes, or until soft but not browned.

3 Stir in the tomatoes, garlic, wine, paprika, salt and pepper and bring to the boil. Reduce the heat and simmer for 5 minutes, stirring occasionally.

4 Stir the red and green peppers into the casserole with the lemon strips and bring to the boil. Lay the cod fillets on top, browned-side up, and season with salt and pepper. Cover the casserole and bake in a preheated oven, 200°C/400°F/Gas Mark 6, for 12–15 minutes, depending on the thickness of the cod, until it is cooked through and flakes easily.

5 Discard the lemon rind just before serving. Serve the cod on a bed of the vegetables and sprinkled with the chopped parsley.

cod with spinach

ingredients

SERVES 4

catalan spinach
55 g/2 oz raisins
55 g/2 oz pine kernels
4 tbsp extra virgin olive oil
3 garlic cloves, crushed
500 g/1 lb 2 oz baby spinach
    leaves, rinsed and
    shaken dry

4 cod fillets, each about
    175 g/6 oz
olive oil
salt and pepper
lemon wedges, to serve

method

1 Put the raisins for the Catalan spinach in a small bowl, cover with hot water, and set aside to soak for 15 minutes; drain well.

2 Meanwhile, put the pine kernels in a dry frying pan over medium–high heat and dry-fry for 1–2 minutes, shaking frequently, until toasted and golden brown: watch closely because they burn quickly.

3 Heat the oil in a large, lidded frying pan over medium–high heat. Add the garlic and cook for 2 minutes or until golden but not brown. Remove with a slotted spoon and discard.

4 Add the spinach to the oil with only the rinsing water clinging to its leaves. Cover and cook for 4–5 minutes until wilted. Uncover, stir in the drained raisins and pine kernels and continue cooking until all the liquid evaporates. Season to taste and keep warm.

5 To cook the cod, brush the fillets lightly with oil and sprinkle with salt and pepper. Place under a preheated hot grill about 10 cm/4 inches from the heat and grill for 8–10 minutes until the flesh is opaque and flakes easily.

6 Divide the spinach between 4 plates and place the cod fillets on top. Serve with the lemon wedges.

italian fish

ingredients

SERVES 4

2 tbsp butter

50 g/1³/₄ oz fresh wholemeal
  breadcrumbs

1 heaped tbsp chopped
  walnuts

grated rind and juice of
  2 lemons

2 fresh rosemary sprigs, stalks
  removed

2 tbsp chopped fresh parsley

4 cod fillets, about
  150 g/5¹/₂ oz each

1 garlic clove, crushed

1 small fresh red chilli, diced

3 tbsp walnut oil

method

1 Melt the butter in a large saucepan over a low heat, stirring constantly. Remove the pan from the heat and add the breadcrumbs, walnuts, the rind and juice of 1 lemon, half the rosemary and half the parsley, stirring until mixed.

2 Press the breadcrumb mixture over the top of the cod fillets. Place the cod fillets in a shallow foil-lined roasting tin and roast in a preheated oven, 200°C/400°F/Gas Mark 6, for 25–30 minutes.

3 Mix the garlic, the remaining lemon rind and juice, rosemary and parsley, and the chilli together in a bowl. Beat in the oil and mix to combine. Drizzle the dressing over the cod steaks as soon as they are cooked.

4 Transfer the fish to warmed serving plates and serve immediately.

nut-crusted halibut

ingredients

SERVES 4

3 tbsp butter, melted

750 g/1 lb 10 oz halibut fillet

55 g/2 oz pistachios, shelled
and very finely chopped

method

1 Brush the melted butter over the halibut fillet. Spread the nuts out on a large, flat plate. Roll the fish in the nuts, pressing down gently.

2 Preheat a ridged griddle pan over a medium heat. Cook the halibut, turning once, for 10 minutes, or until firm but tender – the exact cooking time will depend on the thickness of the fillet.

3 Remove the fish and any loose pistachio pieces from the heat and transfer to a large, warmed serving platter. Serve immediately.

fish parcels with fresh herbs

ingredients

SERVES 4

vegetable oil spray

4 flounder fillets, skinned

6 tbsp chopped fresh herbs,
    such as dill, parsley,
    chives, thyme or marjoram

finely grated rind and
    juice of 2 lemons

1 small onion, thinly sliced

1 tbsp capers, rinsed
    (optional)

salt and pepper

method

1 Cut 4 large squares of aluminium foil, each large enough to hold a fish and form a parcel, and spray with oil.

2 Place each fish fillet on a foil sheet and sprinkle with the herbs, lemon rind and juice, onion, capers, if using, salt and pepper. Fold the foil to make a secure parcel and place on a baking sheet.

3 Bake the parcels in a preheated oven, 190°C/375°F/Gas Mark 5, for 15 minutes, or until tender. Serve the fish piping hot, in their loosely opened parcels.

hake in white wine

ingredients

SERVES 4

about 2 tbsp plain flour

salt and pepper

4 hake fillets, about
   150 g/5½ oz each

4 tbsp extra virgin olive oil

125 ml/4 fl oz dry white wine,
   such as a white Rioja

2 large garlic cloves,
   chopped very finely

6 spring onions, sliced finely

2 tbsp fresh parsley,
   chopped very finely

method

1 Season the flour generously with salt and pepper on a flat plate. Dredge the skin side of the hake fillets in the seasoned flour, then shake off the excess; set aside.

2 Heat a shallow, flameproof casserole over high heat until you can feel the heat rising. Add the oil and heat for about 30 seconds or until a cube of day-old bread sizzles. Add the hake fillets, skin-side down, and cook for 3 minutes or until the skin is golden brown.

3 Turn the fish over and season with salt and pepper to taste. Pour in the wine and add the garlic, spring onions and parsley. Transfer the casserole, uncovered, to a preheated oven, 230°C/450°F/Gas Mark 8, and bake for 5 minutes or until the flesh flakes easily. Serve straight from the casserole.

sole à la meunière

ingredients

SERVES 4

4 tbsp plain flour

1 tsp salt

4 x 400-g/14-oz Dover sole,
    cleaned and skinned

150 g/5$^{1}/_{2}$ oz butter

3 tbsp lemon juice

1 tbsp chopped fresh parsley

$^{1}/_{4}$ of a preserved lemon,
    finely chopped (optional)

fresh parsley sprigs, to garnish

lemon wedges, to serve

method

1 Mix the flour with the salt and place on a large plate. Drop the fish into the flour, one at a time, and shake well to remove any excess. Melt 3 tablespoons of the butter in a small saucepan and use to brush the fish liberally all over. Place the fish under a grill preheated to medium and cook for 5 minutes on each side.

2 Meanwhile, melt the remaining butter in a saucepan. Pour cold water into a bowl that is large enough to take the bottom of the saucepan and keep nearby.

3 Heat the butter until it turns a golden brown and begins to smell nutty. Remove from the heat immediately and immerse the bottom of the saucepan in the cold water, to stop the cooking.

4 Place the fillets on individual plates, drizzle with the lemon juice and sprinkle with the parsley and preserved lemon, if using. Pour over the browned butter, garnish with parsley sprigs and serve immediately with lemon wedges for squeezing over.

skate in mustard & caper sauce

ingredients

SERVES 4

2 skate wings
lemon wedges, to serve

mustard &
caper sauce

2 tbsp olive oil
1 onion, finely chopped
1 garlic clove, finely chopped
150 ml/5 fl oz Greek-style
    yogurt
1 tsp lemon juice
1 tbsp chopped fresh flat-
    leaf parsley, plus extra to
    garnish
1 tbsp capers, roughly
    chopped
1 tbsp wholegrain mustard
salt and pepper

method

1 Cut each skate wing in half and place them in a large frying pan. Cover with salted water, bring to the boil, then simmer for 10–15 minutes, until tender.

2 Meanwhile, make the mustard and caper sauce. Heat the oil in a saucepan, add the onion and garlic and cook for 5 minutes, until softened. Add the yogurt, lemon juice, parsley and capers and cook for 1–2 minutes, until heated through. (Do not boil, or the sauce will curdle.) Stir in the mustard and season with salt and pepper.

3 Drain the skate and put on four warmed serving plates. Pour over the sauce and sprinkle with chopped parsley.

4 Serve hot, with lemon wedges.

sweet-&-sour sea bass

ingredients

SERVES 2

60 g/2¼ oz pak choi,
   shredded
40 g/1½ oz beansprouts
40 g/1½ oz shiitake
   mushrooms, sliced
40 g/1½ oz oyster
   mushrooms, torn
20 g/¾ oz spring onions,
   finely sliced
1 tsp finely grated fresh ginger
1 tbsp finely sliced
   lemon grass
2 x 90-g/3¼-oz sea bass
   fillets, skinned and boned
10 g/¼ oz sesame seeds,
   toasted

sweet-&-sour sauce

90 ml/3 fl oz unsweetened
   pineapple juice
1 tbsp sugar
1 tbsp red wine vinegar
2 star anise, crushed
6 tbsp tomato juice
1 tbsp cornflour, blended with
   a little cold water

method

1 Cut 2 x 38-cm/15-inch squares of baking paper and 2 x 38-cm/15-inch squares of aluminium foil.

2 To make the sauce, heat the pineapple juice, sugar, red wine vinegar, star anise and tomato juice. Simmer for 1–2 minutes, then thicken with the cornflour and water mixture, whisking continuously. Pass through a fine sieve into a small bowl to cool.

3 In a separate large bowl mix together the pak choi, beansprouts, mushrooms and spring onions, then add the ginger and lemon grass. Toss all the ingredients together.

4 Put a square of greaseproof paper on top of a square of foil and fold into a triangle. Open up and place half the vegetable mix in the centre, pour half the sweet and sour sauce over the vegetables and place the sea bass on top. Sprinkle with a few sesame seeds. Close the triangle over the mixture and, starting at the top, fold the right corner and crumple the edges together to form an airtight triangular bag. Repeat to make another bag.

5 Place on a baking sheet and cook in a preheated oven, 200°C/400°F/Gas Mark 6, for 10 minutes, until the foil bags puff with steam. To serve, place on individual plates and snip open at the table.

roast sea bream with fennel

ingredients

SERVES 4

250 g/9 oz dried, uncoloured
    breadcrumbs

2 tbsp milk

1 fennel bulb, thinly sliced,
    fronds reserved for garnish

1 tbsp lemon juice

2 tbsp sambuca

1 tbsp chopped fresh thyme

1 bay leaf, crumbled

1.5 kg/3 lb 5 oz whole sea
    bream, cleaned, scaled
    and boned

salt and pepper

3 tbsp olive oil, plus extra
    for brushing

1 red onion, chopped

300 ml/10 fl oz dry white wine

method

1 Place the breadcrumbs in a bowl, add the milk and set aside for 5 minutes to soak. Place the fennel in another bowl and add the lemon juice, sambuca, thyme and bay leaf. Squeeze the breadcrumbs and add them to the mixture, stirring well.

2 Rinse the fish inside and out under cold running water and pat dry with kitchen paper. Season with salt and pepper. Spoon the fennel mixture into the cavity, then bind the fish with kitchen string.

3 Brush a large ovenproof dish with olive oil and sprinkle the onion over the bottom. Lay the fish on top and pour in the wine – it should come about one third of the way up the fish. Drizzle the sea bream with the olive oil and cook in preheated oven, 240°C/475°F/Gas Mark 9, for 25–30 minutes. Baste the fish occasionally with the cooking juices and if it starts to brown, cover with a piece of foil to protect it.

4 Carefully lift out the fish, remove the string and place on a warmed serving platter. Garnish with the reserved fennel fronds and serve immediately.

chillies stuffed with fish paste

ingredients

SERVES 4–6

225 g/8 oz white fish, minced

2 tbsp lightly beaten egg

4–6 mild red and green
    chillies

vegetable or peanut oil, for
    shallow-frying

2 garlic cloves, finely chopped

1/2 tsp fermented black beans,
    rinsed and lightly mashed

1 tbsp light soy sauce

pinch of sugar

1 tbsp water

marinade

1 tsp finely chopped
    fresh ginger

pinch of salt

pinch of white pepper

1/2 tsp vegetable or peanut oil

method

1 Combine all the ingredients for the marinade in a bowl and marinate the fish for 20 minutes. Add the egg and mix by hand to create a smooth paste.

2 To prepare the chillies, cut in half lengthways and scoop out the seeds and loose flesh. Cut into bite-sized pieces. Spread each piece of chilli with about 1/2 teaspoon of the fish paste.

3 In a preheated wok or deep saucepan, heat plenty of the oil and cook the chilli pieces on both sides until beginning to turn golden brown. Drain and set aside.

4 Heat 1 tablespoon of the oil in a wok or deep saucepan and stir-fry the garlic until aromatic. Stir in the black beans and mix well. Add the light soy sauce and sugar and stir, then add the chilli pieces. Add the water, then cover and simmer over a low heat for 5 minutes. Serve immediately.

grilled red snapper with garlic

ingredients

SERVES 4

2 tbsp lemon juice

4 tbsp olive oil, plus extra
   for oiling

salt and pepper

4 red snapper or mullet,
   scaled and gutted

2 tbsp chopped fresh
   herbs such as oregano,
   marjoram, flat-leaf parsley
   or thyme

2 garlic cloves, finely chopped

2 tbsp chopped fresh
   flat-leaf parsley

lemon wedges, to garnish

method

1 Preheat the grill. Put the lemon juice, oil, salt and pepper in a bowl and whisk together. Brush the mixture inside and on both sides of the fish and sprinkle on the chopped herb of your choice. Place on an oiled grill pan.

2 Grill the fish for about 10 minutes, basting frequently and turning once, until golden brown.

3 Meanwhile, mix together the chopped garlic and chopped parsley. Sprinkle the garlic mixture on top of the cooked fish and serve hot or cold, garnished with lemon wedges.

spiced steamed fish

ingredients

SERVES 4–6

2.5-cm/1-inch piece fresh root
ginger, finely grated

1 lemon grass stem (base
only), thinly sliced

6 fresh red chillies, deseeded
and coarsely chopped

1 small red onion, finely
chopped

1 tbsp Thai fish sauce

900 g/2 lb whole fish, cleaned

2 fresh kaffir lime leaves,
thinly sliced

2 fresh basil sprigs

freshly cooked rice and thin
cucumber sticks, to serve

method

1 Place the ginger, lemon grass, chillies, onion and fish sauce in a food processor. Process to a coarse paste, adding a little water, if needed.

2 Cut 3–4 deep slits crosswise on each side of the fish. Spread over the spice paste, rubbing it well into the slits. Place the fish in a dish deep enough to hold the liquid that collects during steaming. Sprinkle over the lime leaves and basil.

3 Set up a steamer or place a rack into a wok or deep frying pan. Bring about 5 cm/2 inches of water to the boil in the steamer or wok.

4 Place the dish of fish into the steamer or on the rack. Reduce the heat to a simmer, then cover tightly and steam the fish for 15–20 minutes, or until cooked through. Serve with freshly cooked rice and cucumber sticks.

trout in lemon & red wine sauce

ingredients

SERVES 4

4 trout, cleaned, heads
  removed
225 ml/8 fl oz red wine vinegar
300 ml/10 fl oz red wine
150 ml/5 fl oz water
2 bay leaves
4 sprigs fresh thyme
4 sprigs fresh flat-leaf parsley,
  plus extra to garnish
thinly pared rind of 1 lemon
3 shallots, thinly sliced
1 carrot, thinly sliced
12 black peppercorns
8 cloves
salt and pepper
85 g/3 oz unsalted butter,
  diced
1 tbsp chopped fresh flat-leaf
  parsley
1 tbsp snipped fresh dill

method

1 Rinse the fish inside and out under cold running water and pat dry on kitchen paper. Place them in a single layer in a non-metallic dish. Pour the vinegar into a small saucepan and bring to the boil, then pour it over the fish. Set aside to marinate for 30 minutes.

2 Pour the wine and water into a saucepan, add the bay leaves, thyme and parsley sprigs, lemon rind, shallots, carrots, peppercorns and cloves, and season with salt. Bring to the boil over a low heat.

3 Meanwhile, drain the trout and discard the vinegar. Place the fish in a single layer in a large frying pan and strain the wine mixture over them. Cover and simmer over a low heat for 15 minutes, until cooked through and tender. There is no need to turn them.

4 Using a spatula, transfer the trout to individual serving plates and keep warm. Bring the cooking liquid back to the boil and cook until reduced by about three quarters. Gradually beat in the butter, a little at a time, until fully incorporated. Stir in the chopped parsley and dill, taste and adjust the seasoning if necessary. Pour the sauce over the fish, garnish with parsley sprigs and serve immediately.

marseilles-style fish stew

ingredients

SERVES 4–6

large pinch of saffron threads

2 tbsp olive oil

1 large onion, finely chopped

1 bulb of fennel, thinly sliced,
with the feathery green
fronds reserved

2 large garlic cloves, crushed

4 tbsp pastis

1 litre/1³/₄ pints fish stock

2 large sun-ripened tomatoes,
peeled, deseeded and
diced, or 400 g/14 oz
chopped tomatoes, drained

1 tbsp tomato paste

1 bay leaf

pinch of sugar

pinch of dried chilli flakes
(optional)

salt and pepper

24 large raw prawns, peeled

1 squid, cleaned and cut
into 5-mm/¹/₄-inch rings,
tentacles reserved

900 g/2 lb fresh, skinned
and boned Mediterranean
fish, such as sea bass,
monkfish, red snapper,
halibut or haddock,
cut into large chunks

method

1 Put the saffron threads in a small dry frying pan over a high heat and toast, stirring constantly, for 1 minute, or until you can smell the aroma. Immediately tip out of the pan and set aside.

2 Heat the oil in a large flameproof casserole over a medium heat, then add the onion and fennel and sauté for 3 minutes. Add the garlic and sauté for a further 5 minutes, until the onion and fennel are soft, but not coloured.

3 Remove the casserole from the heat. Warm the pastis in a ladle or small saucepan, then ignite and pour it over the onion and fennel to flambé. When the flames die down, return the casserole to the heat and stir in the stock, tomatoes, tomato paste, bay leaf, sugar, chilli flakes, if using, salt and pepper. Slowly bring to the boil, skimming the surface if necessary, then reduce the heat to low and simmer, uncovered, for 15 minutes.

4 Add the prepared prawns and squid rings and simmer until the prawns turn pink and the squid rings are opaque. Do not overcook, or they will be tough. Use a slotted spoon to transfer to serving bowls. Add the fish chunks to the broth and simmer just until the flesh flakes easily. Transfer the seafood and broth to the serving bowls and garnish with the reserved fennel fronds.

catalan fish stew

ingredients

SERVES 4–6

large pinch of saffron threads

6 tbsp olive oil

1 large onion, chopped

2 garlic cloves, chopped finely

1 1/2 tbsp chopped fresh thyme leaves

2 bay leaves

2 red peppers, cored, deseeded and chopped roughly

800 g/1 lb 12 oz canned chopped tomatoes

1 tsp sweet smoked paprika

250 ml/9 fl oz fish stock

140 g/5 oz blanched almonds, toasted and ground finely

salt and pepper

12–16 live mussels with tightly closed shells

12–16 live clams with tightly closed shells

600 g/1 lb 5 oz thick, boned hake or cod fillets, skinned and cut into 5-cm/2-inch chunks

12–16 uncooked prawns, heads and tails removed and deveined

crusty bread, to serve

method

1 Infuse the saffron threads in 4 tablespoons of boiling water in a heatproof bowl.

2 Heat the oil in a heavy-based flameproof casserole over medium–high heat. Reduce the heat to low, add the onion and cook for 10 minutes or until golden but not brown. Stir in the garlic, thyme, bay leaves and red peppers and continue cooking for a further 5 minutes or until the peppers are soft and the onions have softened further. Add the tomatoes and paprika and continue to simmer for 5 minutes, stirring frequently.

3 Stir in the fish stock, reserved saffron water, and ground almonds and bring to the boil, stirring frequently. Reduce the heat and simmer for 5–10 minutes until the sauce reduces and thickens. Season to taste.

4 Meanwhile, prepare the mussels and clams, discarding any with broken shells and any open ones that do not close when tapped. Cut off and discard any beards from the mussels, then scrub any dirty shells.

5 Gently stir in the hake and add the prawns, mussels and clams. Reduce the heat to very low, cover the casserole, and simmer for about 5 minutes until the hake is cooked through, the prawns turn pink and the mussels and clams open; discard any that remain closed. Serve at once with the bread.

fish curry with rice noodles

ingredients

SERVES 4

2 tbsp vegetable or peanut oil

1 large onion, chopped

2 garlic cloves, chopped

75 g/3 oz white mushrooms

225 g/8 oz monkfish, cut into
    cubes, each about
    2.5 cm/1 inch

225 g/8 oz salmon fillets, cut
    into cubes, each about
    2.5 cm/1 inch

225 g/8 oz cod, cut into
    cubes, each about
    2.5 cm/1 inch

2 tbsp Thai red curry paste

400 g/14 oz canned
    coconut milk

handful of fresh coriander,
    chopped

1 tsp soft light brown sugar

1 tsp fish sauce

115 g/4 oz rice noodles

3 spring onions, chopped

55 g/2 oz beansprouts

a few Thai basil leaves

method

1 Heat the oil in a wok or large frying pan and gently sauté the onion, garlic and mushrooms until softened but not browned.

2 Add the fish, curry paste and coconut milk and bring gently to the boil. Simmer for 2–3 minutes, then add half the coriander, the sugar and fish sauce. Keep warm.

3 Meanwhile, soak the noodles for 3–4 minutes (check the packet instructions) or until tender, and drain well through a colander. Put the colander and noodles over a pan of simmering water. Add the spring onions, beansprouts and most of the basil and steam on top of the noodles for 1–2 minutes or until just wilted.

4 Pile the noodles onto warmed serving plates and top with the fish curry. Sprinkle the remaining coriander and basil over the top and serve immediately.

fish in coconut

ingredients

SERVES 4

2 tbsp vegetable or peanut oil

6 spring onions, chopped
coarsely

2.5-cm/1-inch piece fresh root
ginger, grated

2–3 tbsp Thai red curry paste

400 ml/14 fl oz coconut milk

150 ml/5 fl oz fish stock

4 kaffir lime leaves

1 lemon grass stalk, halved

350 g/12 oz skinned white fish
fillets, cut into chunks

225 g/8 oz squid rings and
tentacles

225 g/8 oz large cooked
shelled prawns

1 tbsp fish sauce

2 tbsp Thai soy sauce

4 tbsp chopped fresh
Chinese chives

boiled jasmine rice with
chopped fresh coriander,
to serve

method

1 Heat the oil in a wok or large frying pan and stir-fry the spring onions and ginger for 1–2 minutes. Add the curry paste and stir-fry for 1–2 minutes.

2 Add the coconut milk, fish stock, lime leaves and lemon grass. Bring to the boil, then reduce the heat and simmer for 1 minute.

3 Add the fish, squid and prawns and simmer for 2–3 minutes, until the fish is cooked. Add the fish and soy sauces and stir in the chives. Serve immediately with jasmine rice with fresh coriander stirred through it.

seafood paella with lemon & herbs

ingredients

SERVES 4–6

1/2 tsp saffron threads

2 tbsp hot water

150 g/51/2 oz cod fillet, skinned and rinsed under cold running water

1.3 litres/21/4 pints simmering fish stock

12 large raw prawns, peeled and deveined

450 g/1 lb raw squid, cleaned and cut into rings or bite-sized pieces (or use the same quantity of shucked scallops)

3 tbsp olive oil

1 large red onion, chopped

2 garlic cloves, crushed

1 small fresh red chilli, deseeded and finely chopped

225 g/8 oz tomatoes, peeled and cut into wedges

375 g/13 oz medium-grain paella rice

1 tbsp chopped fresh parsley

2 tsp chopped fresh dill

salt and pepper

1 lemon, cut into halves, to serve

method

1 Put the saffron threads and water in a small bowl for a few minutes to infuse.

2 Add the cod to the saucepan of simmering stock and cook for 5 minutes, then transfer to a colander, rinse under cold running water and drain. Add the prawns and squid to the stock and cook for 2 minutes. Cut the cod into chunks, then transfer, with the other seafood, to a bowl and set aside. Let the stock simmer.

3 Heat the oil in a paella pan and stir the onion over a medium heat until softened. Add the garlic, chilli and saffron and its soaking liquid and cook, stirring, for 1 minute. Add the tomato wedges and cook, stirring, for 2 minutes. Add the rice and herbs and cook, stirring, for 1 minute. Add most of the stock and bring to the boil. Simmer, uncovered, for 10 minutes. Do not stir during cooking, but shake the pan once or twice, and when adding ingredients. Season and cook for 10 minutes, until the rice is almost cooked. Add more stock if necessary. Add the seafood and cook for 2 minutes.

4 When all the liquid has been absorbed and you detect a faint toasty aroma coming from the rice, remove from the heat immediately. Cover with foil and let stand for 5 minutes.

rice with seafood & squid

ingredients

SERVES 4

2 tbsp vegetable or peanut oil

3 shallots, chopped finely

2 garlic cloves, chopped finely

225 g/8 oz jasmine rice

300 ml/10 fl oz fish stock

4 spring onions, chopped

2 tbsp Thai red curry paste

225 g/8 oz baby squid,
    cleaned and sliced thickly

225 g/8 oz white fish fillets,
    skinned and cut into cubes

225 g/8 oz salmon fillets,
    skinned and cut into cubes

4 tbsp chopped fresh
    coriander

method

1 Heat 1 tablespoon of the oil in a wok and stir-fry the shallots and garlic for 2–3 minutes, until softened. Add the rice and stir-fry for 2–3 minutes.

2 Add a ladleful of the stock and simmer, adding more stock as needed, for 12–15 minutes, until tender. Transfer to a dish, let cool and chill overnight.

3 Heat the remaining oil in a wok and stir-fry the spring onions and curry paste for 2–3 minutes. Add the squid and fish and stir-fry gently to avoid breaking up the fish. Stir in the rice and coriander, heat through gently and serve.

spaghetti with prawns

ingredients

SERVES 4

450 g/1 lb dried spaghetti

125 ml/4 fl oz olive oil

6 garlic cloves, sliced thinly

450 g/1 lb raw medium
    prawns, peeled and
    deveined

2 tbsp flat-leaf parsley,
    chopped finely, plus
    2 tbsp extra, to garnish

125 ml/4 fl oz dry white wine

4 tbsp freshly squeezed
    lemon juice

salt and pepper

method

1 Bring a large saucepan of salted water to the boil over high heat. Add the spaghetti, return the water to the boil and boil for 10 minutes, or until tender.

2 Meanwhile, heat the oil in another large saucepan over medium heat. Add the garlic and cook until just golden brown. Add the prawns and 2 tablespoons of chopped parsley and stir. Add the wine and simmer for 2 minutes. Stir in the lemon juice and simmer until the prawns turn pink and curl.

3 Drain the spaghetti, then tip it into the pan with the prawns and toss. Season with salt and pepper.

4 Transfer to a large serving platter and sprinkle with the extra parsley. Serve at once.

seafood omelette

ingredients

SERVES 3

2 tbsp unsalted butter

1 tbsp olive oil

1 onion, very finely chopped

175 g/6 oz courgette, halved lengthways and sliced

1 celery stick, very finely chopped

85 g/3 oz white mushrooms, sliced

55 g/2 oz French beans, cut into 5-cm/2-inch lengths

4 eggs

85 g/3 oz mascarpone cheese

1 tbsp chopped fresh thyme

1 tbsp shredded fresh basil

salt and pepper

200 g/7 oz canned tuna, drained and flaked

115 g/4 oz peeled cooked prawns

method

1 Melt the butter with the olive oil in a heavy-based frying pan with a flameproof handle. If the pan has a wooden handle, protect it with foil because it needs to go under the grill. Add the onion and cook over a low heat, stirring occasionally, for 5 minutes, until softened.

2 Add the courgette, celery, mushrooms and beans and cook, stirring occasionally, for a further 8–10 minutes, until starting to brown.

3 Beat the eggs with the mascarpone, thyme, basil, and salt and pepper to taste.

4 Add the tuna to the pan and stir it into the mixture with a wooden spoon, then add the prawns.

5 Pour the egg mixture into the pan and cook for 5 minutes, until it is just starting to set. Draw the egg from the sides of the pan towards the centre to let the uncooked egg run underneath.

6 Put the pan under a preheated grill and cook until the egg is just set and the surface is starting to brown. Cut the omelette into wedges and serve.

paprika prawns

ingredients

SERVES 4–6

16–24 large, uncooked king
     prawns
6 tbsp extra virgin olive oil
1 large garlic clove, crushed
$1/2$ tsp mild paprika, or to taste
salt
lemon wedges, to serve

method

1 Remove the shell from the centre of the prawns, leaving the heads and tails intact. Devein the prawns.

2 Mix together the oil, garlic, paprika and salt in a shallow dish large enough to hold the prawns in a single layer. Stir together, then add the prawns and turn so they are coated. Cover with clingfilm and marinate in the refrigerator for at least 1 hour.

3 When ready to cook, heat a large, ridged cast-iron griddle pan over medium-high heat until you can feel the heat rising. Add as many prawns as will fit without overcrowding the griddle pan. Cook for about 1 minute until the prawns curl and the shells turn pink. Turn over and continue cooking for a further minute or until cooked through. Drain well on kitchen paper and keep hot while you continue cooking the remainder.

4 Serve at once with lemon wedges for squeezing over the prawns.

curried noodles with prawns & straw mushrooms

ingredients

SERVES 4

1 tbsp vegetable or peanut oil

3 shallots, chopped

1 fresh red chilli, deseeded
and chopped

1 tbsp Thai red curry paste

1 lemon grass stalk (white part
only), chopped finely

225 g/8 oz cooked peeled
prawns

400 g/14 oz canned straw
mushrooms, drained

2 tbsp fish sauce

2 tbsp Thai soy sauce

225 g/8 oz fresh egg noodles

fresh coriander, chopped,
to garnish

method

1 Heat the oil in a wok and stir-fry the shallots and chilli for 2–3 minutes. Add the curry paste and lemon grass and stir-fry for 2–3 minutes.

2 Add the prawns, mushrooms, fish sauce and soy sauce and stir well to mix.

3 Meanwhile, cook the noodles in boiling water for 3–4 minutes, drain and transfer to warmed plates. Top with the prawn curry, sprinkle the coriander over and serve immediately.

prawn pilau

ingredients

SERVES 4

3 tbsp olive oil

1 onion, finely chopped

1 red pepper, cored, deseeded
and thinly sliced

1 garlic clove, crushed

225 g/8 oz long-grain
white rice

750 ml/1¼ pints fish, chicken
or vegetable stock

1 bay leaf

salt and pepper

400 g/14 oz peeled cooked
prawns, thawed and
drained if frozen

grated kefalotiri or romano
cheese and cubes of feta
cheese, to serve

to garnish

whole cooked prawns

lemon wedges

black Greek olives

method

1 Heat the oil in a large, lidded frying pan, add the onion, red pepper and garlic, and fry for 5 minutes, until softened. Add the rice and cook for 2–3 minutes, stirring all the time, until the grains look transparent.

2 Add the stock, bay leaf, salt and pepper. Bring to the boil, cover the pan with a tightly fitting lid, and simmer for about 15 minutes, until the rice is tender and the liquid has been absorbed. Do not stir during cooking. When cooked, very gently stir in the prawns.

3 Remove the lid, cover the frying pan with a clean tea towel, replace the lid and stand in a warm place for 10 minutes to dry out. Stir with a fork to separate the grains.

4 Serve garnished with whole prawns, lemon wedges and black olives. Accompany with grated kefalotiri or romano cheese, for sprinkling on top, and a bowl of feta cubes.

prawn & asparagus risotto

ingredients

SERVES 4

1.2 litres/2 pints vegetable
    stock
375 g/12 oz fresh asparagus
    spears, cut into 5-cm/
    2-inch lengths
2 tbsp olive oil
1 onion, finely chopped
1 garlic clove, finely chopped
350 g/12 oz risotto rice
450 g/1 lb raw jumbo prawns,
    peeled and deveined
2 tbsp olive paste or tapenade
2 tbsp chopped fresh basil
salt and pepper
freshly grated Parmesan
    cheese, to serve
fresh basil sprigs, to garnish

method

1 Bring the stock to the boil in a large saucepan. Add the asparagus and cook for 3 minutes until just tender. Strain, reserving the stock, and refresh the asparagus under cold running water. Drain and set aside.

2 Return the stock to the pan and keep simmering gently over a low heat while you are cooking the risotto.

3 Heat the olive oil in a large heavy-based saucepan. Add the onion and cook over a medium heat, stirring occasionally, for 5 minutes until softened. Add the garlic and cook for a further 30 seconds.

4 Reduce the heat, add the rice and mix to coat in oil. Cook, stirring constantly, for 2–3 minutes, or until the grains are translucent.

5 Gradually add the hot stock, a ladleful at a time. Stir constantly and add more liquid as the rice absorbs each addition. Increase the heat to medium so that the liquid bubbles. Cook for 20 minutes, until all the liquid is absorbed and the rice is creamy. Add the prawns and asparagus with the last ladleful of stock.

6 Remove the pan from the heat, stir in the olive paste and basil and season to taste with salt and pepper. Serve the risotto immediately, sprinkled with Parmesan cheese and garnished with basil sprigs.

spaghetti with clams

ingredients

SERVES 4

1 kg/2 lb 4 oz live clams
175 ml/6 fl oz water
175 ml/6 fl oz dry white wine
350 g/12 oz dried spaghetti
5 tbsp olive oil
2 garlic cloves, finely chopped
4 tbsp chopped fresh flat-leaf
   parsley
salt and pepper

method

1 Place the clams in a large heavy-based saucepan, add the water and wine, cover and cook over a high heat, shaking the saucepan occasionally, for 5 minutes, or until the shells have opened.

2 Remove the clams with a slotted spoon and cool slightly. Strain the cooking liquid into a small saucepan through a sieve lined with muslin. Bring to the boil and cook until reduced by about half, then remove from the heat. Meanwhile, discard any clams that have not opened, then remove the remainder from their shells and reserve until required.

3 Bring a large saucepan of lightly salted water to the boil. Add the pasta, return to the boil and cook for 8–10 minutes, or until tender but still firm to the bite.

4 Meanwhile, heat the olive oil in a large heavy-based frying pan. Add the garlic and cook, stirring frequently, for 2 minutes. Add the parsley and the reduced clam cooking liquid and simmer gently.

5 Drain the pasta and add it to the frying pan with the clams. Season with salt and pepper and cook, stirring constantly, for 4 minutes, or until the pasta is coated and the clams have heated through. Transfer to a warmed serving dish and serve immediately.

fettuccine with scallops & porcini

ingredients

SERVES 4

25 g/1 oz dried porcini
   mushrooms
500 ml/18 fl oz hot water
3 tbsp olive oil
3 tbsp butter
350 g/12 oz scallops, sliced
2 garlic cloves, very finely
   chopped
2 tbsp lemon juice
250 ml/9 fl oz double cream
salt and pepper
350 g/12 oz dried fettuccine
   or pappardelle
2 tbsp chopped fresh flat-leaf
   parsley

method

1 Put the porcini and hot water in a bowl and soak for 20 minutes. Strain the mushrooms, reserving the soaking water, and chop roughly. Line a sieve with kitchen paper and strain the mushroom water into a bowl.

2 Heat the oil and butter in a large frying pan over a medium heat. Add the scallops and cook for 2 minutes, or until just golden. Add the garlic and mushrooms, then stir-fry for another minute.

3 Stir in the lemon juice, cream and 150 ml/ 5 fl oz of the mushroom water. Bring to the boil, then simmer over a medium heat for 2–3 minutes, stirring constantly, until the liquid is reduced by half. Season with salt and pepper. Remove from the heat.

4 Cook the pasta in plenty of boiling salted water until al dente. Drain and transfer to a warm serving dish. Briefly reheat the sauce and pour over the pasta. Sprinkle with the parsley and toss well to mix. Serve immediately.

saffron & lemon risotto with scallops

ingredients

SERVES 4

16 live scallops, shucked

juice of 1 lemon, plus extra
   for seasoning

3 tbsp butter

1 tbsp olive oil, plus extra
   for brushing

1 small onion, finely chopped

280 g/10 oz risotto rice

1 tsp crumbled saffron threads

1.2 litres/2 pints simmering
   fish or vegetable stock

salt and pepper

2 tbsp vegetable oil

115 g/4 oz freshly grated
   Parmesan or Grana
   Padano cheese

1 lemon, cut into wedges

2 tsp grated lemon zest,
   to garnish

method

1 Place the scallops in a non-metallic bowl and mix with the lemon juice. Cover the bowl with clingfilm and chill for 15 minutes.

2 Melt 2 tablespoons of the butter with the oil in a deep saucepan over a medium heat. Add the onion and cook, stirring occasionally, until soft and starting to turn golden. Add the rice and mix to coat in oil and butter. Cook, stirring, until the grains are translucent. Dissolve the saffron in 4 tablespoons of hot stock and add to the rice. Gradually add the remaining stock a ladleful at a time, stirring constantly, until all the liquid is absorbed and the rice is creamy. Season with salt and pepper.

3 When the risotto is nearly cooked, heat a griddle pan over a high heat. Brush the scallops with oil and sear on the griddle pan for 3–4 minutes on each side, depending on their thickness. Take care not to overcook or they will be rubbery.

4 Remove the risotto from the heat and add the remaining butter. Mix well, then stir in the Parmesan until it melts. Season with lemon juice, adding just 1 teaspoon at a time and tasting as you go. Serve the risotto immediately with the scallops and lemon wedges arranged on top, sprinkled with lemon zest.

simple stir-fried scallops

ingredients

SERVES 4

450 g/1 lb scallops

2 tbsp sesame oil

1 tbsp chopped fresh
    coriander

1 tbsp chopped fresh flat-leaf
    parsley

rice noodles, to serve

sauce

2 tbsp lemon juice

2 tbsp soy sauce

1 tbsp honey

1 tbsp grated fresh ginger

1 tbsp fish sauce

1 clove garlic, peeled and
    flattened

method

1 Combine the lemon juice, soy sauce, honey, ginger, fish sauce and garlic in a bowl and stir well to dissolve the honey. Add the scallops and toss to coat.

2 Heat a heavy frying pan or wok over the highest heat for 3 minutes. Add the oil and heat for 30 seconds.

3 Add the scallops with their sauce and the coriander and parsley to the pan. Stir constantly, cooking for about 3 minutes (less time if the scallops are small). Serve immediately with rice noodles.

spicy scallops with lime & chilli

ingredients

SERVES 4

16 large scallops, shelled

1 tbsp butter

1 tbsp vegetable oil

1 tsp crushed garlic

1 tsp grated fresh root ginger

1 bunch of spring onions,
   finely sliced

finely grated rind of 1 lime

1 small fresh red chilli,
   deseeded and very finely
   chopped

3 tbsp lime juice

lime wedges, to garnish

freshly cooked rice, to serve

method

1 Using a sharp knife, trim the scallops to remove any black intestine, then wash and pat dry with kitchen paper. Separate the corals from the white parts, then slice each white part in half horizontally, making 2 circles.

2 Heat the butter and oil in a frying pan or preheated wok. Add the garlic and ginger and stir-fry for 1 minute without browning. Add the spring onions and stir-fry for a further 1 minute.

3 Add the scallops and continue stir-frying over high heat for 4–5 minutes. Stir in the lime rind, chilli and lime juice and cook for a further 1 minute.

4 Transfer the scallops to serving plates, then spoon over the pan juices and garnish with lime wedges. Serve hot with freshly cooked rice.

penne with squid & tomatoes

ingredients

SERVES 4

225 g/8 oz dried penne
350 g/12 oz prepared squid
6 tbsp olive oil
2 onions, sliced
250 ml/8 fl oz fish or
  chicken stock
150 ml/5 fl oz full-bodied
  red wine
400 g/14 oz canned chopped
  tomatoes
2 tbsp tomato purée
1 tbsp chopped fresh
  marjoram
1 bay leaf
salt and pepper
2 tbsp chopped fresh parsley

method

1 Bring a large, heavy-based saucepan of lightly salted water to the boil. Add the pasta, return to the boil and cook for 3 minutes, then drain and set aside until required. With a sharp knife, cut the squid into strips.

2 Heat the olive oil in a large flameproof dish or casserole. Add the onions and cook over low heat, stirring occasionally, for 5 minutes, or until softened. Add the squid and fish stock, bring to the boil and simmer for 3 minutes. Stir in the wine, chopped tomatoes and their can juices, tomato purée, marjoram and bay leaf. Season with salt and pepper. Bring to the boil and cook for 5 minutes, or until slightly reduced.

3 Add the pasta, return to the boil and simmer for 5–7 minutes, or until tender but still firm to the bite. Remove and discard the bay leaf, stir in the parsley and serve at once.

sweet chilli squid

ingredients

SERVES 4

1 tbsp sesame seeds, toasted

2¹/₂ tbsp sesame oil

280 g/10 oz squid, cut into
  strips

2 red peppers, thinly sliced

3 shallots, thinly sliced

85 g/3 oz mushrooms,
  thinly sliced

1 tbsp dry sherry

4 tbsp soy sauce

1 tsp sugar

1 tsp hot chilli flakes,
  or to taste

1 clove of garlic, crushed

freshly cooked rice, to serve

method

1 Place the sesame seeds on a baking sheet, toast under a hot grill and set aside.

2 Heat 1 tablespoon of the oil in a frying pan or wok over a medium heat. Add the squid and cook for 2 minutes, then remove and set aside.

3 Add another 1 tablespoon of the oil to the frying pan and fry the peppers and shallots over a medium heat for 1 minute. Add the mushrooms and fry for a further 2 minutes.

4 Return the squid to the frying pan and add the sherry, soy sauce, sugar, chilli flakes and garlic, stirring thoroughly. Cook for a further 2 minutes.

5 Sprinkle with the toasted sesame seeds, drizzle over the remaining sesame oil and mix. Serve on a bed of freshly cooked rice.

stir-fried squid with hot black bean sauce

ingredients

SERVES 4

750 g/1 lb 10 oz squid, cleaned and tentacles discarded

1 large red pepper, deseeded

115 g/4 oz mangetout

1 head pak choi

3 tbsp black bean sauce

1 tbsp Thai fish sauce

1 tbsp rice wine or dry sherry

1 tbsp dark soy sauce

1 tsp brown sugar

1 tsp cornflour

1 tbsp water

1 tbsp corn oil

1 tsp sesame oil

1 small fresh red Thai chilli, chopped

1 garlic clove, finely chopped

1 tsp grated fresh root ginger

2 spring onions, chopped

method

1 Cut the squid body cavities into quarters lengthways. Use the tip of a small, sharp knife to score a diamond pattern into the flesh, without cutting all the way through. Pat dry with kitchen paper.

2 Cut the pepper into long, thin slices. Cut the mangetout in half diagonally. Coarsely shred the pak choi.

3 Mix the black bean sauce, fish sauce, rice wine, soy sauce and sugar together in a bowl. Blend the cornflour with the water and stir into the other sauce ingredients. Reserve until required.

4 Heat the oils in a preheated wok. Add the chilli, garlic, ginger and spring onions and stir-fry for 1 minute. Add the pepper slices and stir-fry for 2 minutes.

5 Add the squid and stir-fry over high heat for a further 1 minute. Stir in the mangetout and pak choi and stir for a further 1 minute, or until wilted.

6 Stir in the sauce ingredients and cook, stirring constantly, for 2 minutes, or until the sauce thickens and clears. Serve immediately.

black rice

ingredients

SERVES 4–6

400 g/14 oz Spanish short-
　grain rice

6 tbsp olive oil

1 large onion, sliced finely

2 large garlic cloves, crushed

2 tomatoes, grilled, peeled,
　deseeded and chopped
　finely

1 prepared squid body, cut
　into 5-mm/1/4-inch rings
　(tentacles set aside,
　if available)

1 litre/1 3/4 pints fish stock

ink sac from squid, or a sachet
　of squid ink

salt and pepper

12 large uncooked prawns,
　peeled and deveined

2 red peppers, grilled, peeled,
　deseeded and sliced

garlic mayonnaise, to serve

method

1 Put the rice in a sieve and rinse until the water runs clear; set aside.

2 Heat the oil in a large, shallow casserole or frying pan over medium–high heat. Add the onion and cook for 3 minutes, then add the garlic cloves and cook for a further 2 minutes until the onion is soft but not brown. Add the tomatoes and simmer until they are very soft. Add the squid rings and cook quickly until they turn opaque.

3 Add the rice and stir until it is coated in oil. Pour in the stock, squid ink, and salt and pepper to taste and bring to the boil. Reduce the heat and simmer for 15 minutes, uncovered and without stirring but shaking the frying pan frequently, until most of the stock is absorbed and small holes appear on the surface.

4 Lightly stir in the prawns, squid tentacles, if using, and peppers. Cover the frying pan and continue simmering for about 5 minutes until the prawns turn pink and the tentacles turn opaque and curl.

5 Taste and adjust the seasoning. Serve with garlic mayonnaise on the side of each plate.

Almost all common vegetarian ingredients benefit from quick cooking. For example, stir-frying is perfect for retaining the texture and goodness of vegetables, whilst eggs are generally ready in minutes, whatever cooking method you use. Dried beans are the most notable exception as they require prolonged soaking and lengthy cooking but you can skip these stages by using drained and rinsed canned beans. Lentils generally do not need to be soaked and, depending on the type, are usually cooked within 30 minutes.

There is a huge range of vegetables to choose from and most are suited to many different kinds of dishes – from curries to gratins and from pasta sauces to kebabs. They go well with rice, whether in an Italian risotto, a Spanish paella or an Oriental dish. Cheese is a good source of protein in the vegetarian diet and is extremely versatile, partnering many vegetables, as well as being a classic accompaniment to pasta dishes. Chinese and South-east Asian cooks have created an array of superb vegetarian dishes with a wonderful balance of flavours, textures and colours, yet, like most Eastern food, they are characteristically simple and very quick to cook.

With the global increase in food prices plus a growing awareness about healthy eating, it makes sense for meat-eating families to include at least

one vegetarian meal in the weekly menu. There is such a variety of delicious, nutritious, inexpensive dishes that are also easy and quick to prepare and cook that you simply can't go wrong.

sweet-&-sour vegetables with cashews

ingredients

SERVES 4

1 tbsp vegetable or peanut oil

1 tsp chilli oil

2 onions, sliced

2 carrots, thinly sliced

2 courgettes, thinly sliced

115 g/4 oz broccoli, cut into florets

115 g/4 oz white mushrooms, sliced

115 g/4 oz small pak choi, halved

2 tbsp jaggery or brown sugar

2 tbsp Thai soy sauce

1 tbsp rice vinegar

55 g/2 oz cashews

method

1 Heat both the oils in a preheated wok or frying pan, add the onions, and stir-fry for 1–2 minutes until beginning to soften.

2 Add the carrots, courgettes and broccoli and stir-fry for 2–3 minutes. Add the mushrooms, pak choi, sugar, soy sauce and vinegar and stir-fry for 1–2 minutes.

3 Meanwhile, heat a dry, heavy-based frying pan over high heat, add the cashews and cook, shaking the pan frequently, until lightly toasted. Sprinkle the cashews over the stir-fry and serve immediately.

crisp noodle & vegetable stir-fry

ingredients

SERVES 4

peanut or sunflower oil,
   for deep-frying

115 g/4 oz rice vermicelli,
   broken into 7.5-cm/3-inch
   lengths

115 g/4 oz green beans,
   cut into short lengths

2 carrots, cut into thin sticks

2 courgettes, cut into thin
   sticks

115 g/4 oz shiitake
   mushrooms, sliced

2.5-cm/1-inch piece fresh root
   ginger, shredded

1/2 small head Chinese
   cabbage, shredded

4 spring onions, shredded

85 g/3 oz beansprouts

2 tbsp dark soy sauce

2 tbsp Chinese rice wine

large pinch of sugar

2 tbsp coarsely chopped fresh
   coriander

method

1 Half-fill a wok or deep, heavy-based frying pan with oil. Heat to 180–190°C/350–375°F, or until a cube of bread browns in 30 seconds.

2 Add the noodles, in batches, and cook for 1 1/2–2 minutes, or until crisp and puffed up. Remove and drain on kitchen paper. Pour off all but 2 tablespoons of oil from the wok.

3 Heat the remaining oil over high heat. Add the green beans and stir-fry for 2 minutes. Add the carrot and courgette sticks, sliced mushrooms and ginger and stir-fry for a further 2 minutes.

4 Add the shredded cabbage, spring onions and beansprouts and stir-fry for a further minute. Add the soy sauce, rice wine and sugar and cook, stirring constantly, for 1 minute.

5 Add the chopped coriander and toss well. Serve immediately, with the noodles.

chinese vegetables & beansprouts with noodles

ingredients

SERVES 4

1.2 litres/2 pints vegetable
   stock
1 garlic clove, crushed
1-cm/$\frac{1}{2}$-inch piece fresh root
   ginger, finely chopped
225 g/8 oz dried medium
   egg noodles
1 red pepper, deseeded
   and sliced
85 g/3 oz frozen peas
115 g/4 oz broccoli florets
85 g/3 oz shiitake mushrooms,
   sliced
2 tbsp sesame seeds
225 g/8 oz canned water
   chestnuts, drained
   and halved
225 g/8 oz canned bamboo
   shoots, drained
280 g/10 oz Chinese cabbage,
   sliced
140 g/5 oz beansprouts
3 spring onions, sliced
1 tbsp dark soy sauce
pepper

method

1 Bring the stock, garlic and ginger to the boil in a large saucepan. Stir in the noodles, red pepper, peas, broccoli and mushrooms and return to the boil. Reduce the heat, cover, and simmer for 5–6 minutes, or until the noodles are tender.

2 Meanwhile, preheat the grill to medium. Spread the sesame seeds out in a single layer on a baking sheet and toast under the preheated grill, turning to brown evenly – watch constantly because they brown very quickly. Tip the sesame seeds into a small dish and set aside.

3 Once the noodles are tender, add the water chestnuts, bamboo shoots, cabbage, beansprouts and spring onions to the pan. Return the stock to the boil, stir to mix the ingredients and simmer for a further 2–3 minutes to heat through thoroughly.

4 Carefully drain off 300 ml/10 fl oz of the stock into a small heatproof jug and set aside. Drain and discard any remaining stock and turn the noodles and vegetables into a warmed serving dish. Quickly mix the soy sauce with the reserved stock and pour over the noodles and vegetables. Season with pepper and serve at once.

stir-fried rice with green vegetables

ingredients

SERVES 4

225 g/8 oz jasmine rice

2 tbsp vegetable or peanut oil

1 tbsp Thai green curry paste

6 spring onions, sliced

2 garlic cloves, crushed

1 courgette, cut into thin sticks

115 g/4 oz green beans

175 g/6 oz asparagus,
   trimmed

3–4 fresh Thai basil leaves

method

1 Cook the rice in lightly salted boiling water for 12–15 minutes, drain well, then cool thoroughly and chill overnight.

2 Heat the oil in a wok and stir-fry the curry paste for 1 minute. Add the spring onions and garlic and stir-fry for 1 minute.

3 Add the courgette, beans and asparagus and stir-fry for 3–4 minutes, until just tender. Break up the rice and add it to the wok. Cook, stirring constantly for 2–3 minutes, until the rice is hot. Stir in the basil leaves. Serve hot.

classic stir-fried vegetables

ingredients

SERVES 4

3 tbsp sesame oil

6 spring onions, finely
chopped, plus 2 spring
onions, finely chopped,
to garnish

1 garlic clove, crushed

1 tbsp grated fresh ginger

1 head of broccoli,
cut into florets

1 orange or yellow pepper,
roughly chopped

125 g/4^1/$_2$ oz red cabbage,
shredded

125 g/4^1/$_2$ oz baby corn

175 g/6 oz portobello or large
cup mushrooms, thinly
sliced

200 g/7 oz fresh beansprouts

250 g/9 oz canned water
chestnuts, drained

4 tsp soy sauce, or to taste

cooked wild rice, to serve

method

1 Heat 2 tablespoons of the oil in a large
frying pan or wok over a high heat. Stir-fry the
6 chopped spring onions with the garlic and
ginger for 30 seconds.

2 Add the broccoli, pepper and red cabbage
and stir-fry for 1–2 minutes. Mix in the baby
corn and mushrooms and stir-fry for a further
1–2 minutes.

3 Finally, add the beansprouts and water
chestnuts and cook for 2 minutes. Pour in
the soy sauce and stir well.

4 Serve immediately over cooked wild rice,
garnished with the remaining spring onions.

thai potato stir-fry

ingredients

SERVES 4

900 g/2 lb waxy potatoes, cut
  into small dice
2 tbsp vegetable oil
1 yellow pepper, deseeded
  and diced
1 red pepper, deseeded
  and diced
1 carrot, cut into thin strips
1 courgette, cut into thin strips
2 garlic cloves, crushed
1 red chilli, sliced
1 bunch spring onions,
  halved lengthways
125 ml/4 fl oz coconut milk
1 tsp chopped lemon grass
2 tsp lime juice
finely grated zest of 1 lime
1 tbsp chopped fresh
  coriander

method

1 Bring a large saucepan of water to the boil
and cook the diced potatoes for 5 minutes.
Drain thoroughly.

2 Heat the vegetable oil in a wok or large frying
pan, swirling the oil around the base of the wok
until it is really hot.

3 Add the potatoes, peppers, carrot, courgette,
garlic and chilli to the wok and stir-fry the
vegetables for 2–3 minutes.

4 Stir in the spring onions, coconut milk,
chopped lemon grass and lime juice and stir-fry
the mixture for a further 2 minutes. Add
the lime zest and coriander and stir-fry for
1 minute. Serve hot.

tofu & green vegetable curry

ingredients

SERVES 4

vegetable oil, for deep-frying
225 g/8 oz firm tofu, cubed
2 tbsp vegetable or peanut oil
1 tbsp chilli oil
2 fresh green chillies,
    deseeded and sliced
2 garlic cloves, crushed
6 spring onions, sliced
2 medium courgettes, cut into
    sticks
1/2 cucumber, peeled,
    deseeded and sliced
1 green pepper, deseeded and
    sliced
1 small head of broccoli,
    cut into florets
55 g/2 oz fine green beans,
    halved
55 g/2 oz frozen peas, thawed
300 ml/10 fl oz vegetable
    stock
55 g/2 oz creamed coconut,
    chopped
2 tbsp Thai soy sauce
1 tsp soft light brown sugar
4 tbsp chopped fresh parsley

method

1 Heat the oil for deep-frying in a frying pan and carefully lower in the tofu cubes, in batches, and cook for 2–3 minutes, until golden brown. Remove with a slotted spoon and drain on kitchen paper.

2 Heat the other oils in a wok and stir-fry the chillies, garlic and spring onions for 2–3 minutes. Add the courgettes, cucumber, green pepper, broccoli and green beans and stir-fry for a further 2–3 minutes.

3 Add the peas, stock, creamed coconut, soy sauce and sugar. Cover and simmer for 2–3 minutes, until all the vegetables are tender and the coconut has dissolved.

4 Stir in the tofu and serve immediately, sprinkled with the chopped fresh parsley.

spicy tofu

ingredients

SERVES 4

250 g/9 oz firm tofu, rinsed
   and drained thoroughly
   and cut into 1-cm/$\frac{1}{2}$-inch
   cubes
4 tbsp peanut oil
1 tbsp grated fresh ginger
3 garlic cloves, crushed
4 spring onions, thinly sliced
1 head of broccoli, cut into
   florets
1 carrot, cut into batons
1 yellow pepper, thinly sliced
250 g/9 oz shiitake
   mushrooms, thinly sliced
steamed rice, to serve

marinade
5 tbsp vegetable stock
2 tsp cornflour
2 tbsp soy sauce
1 tbsp caster sugar
pinch of chilli flakes

method

1 Combine all the ingredients for the marinade in a large bowl. Add the tofu and toss well to cover in the marinade. Set aside to marinate for 20 minutes.

2 In a large frying pan or wok, heat 2 tablespoons of the peanut oil and stir-fry the tofu with its marinade until brown and crispy. Remove from the frying pan and set aside.

3 Heat the remaining 2 tablespoons of peanut oil in the frying pan and stir-fry the ginger, garlic and spring onions for 30 seconds. Add the broccoli, carrot, yellow pepper and mushrooms to the frying pan and cook for 5–6 minutes. Return the tofu to the frying pan and stir-fry to reheat. Serve immediately over steamed rice.

mixed vegetables with quick-fried basil

ingredients

SERVES 4

2 tbsp vegetable or peanut oil

2 garlic cloves, chopped

1 onion, sliced

115 g/4 oz baby corn, cut in half diagonally

$^1/_2$ cucumber, peeled, halved, deseeded and sliced

225 g/8 oz canned water chestnuts, drained and rinsed

60 g/2$^1/_4$ oz mangetout, trimmed

115 g/4 oz shiitake mushrooms

1 red pepper, deseeded and sliced thinly

1 tbsp soft light brown sugar

3 tbsp Thai soy sauce

1 tbsp rice vinegar

boiled rice, to serve

quick-fried basil

vegetable or peanut oil, for cooking

8–12 sprigs fresh Thai basil

method

1 Heat the oil in a wok and stir-fry the garlic and onion for 1–2 minutes. Add the corn, cucumber, water chestnuts, mangetout, mushrooms and red pepper and stir-fry for 2–3 minutes, until starting to soften.

2 Add the sugar, soy sauce and vinegar and gradually bring to the boil. Simmer for 1–2 minutes.

3 Meanwhile, heat the oil for the basil in a wok or frying pan and, when hot, add the basil sprigs. Cook for 20–30 seconds, until crisp. Remove with a slotted spoon and drain thoroughly on kitchen paper.

4 Garnish the vegetable stir-fry with the crispy basil and serve immediately, with the boiled rice.

cauliflower & beans with cashews

ingredients

SERVES 4

1 tbsp vegetable or peanut oil

1 tbsp chilli oil

1 onion, chopped

2 garlic cloves, chopped

2 tbsp Thai red curry paste

1 small cauliflower, cut into
   florets

175 g/6 oz green beans, cut
   into 7.5-cm/3-inch lengths

150 ml/5 fl oz vegetable stock

2 tbsp Thai soy sauce

50 g/1¾ oz toasted cashews,
   to garnish

method

1 Heat both the oils in a wok and stir-fry the onion and garlic until softened. Add the curry paste and stir-fry for 1–2 minutes.

2 Add the cauliflower and beans and stir-fry for 3–4 minutes, until softened. Pour in the stock and soy sauce and simmer for 1–2 minutes. Serve immediately, garnished with the cashews.

aubergine & bean curry

ingredients

SERVES 4

2 tbsp vegetable or peanut oil

1 onion, chopped

2 garlic cloves, crushed

2 fresh red chillies, deseeded
and chopped

1 tbsp Thai red curry paste

1 large aubergine, cut into
chunks

115 g/4 oz pea or small
aubergines

115 g/4 oz baby broad beans

115 g/4 oz fine green beans

300 ml/10 fl oz vegetable
stock

55 g/2 oz creamed coconut,
chopped

3 tbsp Thai soy sauce

1 tsp jaggery or soft light
brown sugar

3 kaffir lime leaves, torn
coarsely

4 tbsp chopped fresh
coriander

method

1 Heat the oil in a wok or large frying pan and sauté the onion, garlic and chillies for 1–2 minutes. Stir in the curry paste and cook for 1–2 minutes.

2 Add the aubergines and cook for 3–4 minutes, until starting to soften. (You may need to add a little more oil as aubergines soak it up quickly.) Add the beans and stir-fry for 2 minutes.

3 Pour in the stock and add the creamed coconut, soy sauce, sugar and lime leaves. Bring gently to the boil and cook until the coconut has dissolved. Stir in the coriander and serve hot.

vegetable & coconut curry

ingredients

SERVES 4

1 onion, roughly chopped

3 garlic cloves, thinly sliced

2.5-cm/1-inch piece fresh
ginger, thinly sliced

2 fresh green chillies,
deseeded and finely
chopped

1 tbsp vegetable oil

1 tsp ground turmeric

1 tsp ground coriander

1 tsp ground cumin

1 kg/2 lb 4 oz mixed
vegetables, such as
cauliflower, courgettes,
potatoes, carrots and green
beans, cut into chunks

200 g/7 oz coconut cream or
coconut milk

salt and pepper

2 tbsp chopped fresh
coriander, to garnish

freshly cooked rice, to serve

method

1 Put the onion, garlic, ginger and chillies in a food processor and process until almost smooth.

2 Heat the oil in a large, heavy-based saucepan over a medium–low heat, add the onion mixture and cook, stirring constantly, for 5 minutes.

3 Add the turmeric, coriander and cumin and cook, stirring frequently, for 3–4 minutes. Add the vegetables and stir to coat in the spice paste.

4 Add the coconut cream to the vegetables, cover and simmer for 30–40 minutes until the vegetables are tender.

5 Season with salt and pepper, garnish with the chopped fresh coriander and serve with freshly cooked rice.

spinach with chickpeas

ingredients

SERVES 4–6

2 tbsp olive oil

1 large garlic clove, cut in half

1 medium onion, chopped finely

1/2 tsp cumin

pinch cayenne pepper

pinch turmeric

800 g/1 lb 12 oz canned chickpeas, drained and rinsed

500 g/1 lb 2 oz baby spinach leaves, rinsed and shaken dry

2 pimientos del piquillo, drained and sliced

salt and pepper

method

1 Heat the oil in a large, lidded frying pan over medium–high heat. Add the garlic and cook for 2 minutes, or until golden but not brown. Remove with a slotted spoon and discard.

2 Add the onion and cumin, cayenne and turmeric and cook, stirring, for about 5 minutes until soft. Add the chickpeas and stir around until they are lightly coloured with the turmeric and cayenne.

3 Stir in the spinach with just the water clinging to its leaves. Cover and cook for 4–5 minutes until wilted. Uncover, stir in the pimientos del piquillo and continue cooking, stirring gently, until all the liquid evaporates. Season with salt and pepper and serve.

chickpea curry

ingredients

SERVES 4

6 tbsp vegetable oil

2 onions, sliced

1 tsp finely chopped fresh root
    ginger

1 tsp ground cumin

1 tsp ground coriander

1 tsp fresh garlic, crushed

1 tsp chilli powder

2 fresh green chillies

2–3 tbsp fresh coriander
    leaves

150 ml/5 fl oz water

1 large potato

400 g/14 oz canned
    chickpeas, drained

1 tbsp lemon juice

method

1 Heat the vegetable oil in a large, heavy-based saucepan. Add the onions and cook, stirring occasionally, until golden. Reduce the heat, add the ginger, ground cumin, ground coriander, garlic, chilli powder, fresh green chillies and fresh coriander leaves and stir-fry for 2 minutes.

2 Add the water to the mixture in the pan and stir to mix.

3 Using a sharp knife, cut the potato into dice, then add, with the chickpeas, to the pan. Cover and simmer, stirring occasionally, for 5–7 minutes.

4 Sprinkle the lemon juice over the curry. Transfer the chickpea curry to serving dishes and serve hot.

potato & spinach yellow curry

ingredients

SERVES 4

2 garlic cloves, finely chopped

3-cm/1¼-inch piece fresh galangal, finely chopped

1 lemon grass stem, finely chopped

1 tsp coriander seeds

3 tbsp vegetable oil

2 tsp Thai red curry paste

½ tsp ground turmeric

175 ml/6 fl oz coconut milk

250 g/9 oz potatoes, cut into 2-cm/¾-inch cubes

300 ml/10 fl oz vegetable stock

200 g/7 oz fresh young spinach leaves

1 small onion, thinly sliced

method

1 Place the garlic, galangal, lemon grass and coriander seeds in a mortar and, using a pestle, grind to make a smooth paste.

2 Heat 2 tablespoons of the oil in a frying pan or preheated wok. Stir in the garlic paste mixture and stir-fry for 30 seconds. Stir in the curry paste and turmeric, then add the coconut milk and bring to the boil.

3 Add the potatoes and stock. Return to the boil, then reduce the heat and simmer, uncovered, for 10–12 minutes, or until the potatoes are almost tender.

4 Stir in the spinach and simmer until the leaves are wilted.

5 Meanwhile, heat the remaining oil in a separate frying pan. Add the onion and cook until crisp and golden brown. Place the crispy fried onions on top of the curry just before serving.

carrot & pumpkin curry

ingredients

SERVES 4

150 ml/5 fl oz vegetable stock
2.5-cm/1-inch piece fresh
    galangal, sliced
2 garlic cloves, chopped
1 lemon grass stalk (white part
    only), chopped finely
2 fresh red chillies, deseeded
    and chopped
4 carrots, peeled and cut into
    chunks
225 g/8 oz pumpkin, peeled,
    deseeded and cut into
    cubes
2 tbsp vegetable or peanut oil
2 shallots, chopped finely
3 tbsp Thai yellow curry paste
400 ml/14 fl oz coconut milk
4–6 sprigs fresh Thai basil
25 g/1 oz toasted pumpkin
    seeds, to garnish

method

1 Pour the stock into a large saucepan and bring to the boil. Add the galangal, half the garlic, the lemon grass and chillies and simmer for 5 minutes. Add the carrots and pumpkin and simmer for 5–6 minutes, until tender.

2 Meanwhile, heat the oil in a wok or frying pan and stir-fry the shallots and the remaining garlic for 2–3 minutes. Add the curry paste and stir-fry for 1–2 minutes.

3 Stir the shallot mixture into the pan and add the coconut milk and basil. Simmer for 2–3 minutes. Serve hot, sprinkled with the toasted pumpkin seeds.

lentil & rice casserole

ingredients

SERVES 4

225 g/8 oz red split lentils, rinsed

55 g/2 oz long-grain rice

1.2 litres/2 pints vegetable stock

1 leek, cut into chunks

3 garlic cloves, crushed

400 g/14 oz canned chopped tomatoes

1 tsp each of ground cumin, chilli powder and garam masala

1 red pepper, deseeded and sliced

100 g/3½ oz small broccoli florets

8 baby corn cobs, halved lengthways

55 g/2 oz green beans, halved

1 tbsp shredded fresh basil

salt and pepper

fresh basil sprigs, to garnish

method

1 Place the lentils, rice and vegetable stock in a flameproof casserole and cook over low heat, stirring occasionally, for 20 minutes.

2 Add the leek and garlic to the pan with the tomatoes and their juices, ground spices, pepper, broccoli, baby corn and green beans and stir well to mix.

3 Bring the mixture to the boil, then reduce the heat, cover and simmer for a further 10–15 minutes or until the vegetables are tender. Add the shredded basil and season to taste with salt and pepper. Garnish with basil sprigs and serve.

celeriac, chestnut, spinach & feta filo pies

ingredients

SERVES 4

4 tbsp olive oil

2 garlic cloves, crushed

1/2 large or 1 whole small head celeriac, cut into short thin sticks

250 g/9 oz baby spinach leaves

85 g/3 oz cooked, peeled chestnuts, coarsely chopped

200 g/7 oz feta cheese (drained weight), crumbled

1 egg

2 tbsp pesto sauce

1 tbsp finely chopped fresh parsley

pepper

4 sheets filo pastry, about 33 x 18 cm/ 13 x 7 inches each

method

1 Heat 1 tablespoon of the oil in a large frying pan over medium heat, add the garlic and cook for 1 minute, stirring constantly. Add the celeriac and cook for 5 minutes, or until soft and browned. Remove from the pan and keep warm.

2 Add 1 tablespoon of the remaining oil to the frying pan, then add the spinach, cover and cook for 2–3 minutes, or until the spinach has wilted. Uncover and cook until any liquid has evaporated.

3 Mix the garlic and celeriac, spinach, chestnuts, cheese, egg, pesto, parsley and pepper in a large bowl. Divide the mixture between 4 individual gratin dishes or put it all into 1 medium gratin dish.

4 Brush each sheet of filo with the remaining oil and arrange, slightly scrunched, on top of the celeriac mixture. Bake in a preheated oven, 190°C/375°F/Gas Mark 5, for 15–20 minutes, or until browned. Serve at once.

aubergine gratin

ingredients

SERVES 4

4 tbsp olive oil

2 onions, finely chopped

2 garlic cloves, very
    finely chopped

2 aubergines, thickly sliced

3 tbsp chopped fresh
    flat-leaf parsley

1/2 tsp dried thyme

salt and pepper

400 g/14 oz canned
    chopped tomatoes

175 g/6 oz mozzarella cheese,
    coarsely grated

6 tbsp freshly grated
    Parmesan cheese

method

1 Heat the oil in a frying pan over a medium heat. Add the onion and cook for 5 minutes, or until softened. Add the garlic and cook for a few seconds, or until just beginning to colour. Using a slotted spoon, transfer the onion mixture to a plate. Cook the aubergine slices in batches in the same frying pan until they are just lightly browned.

2 Arrange a layer of aubergine slices in a shallow ovenproof dish. Sprinkle with some of the parsley, thyme, salt and pepper. Add a layer of onion, tomatoes and mozzarella and a sprinkling of parsley, thyme, salt and pepper.

3 Continue layering, sprinkling parsley, thyme, salt and pepper over each layer and finishing with a layer of aubergine slices. Sprinkle with the Parmesan cheese. Bake, uncovered, in a preheated oven, 200°C/400°F/Gas Mark 6, for 20–30 minutes, or until the top is golden and the aubergines are tender. Serve hot.

roasted summer vegetables

ingredients

SERVES 4

2 tbsp olive oil

1 fennel bulb

2 red onions

2 beefsteak tomatoes

1 aubergine

2 courgettes

1 yellow pepper

1 red pepper

1 orange pepper

4 garlic cloves, peeled but
    left whole

4 fresh rosemary sprigs

pepper

crusty bread, to serve
    (optional)

method

1 Brush a large ovenproof dish with a little of the oil. Prepare the vegetables. Cut the fennel bulb, red onions, and tomatoes into wedges. Slice the aubergine and courgettes thickly, then deseed all the peppers and cut into chunks. Arrange the vegetables in the dish and tuck the garlic cloves and rosemary sprigs among them. Drizzle with the remaining oil and season with pepper.

2 Roast the vegetables in a preheated oven, 200°C/400°F/Gas Mark 6, for 10 minutes. Remove the dish from the oven and turn the vegetables over using a slotted spoon. Return the dish to the oven and roast for a further 10–15 minutes, or until the vegetables are tender and starting to turn golden brown.

3 Serve the vegetables straight from the dish or transfer them to a warmed serving plate. For a vegetarian main course, serve with crusty bread, if you like.

roasted red peppers with halloumi

ingredients

SERVES 4

6 small red peppers

2 tbsp olive oil, plus extra for oiling

3 garlic cloves, thinly sliced

250 g/9 oz halloumi or feta cheese, thinly sliced

12 fresh mint leaves grated rind and juice of 1 lemon

1 tbsp chopped fresh thyme

3 tbsp pine kernels

pepper

method

1 Cut the peppers in half lengthways and remove the cores and seeds. Rub the skins of the peppers with a little of the oil, then arrange the peppers, skin-side down, on a large oiled baking sheet.

2 Scatter half the garlic into the peppers. Add the cheese, then the mint leaves, lemon rind, remaining garlic, thyme, pine kernels and pepper. Drizzle over the remaining oil and the lemon juice.

3 Roast the peppers in a preheated oven, 200°C/400°F/Gas Mark 6, for 30 minutes, until tender and beginning to char around the edges. Serve warm.

stuffed courgettes with walnuts & feta

ingredients

SERVES 4

4 fat, medium courgettes
3 tbsp olive oil
1 onion, finely chopped
1 garlic clove, finely chopped
55 g/2 oz feta cheese,
    crumbled
25 g/1 oz walnut pieces,
    chopped
55 g/2 oz white breadcrumbs
1 egg, beaten
1 tsp chopped fresh dill
salt and pepper

method

1 Put the courgettes in a saucepan of boiling water, return to the boil, then boil for 3 minutes. Drain, rinse under cold water and drain again. Let cool.

2 When the courgettes are cool enough to handle, cut a thin strip off the top side of each one with a sharp knife. Using a teaspoon, carefully scoop out the flesh, leaving a shell to hold the stuffing. Chop the courgette flesh.

3 Heat 2 tablespoons of the oil in a saucepan. Add the onion and garlic and fry for 5 minutes, until softened. Add the courgette flesh and fry for 5 minutes, until the onion is golden brown. Remove from the heat and cool slightly. Stir in the cheese then the walnuts, breadcrumbs, egg, dill, salt and pepper.

4 Use the stuffing to fill the courgette shells, and place side by side in an ovenproof dish. Drizzle over the remaining oil.

5 Cover the dish with foil and bake in a preheated oven, 190°C/375°F/Gas Mark 5, for 30 minutes. Remove the foil and bake for another 10–15 minutes or until golden brown. Serve hot.

stuffed portobello mushrooms

ingredients

SERVES 4

12 large portobello
mushrooms, wiped over
and stems removed

2 tbsp corn oil, plus extra
for oiling

1 fennel bulb, stalks removed,
finely chopped

100 g/3^1/$_2$ oz sun-dried
tomatoes, finely chopped

2 garlic cloves, crushed

125 g/4^1/$_2$ oz grated fontina
cheese

50 g/1^3/$_4$ oz freshly grated
Parmesan cheese

3 tbsp chopped fresh basil

salt and pepper

1 tbsp olive oil

fresh Parmesan cheese
shavings and chopped
fresh parsley, to serve

method

1 Place 8 of the mushrooms, cup-side up, in a large, lightly oiled ovenproof dish and chop the remaining 4 mushrooms finely.

2 Heat the corn oil in a non-stick frying pan, add the chopped mushrooms, fennel, sun-dried tomatoes and garlic and cook over low heat until the vegetables are soft, but not browned. Remove from the heat and let cool.

3 When cool, add the cheeses, basil, salt and pepper. Mix well. Brush the mushrooms lightly with the olive oil and fill each cavity with a spoonful of the vegetable filling. Bake in a preheated oven, 180°C/350°F/Gas Mark 4, for 20–25 minutes, or until the mushrooms are tender and the filling is heated through.

4 Top with Parmesan shavings and parsley and serve at once, allowing 2 mushrooms for each person.

halloumi cheese & vegetable kebabs

ingredients

SERVES 4

kebabs

225 g/8 oz halloumi cheese

12 button mushrooms

8 baby onions

12 cherry tomatoes

2 courgettes, cut into small
    chunks

1 red pepper, deseeded and
    cut into small chunks

chopped fresh coriander,
    to garnish

freshly cooked rice or fresh
    mixed salad leaves and
    fresh crusty bread, to serve

marinade

4 tbsp extra virgin olive oil

2 tbsp balsamic vinegar

2 garlic cloves, finely chopped

1 tbsp chopped fresh
    coriander

salt and pepper

method

1 If using wooden skewers, soak them in cold water for 30 minutes before use.

2 Put the oil, vinegar, garlic and coriander into a large bowl. Season with salt and pepper and mix until well combined.

3 Cut the halloumi cheese into bite-sized cubes. Thread the cubes onto skewers, alternating them with whole button mushrooms, baby onions and cherry tomatoes, and chunks of courgette and red pepper. When the skewers are full (leave a small space at either end), transfer them to the bowl and turn them in the marinade until they are well coated. Cover with clingfilm and place in the refrigerator to marinate for at least 2 hours.

4 When the skewers are thoroughly marinated, barbecue them over hot coals for 5–10 minutes, or until they are cooked to your taste, turning frequently, and basting with the remaining marinade. Arrange the skewers on a bed of freshly cooked rice or fresh mixed salad leaves, garnish with coriander leaves and serve with fresh crusty bread.

lentil bolognese

ingredients

SERVES 4

1 tsp vegetable oil

1 tsp crushed garlic

25 g/1 oz onion, finely
chopped

25 g/1 oz leek, finely chopped

25 g/1 oz celery, finely
chopped

25 g/1 oz green pepper,
deseeded and finely
chopped

25 g/1 oz carrot, finely
chopped

25 g/1 oz courgette, finely
chopped

85 g/3 oz flat mushrooms,
diced

4 tbsp red wine

pinch of dried thyme

400 g/14 oz canned tomatoes,
chopped, strained through
a colander, and the
juice and pulp reserved
separately

4 tbsp dried Puy or green
lentils, cooked

pepper, to taste

2 tsp lemon juice

1 tsp sugar

3 tbsp chopped fresh basil,
plus extra sprigs to garnish

freshly cooked spaghetti,
to serve

method

1 Heat a saucepan over low heat, add the oil and garlic and cook, stirring, until golden brown. Add all the vegetables, except the mushrooms, increase the heat to medium and cook, stirring occasionally, for 10–12 minutes, or until softened and there is no liquid from the vegetables left in the pan.

2 Add the mushrooms, increase the heat to high, add the wine and cook for 2 minutes. Add the thyme and the juice from the tomatoes and cook until reduced by half.

3 Add the lentils and pepper, stir in the tomatoes and cook for a further 3–4 minutes. Remove the pan from the heat and stir in the lemon juice, sugar and basil.

4 Serve the sauce with freshly cooked spaghetti, garnished with basil sprigs.

mushroom stroganoff

ingredients

SERVES 4

550 g/1 lb 4 oz mixed fresh
   mushrooms, such as
   chestnut, chanterelles,
   cèpes and oyster
1 red onion, diced
2 garlic cloves, crushed
425 ml/15 fl oz vegetable
   stock
1 tbsp tomato paste
2 tbsp lemon juice
scant 1 tbsp cornflour
2 tbsp cold water
115 g/4 oz low-fat plain yogurt
3 tbsp chopped fresh parsley
pepper
boiled brown or white rice and
   crisp green salad, to serve

method

1 Put the mushrooms, onion, garlic, stock, tomato paste and lemon juice into a saucepan and bring to the boil. Reduce the heat, cover and simmer for 15 minutes, or until the onion is tender.

2 Blend the cornflour with the water in a small bowl and stir into the mushroom mixture. Return to the boil, stirring constantly, and cook until the sauce thickens. Reduce the heat and simmer for a further 2–3 minutes, stirring occasionally.

3 Just before serving, remove the pan from the heat, and stir in the yogurt, making sure that the stroganoff is not boiling or it may separate and curdle. Stir in 2 tablespoons of the parsley and season with pepper. Transfer the stroganoff to a warmed serving dish, sprinkle over the remaining parsley and serve at once with boiled brown or white rice and a crisp green salad.

spaghetti olio e aglio

ingredients

SERVES 4

450 g/1 lb dried spaghetti

125 ml/4 fl oz extra virgin
    olive oil

3 garlic cloves, finely chopped

salt and pepper

3 tbsp chopped fresh flat-leaf
    parsley

method

1 Bring a large, heavy-based saucepan of lightly salted water to the boil. Add the spaghetti, return to the boil and cook for 8–10 minutes, or until tender but still firm to the bite.

2 Meanwhile, heat the olive oil in a heavy-based frying pan. Add the garlic and a pinch of salt and cook over low heat, stirring constantly, for 3–4 minutes, or until golden. Do not allow the garlic to brown or it will taste bitter. Remove the pan from the heat.

3 Drain the pasta and transfer to a warmed serving dish. Pour in the garlic-flavoured olive oil, then add the chopped parsley and season with salt and pepper. Toss well and serve immediately.

fettuccine alfredo

ingredients

SERVES 4

25 g/1 oz butter
225 ml/8 fl oz double cream
450 g/1 lb fresh fettuccine
1 tbsp olive oil
90 g/3¼ oz freshly grated
   Parmesan cheese, plus
   extra to serve
pinch of freshly grated nutmeg
salt and pepper
fresh flat-leaf parsley sprigs,
   to garnish

method

1 Place the butter and 150 ml/5 fl oz of the cream in a large saucepan and bring the mixture to the boil over medium heat. Reduce the heat and simmer gently for about 1½ minutes, or until slightly thickened.

2 Meanwhile, bring a large saucepan of lightly salted water to the boil. Add the fettuccine and oil, return to the boil and cook for 2–3 minutes until tender but still firm to the bite. Drain the fettuccine, return it to the pan and pour the sauce over it. Return the pan to low heat and toss the fettuccine in the sauce until coated.

3 Add the remaining cream, the Parmesan cheese and nutmeg to the fettuccine mixture and season with salt and pepper. Toss thoroughly to coat while gently heating through.

4 Transfer the fettuccine mixture to a warmed serving plate and garnish with parsley sprigs. Serve immediately, with extra grated Parmesan cheese.

spaghetti with tomato, garlic & basil sauce

ingredients

SERVES 4

5 tbsp extra virgin olive oil
1 onion, chopped finely
800 g/1 lb 12 oz canned
  chopped tomatoes
4 garlic cloves, cut into
  quarters
salt and pepper
450 g/1 lb dried spaghetti
large handful fresh basil
  leaves, shredded
fresh Parmesan cheese
  shavings, to serve

method

1 Heat the oil in a large saucepan over medium heat. Add the onion and fry gently for 5 minutes until soft. Add the tomatoes and garlic. Bring to the boil, then simmer over medium–low heat for 25–30 minutes until the oil separates from the tomato. Season with salt and pepper.

2 Cook the pasta in plenty of boiling salted water until tender but still firm to the bite. Drain and transfer to a warmed serving dish.

3 Pour the sauce over the pasta. Add the basil and toss well to mix. Serve with the Parmesan cheese shavings.

tagliatelle with asparagus & gorgonzola sauce

ingredients

SERVES 4

450 g/1 lb asparagus tips
olive oil
salt and pepper
225 g/8 oz Gorgonzola,
    crumbled
175 ml/6 fl oz double cream
350 g/12 oz dried tagliatelle

method

1 Place the asparagus tips in a single layer in a shallow ovenproof dish. Sprinkle with a little olive oil and season with salt and pepper. Turn to coat in the oil and seasoning. Roast in a preheated oven, 230°C/450°F/Gas Mark 8, for 10–12 minutes, until slightly browned and just tender. Set aside and keep warm.

2 Combine the crumbled cheese with the cream in a bowl. Season with salt and pepper.

3 Cook the pasta in plenty of boiling salted water until tender but still firm to the bite. Drain and transfer to a warmed serving dish.

4 Immediately add the asparagus and the cheese mixture. Toss well until the cheese has melted and the pasta is coated with the sauce. Serve at once.

chilli broccoli pasta

ingredients

SERVES 4

225 g/8 oz dried penne or macaroni

225 g/8 oz broccoli, cut into florets

50 ml/2 fl oz extra virgin olive oil

2 large garlic cloves, chopped

2 fresh red chillies, deseeded and diced

8 cherry tomatoes (optional)

fresh basil leaves, to garnish

method

1 Bring a large saucepan of salted boiling water to the boil. Add the pasta, return to the boil and cook for 8–10 minutes until tender but still firm to the bite. Drain the pasta, refresh under cold running water and drain again. Set aside.

2 Bring a separate saucepan of salted water to the boil, add the broccoli and cook for 5 minutes. Drain, refresh under cold running water and drain again.

3 Heat the oil in a large saucepan over high heat. Add the garlic, chillies and tomatoes, if using, and cook, stirring, for 1 minute.

4 Add the broccoli and mix well. Cook for 2 minutes, stirring, to heat through. Add the pasta and mix well again. Cook for a further minute. Transfer the pasta to a large, warmed serving bowl and serve garnished with basil leaves.

pasta with pesto

ingredients

SERVES 4

450 g/1 lb dried tagliatelle
fresh basil sprigs, to garnish

pesto
2 garlic cloves
25 g/1 oz pine kernels
salt
115 g/4 oz fresh basil leaves
55 g/2 oz freshly grated
    Parmesan cheese
125 ml/4 fl oz olive oil

method

1 To make the pesto, put the garlic, pine kernels, a large pinch of salt and the basil into a mortar and pound to a paste with a pestle. Transfer to a bowl and gradually work in the Parmesan cheese with a wooden spoon, followed by the olive oil, to make a thick, creamy sauce. Taste and adjust the seasoning if necessary.

2 Alternatively, put the garlic, pine kernels and a large pinch of salt into a food processor or blender and process briefly. Add the basil leaves and process to a paste. With the motor still running, gradually add the olive oil. Scrape into a bowl and beat in the Parmesan cheese.

3 Bring a large pan of lightly salted water to the boil. Add the pasta, return to the boil and cook for 8–10 minutes, or until tender but still firm to the bite. Drain the pasta well, return to the pan, and toss with half the pesto, then divide between warmed serving plates and top with the remaining pesto. Garnish with basil sprigs and serve immediately.

creamy spinach & mushroom pasta

ingredients

SERVES 4

300 g/10¹/₂ oz dried penne or
   pasta of your choice
2 tbsp olive oil
250 g/9 oz mushrooms, sliced
1 tsp dried oregano
275 ml/9 fl oz vegetable stock
1 tbsp lemon juice
6 tbsp cream cheese
200 g/7 oz frozen spinach
   leaves
salt and pepper

method

1 Cook the pasta in a large pan of lightly salted boiling water, according to the packet instructions. Drain, reserving 175 ml/6 fl oz of the cooking liquid.

2 Meanwhile, heat the oil in a large, heavy-based frying pan over medium heat, add the mushrooms and cook, stirring frequently, for 8 minutes, or until almost crisp. Stir in the oregano, stock and lemon juice and cook for 10–12 minutes, or until the sauce is reduced by half.

3 Stir in the cream cheese and spinach and cook over medium–low heat for 3–5 minutes. Add the reserved cooking liquid, then the cooked pasta. Stir well, season to taste with salt and pepper and heat through gently before serving.

penne in a creamy mushroom sauce

ingredients

SERVES 4

4 tbsp butter

1 tbsp olive oil

6 shallots, sliced

450 g/1 lb chestnut
    mushrooms, sliced

salt and pepper

1 tsp plain flour

150 ml/5 fl oz double cream
    or panna da cucina

2 tbsp port

115 g/4 oz sun-dried tomatoes
    in oil, drained and chopped

pinch of freshly grated nutmeg

350 g/12 oz dried penne

2 tbsp chopped fresh flat-leaf
    parsley

method

1 Melt the butter with the olive oil in a large heavy-based frying pan. Add the shallots and cook over a low heat, stirring occasionally, for 4–5 minutes, or until softened. Add the mushrooms and cook over a low heat for a further 2 minutes. Season to taste with salt and pepper, sprinkle in the flour and cook, stirring, for 1 minute.

2 Remove the pan from the heat and gradually stir in the cream and port. Return to the heat, add the sun-dried tomatoes and grated nutmeg and cook over a low heat, stirring occasionally, for 8 minutes.

3 Meanwhile, bring a large heavy-based saucepan of lightly salted water to the boil. Add the pasta, return to the boil and cook for 8–10 minutes, or until tender but still firm to the bite. Drain the pasta well and add to the mushroom sauce. Cook for 3 minutes, then transfer to a warmed serving dish. Sprinkle with the parsley and serve immediately.

penne with pepper & goat's cheese sauce

ingredients

SERVES 4

2 tbsp olive oil

1 tbsp butter

1 small onion, finely chopped

4 peppers, yellow and red, deseeded and cut into 2-cm/³/₄-inch squares

3 garlic cloves, thinly sliced

salt and pepper

450 g/1 lb dried rigatoni or penne

125 g/4¹/₂ oz goat's cheese, crumbled

15 fresh basil leaves, shredded

10 black olives, stoned and sliced

method

1 Heat the oil and butter in a large frying pan over a medium heat. Add the onion and cook until soft. Raise the heat to medium–high and add the peppers and garlic. Cook for 12–15 minutes, stirring, until the peppers are tender but not mushy. Season with salt and pepper. Remove from the heat.

2 Cook the pasta in plenty of boiling salted water until al dente. Drain and transfer to a warm serving dish. Add the goat's cheese and toss to mix.

3 Briefly reheat the sauce. Add the basil and olives. Pour over the pasta and toss well to mix. Serve immediately.

spaghetti with roasted garlic & pepper sauce

ingredients

SERVES 4

6 large garlic cloves, unpeeled

400 g/14 oz bottled roasted
   red peppers, drained and
   sliced

200 g/7 oz canned chopped
   tomatoes

3 tbsp olive oil

1/4 tsp dried chilli flakes

1 tsp chopped fresh thyme or
   oregano

salt and pepper

350 g/12 oz dried spaghetti,
   bucatini or linguine

freshly grated Parmesan,
   to serve

method

1 Place the unpeeled garlic cloves in a shallow, ovenproof dish. Roast in a preheated oven, 200°C/400°F/Gas Mark 6, for 7–10 minutes, or until the cloves feel soft.

2 Put the peppers, tomatoes and oil in a food processor or blender, then purée. Squeeze the garlic flesh into the purée. Add the chilli flakes and oregano. Season with salt and pepper. Blend again, then scrape into a saucepan and set aside.

3 Cook the pasta in plenty of boiling salted water until al dente. Drain and transfer to a warm serving dish.

4 Reheat the sauce and pour over the pasta. Toss well to mix. Serve immediately with Parmesan.

fusilli with courgettes, lemon & rosemary

ingredients

SERVES 4

6 tbsp olive oil

1 small onion, sliced very thinly

2 garlic cloves, chopped very finely

2 tbsp chopped fresh rosemary

1 tbsp chopped fresh flat-leaf parsley

450 g/1 lb small courgettes, cut into 4-cm/1½-inch lengths

finely grated rind of 1 lemon

salt and pepper

450 g/1 lb fusilli tricolore

4 tbsp freshly grated Parmesan cheese

method

1 Heat the olive oil in a large frying pan over medium–low heat. Add the onion and gently fry, stirring occasionally, for about 10 minutes until golden.

2 Raise the heat to medium–high. Add the garlic, rosemary and parsley and cook for a few seconds, stirring. Add the courgettes and lemon rind. Cook for 5–7 minutes, stirring occasionally, until the courgettes are just tender. Season with salt and pepper. Remove from the heat.

3 Cook the pasta in plenty of boiling salted water until tender but still firm to the bite. Drain and transfer to a warmed serving dish.

4 Briefly reheat the courgettes. Pour over the pasta and toss well to mix. Sprinkle with the Parmesan cheese and serve immediately.

potato & spinach gnocchi

ingredients

SERVES 4

300 g/10^1/$_2$ oz diced floury
   potatoes
175 g/6 oz spinach
1 egg yolk
1 tsp olive oil
125 g/4^1/$_2$ oz plain flour
salt and pepper
spinach leaves, to garnish

s a u c e
1 tbsp olive oil
2 shallots, chopped
1 garlic clove, crushed
300 ml/10 fl oz passata
2 tsp soft light brown sugar

method

1 Cook the diced potatoes in a saucepan of boiling water for 10 minutes, or until cooked through. Drain and mash the potatoes.

2 Meanwhile, in a separate saucepan, blanch the spinach in a little boiling water for 1–2 minutes. Drain and shred the leaves.

3 Transfer the mashed potato to a lightly floured cutting board and make a well in the centre. Add the egg yolk, olive oil, spinach and a little of the flour. Quickly mix the ingredients into the potato, adding more flour as you go, to make a smooth, firm dough. Divide the mixture into very small dumplings.

4 Cook the gnocchi, in batches, in a saucepan of lightly salted, boiling water for about 5 minutes or until they rise to the surface.

5 Meanwhile, make the sauce. Put the oil, shallots, garlic, passata and sugar into a saucepan and cook over low heat for 10–15 minutes or until the sauce has thickened and reduced.

6 Drain the gnocchi using a slotted spoon and transfer to warm serving dishes. Spoon the sauce over the gnocchi and garnish with the fresh spinach leaves.

risotto primavera

ingredients

SERVES 6–8

225 g/8 oz fresh thin
    asparagus spears
4 tbsp olive oil
175 g/6 oz young green
    beans, cut into 2.5-cm/
    1-inch lengths
175 g/6 oz young courgettes,
    quartered and cut into
    2.5-cm/1-inch lengths
225 g/8 oz shelled fresh peas
1 onion, finely chopped
1–2 garlic cloves, finely
    chopped
350 g/12 oz Arborio rice
1.5 litres/2¾ pints simmering
    vegetable stock
4 spring onions, cut into
    2.5-cm/1-inch lengths
salt and pepper
55 g/2 oz butter
115 g/4 oz freshly grated
    Parmesan cheese
2 tbsp snipped fresh chives
2 tbsp shredded fresh basil
spring onions, to garnish
    (optional)

method

1 Trim the woody ends of the asparagus and cut off the tips. Cut the stems into 2.5-cm/1-inch pieces and set aside with the tips.

2 Heat 2 tablespoons of the oil in a large frying pan over high heat until very hot. Add the asparagus, beans, courgettes and peas and stir-fry for 3–4 minutes until they are bright green and just starting to soften. Set aside.

3 Heat the remaining oil in a large, heavy-based pan over medium heat. Add the onion and cook, stirring occasionally, for 3 minutes, or until it starts to soften. Stir in the garlic and cook, while stirring, for 30 seconds. Reduce the heat, add the rice and mix to coat in oil. Cook, stirring constantly, for 2–3 minutes, or until the grains are translucent.

4 Gradually add the hot stock, a ladleful at a time. Stir constantly and add more liquid as the rice absorbs each addition. Increase the heat to medium so that the liquid bubbles. Cook for 20 minutes, or until all but 2 tablespoons of the liquid is absorbed and the rice is creamy.

5 Stir in the stir-fried vegetables, onion mixture and spring onions with the remaining stock. Cook for 2 minutes, stirring frequently, then season with salt and pepper. Stir in the butter, Parmesan, chives and basil. Remove the pan from the heat and serve the risotto at once, garnished with spring onions, if liked.

wild mushroom risotto

ingredients

SERVES 6

55 g/2 oz dried porcini or morel mushrooms

about 500 g/1 lb 2 oz mixed fresh wild mushrooms, such as porcini, field mushrooms and chanterelles, halved if large

4 tbsp olive oil

3–4 garlic cloves, finely chopped

55 g/2 oz butter

1 onion, finely chopped

350 g/12 oz risotto rice

50 ml/2 fl oz dry white vermouth

1.2 litres/2 pints simmering chicken or vegetable stock

salt and pepper

115 g/4 oz freshly grated Parmesan cheese

4 tbsp chopped fresh flat-leaf parsley

method

1 Place the dried mushrooms in a heatproof bowl and add boiling water to cover. Set aside to soak for 30 minutes, then carefully lift out and pat dry. Strain the soaking liquid through a sieve lined with kitchen paper and set aside.

2 Trim the fresh mushrooms and gently brush clean. Heat 3 tablespoons of the oil in a large frying pan. Add the fresh mushrooms and stir-fry for 1–2 minutes. Add the garlic and the soaked mushrooms and cook, stirring frequently, for 2 minutes. Transfer to a plate.

3 Heat the remaining oil and half the butter in a large heavy-based saucepan. Add the onion and cook over a medium heat, stirring occasionally, for 2 minutes, until softened.

4 Reduce the heat, stir in the rice and cook, stirring constantly, for 2–3 minutes, until the grains are translucent. Add the vermouth and cook, stirring, for 1 minute until reduced.

5 Gradually add the hot stock, a ladleful at a time, until all the liquid is absorbed and the rice is creamy. Add half the reserved mushroom soaking liquid to the risotto and stir in the mushrooms. Season to taste and add more mushroom liquid, if necessary.

6 Remove the pan from the heat and stir in the remaining butter, grated Parmesan and chopped parsley. Serve immediately.

minted green risotto

ingredients

SERVES 4

2 tbsp butter

225 g/8 oz shelled fresh peas
or thawed frozen peas

250 g/9 oz fresh young
spinach leaves, washed
and drained

1 bunch of fresh mint, leaves
stripped from stalks

2 tbsp chopped fresh basil

2 tbsp chopped fresh oregano

pinch of freshly grated nutmeg

4 tbsp mascarpone cheese

2 tbsp vegetable oil

1 onion, finely chopped

2 celery sticks, including
leaves, finely chopped

2 garlic cloves, finely chopped

$1/2$ tsp dried thyme

300 g/$10^1/2$ oz risotto rice

50 ml/2 fl oz dry white
vermouth

1 litre/$1^3/4$ pints simmering
chicken or vegetable stock

85 g/3 oz freshly grated
Parmesan cheese

method

1 Heat half the butter in a deep frying pan over a medium–high heat until sizzling. Add the peas, spinach, mint leaves, basil and oregano and season with the nutmeg. Cook, stirring, for 3 minutes, until the spinach and mint leaves are wilted. Cool slightly.

2 Pour the spinach mixture into a food processor and process for 15 seconds. Add the mascarpone and process again for 1 minute. Transfer to a bowl and set aside.

3 Heat the oil and remaining butter in a large heavy-based saucepan over a medium heat. Add the onion, celery, garlic and thyme and cook, stirring occasionally, for 2 minutes, or until the vegetables are softened.

4 Reduce the heat, add the rice and mix to coat in oil and butter. Cook, stirring constantly, for 2–3 minutes, or until the grains are translucent. Add the vermouth and cook, stirring constantly, until it has reduced.

5 Gradually add the hot stock, a ladleful at a time. Stir constantly and add more liquid as the rice absorbs each addition. Increase the heat to medium so that the liquid bubbles. Cook for 20 minutes, or until the liquid is absorbed and the rice is creamy.

6 Stir in the spinach and mascarpone mixture and the Parmesan. Transfer to warmed plates and serve immediately.

crunchy walnut risotto

ingredients

SERVES 4

1 tbsp olive oil

70 g/2^1/$_2$ oz butter

1 small onion, finely chopped

280 g/10 oz Arborio rice

1.2 litres/2 pints simmering
   vegetable stock

salt and pepper

115 g/4 oz walnut halves

85 g/3 oz freshly grated
   Parmesan or Grana
   Padano cheese

55 g/2 oz Mascarpone cheese

55 g/2 oz Gorgonzola cheese,
   diced

method

1 Heat the oil with 2 tablespoons of the butter in a deep pan over medium heat until the butter has melted. Add the onion and cook, stirring occasionally, for 5–7 minutes, or until soft and starting to turn golden. Do not brown.

2 Reduce the heat, add the rice and mix to coat in oil and butter. Cook, stirring constantly, for 2–3 minutes, or until the grains are translucent.

3 Gradually add the hot stock, a ladleful at a time. Stir constantly and add more liquid as the rice absorbs each addition. Increase the heat to medium so that the liquid bubbles. Cook for 20 minutes, or until all the liquid is absorbed and the rice is creamy. Season with salt and pepper.

4 Melt 2 tablespoons of the remaining butter in a frying pan over medium heat. Add the walnuts and toss for 2–3 minutes, or until just starting to brown.

5 Remove the risotto from the heat and add the remaining butter. Mix well, then stir in the Parmesan, Mascarpone and Gorgonzola until they melt, along with most of the walnuts. Spoon the risotto onto warmed plates, sprinkle with the remaining walnuts and serve.

kidney bean risotto

ingredients

SERVES 4

4 tbsp olive oil

1 onion, chopped

2 garlic cloves, finely chopped

175 g/6 oz brown rice

600 ml/1 pint vegetable stock

salt and pepper

1 red pepper, deseeded
and chopped

2 celery stalks, sliced

225 g/8 oz chestnut
mushrooms, thinly sliced

425 g/15 oz canned red
kidney beans, drained
and rinsed

3 tbsp chopped fresh parsley,
plus extra to garnish

55 g/2 oz cashews

method

1 Heat half the oil in a large, heavy-based saucepan. Add the onion and cook, stirring occasionally, for 5 minutes, or until softened. Add half the garlic and cook, stirring frequently, for 2 minutes, then add the rice and stir for 1 minute, or until the grains are thoroughly coated with the oil.

2 Add the stock and a pinch of salt and bring to the boil, stirring constantly. Reduce the heat, cover and simmer for 35–40 minutes, or until all the liquid has been absorbed.

3 Meanwhile, heat the remaining oil in a heavy-based frying pan. Add the pepper and celery and cook, stirring frequently, for 5 minutes. Add the sliced mushrooms and the remaining garlic and cook, stirring frequently, for 4–5 minutes.

4 Stir the rice into the frying pan. Add the beans, parsley and cashews. Season with salt and pepper and cook, stirring constantly, until hot. Transfer to a warmed serving dish, sprinkle with extra parsley, and serve at once.

red wine, herb & sun-dried tomato risotto

ingredients

SERVES 4

1 litre/1¾ pints vegetable stock

1 litre/1¾ pints strong Italian red wine

1 tbsp olive oil

3 tbsp butter

1 small onion, finely chopped

450 g/1 lb risotto rice

6 sun-dried tomatoes in olive oil, drained and finely chopped

1 tbsp chopped fresh thyme, plus extra sprigs to garnish

1 tbsp chopped fresh parsley

salt and pepper

55 g/2 oz freshly grated Parmesan or Grana Padano cheese, plus extra shavings

10–12 fresh basil leaves, shredded, to garnish

method

1 Bring the stock and wine to the boil in a saucepan, then reduce the heat and simmer gently over low heat while you are cooking the risotto.

2 Heat the oil with 2 tablespoons of the butter in a deep saucepan over medium heat until the butter is melted. Add the onion and cook, stirring frequently, for 5 minutes or until softened but not browned.

3 Add the rice, stir to coat in the butter and oil and cook, stirring constantly, for 2–3 minutes until the grains are translucent. Gradually add the hot stock, a ladleful at a time, stirring constantly. Stir in the sun-dried tomatoes, then continue to add the stock, a ladleful at a time. Cook for 20 minutes or until all the stock has been absorbed, carefully folding in the chopped thyme and parsley 5 minutes before the end of cooking time. When the risotto is creamy but still with a little bite to the rice, season to taste.

4 Remove the risotto from the heat and add the remaining butter. Mix well, then stir in the Parmesan cheese until it has melted. Serve immediately, garnished with Parmesan cheese shavings, shredded basil leaves and thyme sprigs.

vegetarian paella

ingredients

SERVES 4–6

1/2 tsp saffron threads

2 tbsp hot water

6 tbsp olive oil

1 Spanish onion, sliced

3 garlic cloves, crushed

1 red pepper, deseeded and
   sliced

1 orange pepper, deseeded
   and sliced

1 large aubergine, cubed

200 g/7 oz medium-grain
   paella rice

600 ml/1 pint vegetable stock

450 g/1 lb tomatoes, peeled
   and chopped

salt and pepper

115 g/4 oz mushrooms, sliced

115 g/4 oz green beans,
   halved

400 g/14 oz canned
   borlotti beans

method

1 Put the saffron threads and water in a small bowl or cup and infuse for a few minutes.

2 Meanwhile, heat the oil in a paella pan or wide, shallow frying pan and cook the onion over medium heat, stirring, for 2–3 minutes, or until softened. Add the garlic, peppers and aubergine and cook, stirring frequently, for 5 minutes.

3 Add the rice and cook, stirring constantly, for 1 minute, or until glossy and coated. Pour in the stock and add the tomatoes, saffron and its soaking water, salt and pepper. Bring to the boil, then reduce the heat and simmer, shaking the pan frequently and stirring occasionally, for 15 minutes.

4 Stir in the mushrooms, green beans and borlotti beans with their can juices. Cook for a further 10 minutes, then serve immediately.

artichoke paella

ingredients

SERVES 4–6

1/2 tsp saffron threads

2 tbsp hot water

3 tbsp olive oil

1 large onion, chopped

1 courgette, coarsely chopped

2 garlic cloves, crushed

1/4 tsp cayenne pepper

225 g/8 oz tomatoes, peeled
    and cut into wedges

425 g/15 oz canned
    chickpeas, drained

425 g/15 oz canned
    artichokes hearts, drained
    and coarsely sliced

350 g/12 oz medium-grain
    paella rice

1.3 litres/21/4 pints simmering
    vegetable stock

150 g/51/2 oz green beans,
    blanched

salt and pepper

1 lemon, cut into wedges,
    to serve

method

1 Put the saffron threads and water in a small bowl and infuse for a few minutes.

2 Meanwhile, heat the oil in a paella pan and cook the onion and courgette over medium heat, stirring, for 2–3 minutes, or until softened. Add the garlic, cayenne pepper and saffron and its soaking liquid and cook, stirring constantly, for 1 minute. Add the tomato wedges, chickpeas and artichokes and cook, stirring, for a further 2 minutes.

3 Add the rice and cook, stirring constantly, for 1 minute, or until the rice is glossy and coated. Pour in most of the hot stock and bring to the boil, then simmer, uncovered, for 10 minutes. Do not stir during cooking, but shake the pan once or twice. Add the green beans and season. Shake the pan and cook for a further 10–15 minutes, or until the rice grains are plump and cooked. If the liquid is absorbed too quickly, pour in a little more hot stock, then shake the pan to spread the liquid through the paella.

4 When all the liquid has been absorbed and you detect a faint toasty aroma coming from the rice, remove from the heat immediately to prevent burning. Cover the pan with a clean tea towel or foil and let stand for 5 minutes. Serve direct from the pan with the lemon wedges to squeeze over the rice.

brown rice vegetable pilau

ingredients

SERVES 4

4 tbsp vegetable oil

1 red onion, finely chopped

2 tender celery stalks, leaves included, quartered lengthways and diced

2 carrots, coarsely grated

1 fresh green chilli, deseeded and finely chopped

3 spring onions, green part included, finely chopped

40 g/1½ oz whole almonds, sliced lengthways

350 g/12 oz cooked brown basmati rice

150 g/5½ oz split red lentils, cooked

175 ml/6 fl oz vegetable stock

5 tbsp fresh orange juice

salt and pepper

fresh celery leaves, to garnish

method

1 Heat 2 tablespoons of the oil, in a high-sided frying pan with a lid, over medium heat. Add the onion. Cook for 5 minutes, or until softened.

2 Add the celery, carrots, chilli, spring onions and almonds. Stir-fry for 2 minutes, or until the vegetables are al dente but still brightly coloured. Transfer to a bowl and set aside until required.

3 Add the remaining oil to the pan. Stir in the rice and lentils. Cook over medium–high heat, stirring, for 1–2 minutes, or until heated through. Reduce the heat. Stir in the stock and orange juice. Season with salt and pepper.

4 Return the vegetables to the pan. Toss with the rice for a few minutes until heated through. Transfer to a warmed dish, garnish with celery leaves and serve.

egg fu yung

ingredients

SERVES 4–6

2 eggs

1/2 tsp salt

pinch of white pepper

1 tsp melted butter

2 tbsp vegetable or peanut oil

1 tsp finely chopped garlic

1 small onion, finely sliced

1 green pepper, finely sliced

450 g/1 lb cooked rice, chilled

1 tbsp light soy sauce

1 tbsp finely chopped
    spring onions

150 g/5 oz beansprouts,
    trimmed

2 drops of sesame oil

method

1 Beat the eggs with the salt and pepper. Heat the butter in a frying pan and pour in the eggs. Cook as an omelette, until set, then remove from the pan and cut into slivers.

2 In a preheated wok or deep saucepan, heat the oil and stir-fry the garlic until fragrant. Add the onion and stir-fry for 1 minute, then add the green pepper and stir-fry for a further 1 minute. Stir in the rice and, when the grains are separated, stir in the light soy sauce and cook for 1 minute.

3 Add the spring onions and egg strips and stir well, then finally add the beansprouts and sesame oil. Stir-fry for 1 minute and serve.

egg-fried rice with peas

ingredients

SERVES 4

150 g/5¹/₂ oz long-grain rice

3 eggs, beaten

2 tbsp vegetable oil

2 garlic cloves, crushed

4 spring onions, chopped

125 g/4¹/₂ oz cooked peas

1 tbsp light soy sauce

pinch of salt

shredded spring onions,
   to garnish

method

1 Cook the rice in a saucepan of boiling water for 10–12 minutes until almost cooked, but not soft. Drain well, rinse under cold running water and drain thoroughly.

2 Place the beaten eggs in a saucepan and cook over a low heat, stirring constantly, until softly scrambled. Remove the pan from the heat and set aside.

3 Preheat a wok over a medium heat. Add the oil and swirl it around to coat the sides of the wok. When the oil is hot, add the garlic, spring onions and peas and sauté, stirring occasionally, for 1–2 minutes.

4 Stir the rice into the mixture in the wok, mixing to combine. Add the eggs, soy sauce and salt to the wok and stir to mix in the eggs thoroughly.

5 Transfer to serving dishes and serve garnished with the shredded spring onions.

egg-fried rice with vegetables & crispy onions

ingredients

SERVES 4

4 tbsp vegetable or peanut oil

2 garlic cloves, chopped finely

2 fresh red chillies, deseeded
    and chopped

115 g/4 oz mushrooms, sliced

55 g/2 oz mangetout, halved

55 g/2 oz baby corn, halved

3 tbsp Thai soy sauce

1 tbsp jaggery or soft light
    brown sugar

a few Thai basil leaves

350 g/12 oz rice, cooked and
    cooled

2 eggs, beaten

2 onions, sliced

method

1 Heat half the oil in a wok or large frying pan and sauté the garlic and chillies for 2–3 minutes.

2 Add the mushrooms, mangetout and baby corn and stir-fry for 2–3 minutes, then add the soy sauce, sugar and basil. Stir in the rice.

3 Push the mixture to one side of the wok and add the eggs to the bottom. Stir until lightly set before combining into the rice mixture.

4 Heat the remaining oil in another pan and sauté the onions until crispy and brown. Serve the rice topped with the onions.

baked portobello mushrooms

ingredients

SERVES 4

4 large portobello mushrooms

200 g/7 oz canned red kidney beans, drained and rinsed

4 spring onions, chopped

1 fresh red jalapeño chilli, deseeded and finely chopped

1 tbsp finely grated lemon rind

1 tbsp chopped fresh flat-leaf parsley, plus extra sprigs to garnish

salt and pepper

85 g/3 oz courgette, coarsely grated

85 g/3 oz carrots, coarsely grated

55 g/2 oz pine kernels, toasted

40 g/1¹/₂ oz raisins

300 ml/10 fl oz vegetable stock

s a u c e

150 ml/5 fl oz Greek-style yogurt

1 tbsp chopped fresh parsley, plus extra to garnish

1 tbsp grated lemon rind

salt and pepper

method

1 Peel the mushrooms and carefully remove the stalks. Trim and rinse the stalks.

2 Put the mushroom stalks, beans, spring onions, chilli, lemon rind, parsley, salt and pepper into a food processor and process for 2 minutes.

3 Scrape the mixture into a bowl and add the courgette, carrots, pine kernels and raisins. Mix well and use to stuff the mushroom cups.

4 Arrange the stuffed mushrooms in an ovenproof dish, pour the stock around them, and cover with foil. Bake in a preheated oven, 180°C/350°F/Gas Mark 4, for 30 minutes, removing the foil for the last 10 minutes of the cooking time.

5 Meanwhile, to make the sauce, blend all the ingredients together in a small serving dish.

6 Serve the mushrooms hot with the sauce, garnished with parsley sprigs.

spinach & mushroom tortilla

ingredients

SERVES 4

2 tbsp olive oil

3 shallots, finely chopped

350 g/12 oz mushrooms, sliced

280 g/10 oz fresh spinach leaves, coarse stems removed

55 g/2 oz toasted flaked almonds

5 eggs

2 tbsp chopped fresh parsley

2 tbsp cold water

85 g/3 oz mature Mahon, Manchego or Parmesan cheese, grated

salt and pepper

method

1 Heat the olive oil in a frying pan that can safely be placed under the grill. Add the shallots and cook over low heat, stirring occasionally, for 5 minutes or until softened. Add the mushrooms and cook, stirring frequently, for a further 4 minutes. Add the spinach, then increase the heat to medium and cook, stirring frequently, for 3–4 minutes or until wilted. Reduce the heat, then season to taste with salt and pepper and stir in the flaked almonds.

2 Beat the eggs with the parsley, water and salt and pepper to taste in a bowl. Pour the mixture into the frying pan and cook for 5–8 minutes or until the underside is set. Lift the edge of the tortilla occasionally to let the uncooked egg run underneath. Meanwhile, preheat the grill to high.

3 Sprinkle the grated cheese over the tortilla and cook under the preheated hot grill for 3 minutes or until the top is set and the cheese has melted. Serve, lukewarm or cold, cut into thin wedges.

sweet treats

When you're cooking family meals and time is tight, making dessert can seem like one chore too many. Fresh fruit or pots of yogurt are convenient and healthy options but will quickly become boring, so it's worth pushing the boat out occasionally – perhaps at weekends – to give the family a sweet treat. Equally, when you're entertaining you don't have to struggle for hours in the kitchen or be a professional pastry cook to produce an impressive dessert as the crowning glory of the meal.

The hot desserts in this chapter include many family favourites, such as fruit crumble, as well as baked and grilled fruit and delicious filled crêpes. Pies and tarts are easy to prepare in advance and then can be popped into the oven to cook while you're eating your main course. Cold desserts, even luxurious mousses and cheesecakes, are surprisingly straightforward and the only time-consuming part is leaving them to chill and set – perfect for a special occasion or a dinner party when you want to make as much as possible in advance.

Home baking is incredibly satisfying and you may be surprised to discover that it takes only minutes to rustle up a batch of muffins, cupcakes, brownies or fabulous cookies. This is fortunate because it will take the family only minutes to demolish them if they get the chance! All these

small bites are ideal for adding to lunch boxes, as after-school snacks, as a pick-me-up with morning coffee or even, in some cases, serving with ready-made ice cream to make it a more special dessert.

cappuccino soufflé puddings

ingredients

SERVES 4

butter, for greasing

2 tbsp golden caster sugar, plus extra for coating

6 tbsp whipping cream

2 tsp instant espresso coffee granules

2 tbsp Kahlua

3 large eggs, separated, plus 1 extra egg white

150 g/5½ oz plain chocolate, melted and cooled

cocoa powder, for dusting

vanilla ice cream, to serve

method

1 Lightly grease the sides of 6 x 175-ml/6-fl oz ramekins with butter and coat with caster sugar. Place the ramekins on a baking sheet.

2 Place the cream in a small, heavy-based saucepan and heat gently. Stir in the coffee until it has dissolved, then stir in the Kahlua. Divide the coffee mixture between the prepared ramekins.

3 Place the egg whites in a clean, grease-free bowl and whisk until soft peaks form, then gradually whisk in the sugar until stiff but not dry. Stir the egg yolks and melted chocolate together in a separate bowl, then stir in a little of the whisked egg whites. Gradually fold in the remaining egg whites.

4 Divide the mixture between the dishes. Bake in a preheated oven, 190°C/375°F/Gas Mark 5 for 15 minutes or until just set. Dust with cocoa powder and serve immediately with vanilla ice cream.

sticky coffee & walnut sponges

ingredients

SERVES 6

1 tbsp instant coffee powder
150 g/5½ oz self-raising flour
1 tsp ground cinnamon
55 g/2 oz butter, softened,
　　plus extra for greasing
55 g/2 oz brown sugar, sifted
2 large eggs, beaten
55 g/2 oz finely chopped
　　walnuts

butterscotch sauce

25 g/1 oz roughly chopped
　　walnuts
55 g/2 oz butter
55 g/2 oz brown sugar
150 ml/5 fl oz double cream

method

1 Dissolve the coffee powder in 2 tablespoons of boiling water and set aside. Sift the flour and cinnamon into a bowl. Place the butter and sugar in a separate bowl and beat together until light and fluffy. Gradually beat in the eggs. Add a little flour if the mixture shows signs of curdling. Fold in half the flour and cinnamon mixture, then fold in the remaining flour and cinnamon, alternately with the coffee. Stir in the walnuts.

2 Divide the batter between 6 greased individual metal pudding bowls. Place a piece of buttered foil over each bowl and secure with an elastic band. Stand the bowls in a roasting tin and pour in enough boiling water to reach halfway up the sides of the bowls. Cover the roasting tin with a tent of foil, folding it under the rim.

3 Bake the sponges in a preheated oven, 190°C/375°F/Gas Mark 5, for 30–40 minutes or until well risen and firm to the touch.

4 Meanwhile, make the sauce. Place all the ingredients in a saucepan over low heat and stir until melted and blended. Bring to a simmer, then remove from the heat. Turn the sponges out onto a serving plate, spoon over the hot sauce and serve.

individual chocolate fondant puddings

ingredients

SERVES 4

100 g/3½ oz butter,
    plus extra for greasing
100 g/3½ oz plain chocolate,
    broken into pieces
2 large eggs
1 tsp vanilla essence
100 g/3½ oz golden caster
    sugar, plus extra for coating
2 tbsp plain flour
icing sugar, for dusting
vanilla ice cream, to serve

method

1 Place the butter and chocolate in a heatproof bowl and set over a saucepan of gently simmering water until melted. Stir until smooth, then set aside to cool.

2 Place the eggs, vanilla essence, caster sugar and flour in a bowl and whisk together. Stir in the melted chocolate. Pour the mixture into 4 lightly greased 175-ml/6-fl oz ovenproof bowls or ramekins coated with caster sugar and place on a baking sheet. Bake in a preheated oven, 200°C/400°F/Gas Mark 6, for 12–15 minutes or until the puddings are well risen and set on the outside but still molten inside.

3 Stand for 1 minute, then turn the puddings out onto 4 individual serving plates. Dust with icing sugar and serve immediately with vanilla ice cream.

zabaglione

ingredients

SERVES 4

4 egg yolks

60 g/2¼ oz caster sugar

5 tbsp Marsala

amaretti biscuits, to serve

method

1 Whisk the egg yolks with the sugar in a heatproof bowl for about 1 minute.

2 Gently whisk in the Marsala. Set the bowl over a pan of barely simmering water and whisk vigorously for 10–15 minutes, until thick, creamy and foamy.

3 Immediately pour into serving glasses and serve with amaretti biscuits.

peach cobbler

ingredients

SERVES 4–6

filling

6 peaches, peeled and sliced

4 tbsp caster sugar

1/2 tbsp lemon juice

1 1/2 tsp cornflour

1/2 tsp almond or vanilla
    essence

vanilla or pecan ice cream,
    to serve

topping

185 g/6 1/2 oz plain flour

115 g/4 oz caster sugar

1 1/2 tsp baking powder

1/2 tsp salt

85 g/3 oz butter, diced

1 egg

6 tbsp milk

method

1 Place the peaches in a 23-cm/9-inch square ovenproof dish. Add the sugar, lemon juice, cornflour and almond essence and toss together. Bake in a preheated oven, 220°C/425°F/Gas Mark 7, for 20 minutes.

2 Meanwhile, to make the topping, sift the flour, all but 2 tablespoons of the sugar, the baking powder and the salt into a bowl. Rub in the butter with the fingertips until the mixture resembles breadcrumbs. Mix the egg and 5 tablespoons of the milk in a jug, then mix into the dry ingredients with a fork until a soft, sticky dough forms. If the dough seems too dry, stir in the extra tablespoon of milk.

3 Reduce the oven temperature to 200°C/400°F/Gas Mark 6. Remove the peaches from the oven and drop spoonfuls of the topping over the surface, without smoothing. Sprinkle with the remaining sugar, return to the oven and bake for a further 15 minutes or until the topping is golden brown and firm – the topping will spread as it cooks. Serve hot or at room temperature, with ice cream.

apple & blackberry crumble

ingredients

SERVES 4

450 g/1 lb cooking apples
450 g/1 lb blackberries
115 g/4 oz caster sugar
4 tbsp water
cream, yogurt or custard,
   to serve

topping

175 g/6 oz wholemeal flour
6 tbsp unsalted butter
85 g/3 oz light brown sugar
1 tsp mixed spice

method

1 Prepare the apples by cutting them into quarters, then peeling and coring them. Thinly slice them into an ovenproof dish. Add the blackberries and stir in the sugar, then pour in the water.

2 Make the topping by placing the flour in a mixing bowl and rubbing in the butter until the mixture resembles breadcrumbs. Stir in the sugar and mixed spice. Spread the topping evenly over the fruit and use a fork to press down lightly.

3 Place the dish on a baking sheet and bake in the centre of a preheated oven, 190°C/375°F/Gas Mark 5, for 25–30 minutes or until the crumble is golden brown.

4 Serve warm with cream, yogurt or custard.

peach & preserved ginger tarte tatin

ingredients

SERVES 6

250 g/9 oz ready-made puff
    pastry
flour, for dusting

filling

6–8 just ripe peaches
100 g/3½ oz golden caster
    sugar
3 heaped tbsp unsalted butter
3 pieces preserved ginger in
    syrup, chopped
1 tbsp ginger syrup from the
    preserved ginger jar
1 egg, beaten
thick cream or ice cream,
    to serve

method

1 Plunge the peaches into boiling water, then drain and peel. Cut each in half. Put the sugar in a 25-cm/10-inch heavy, ovenproof frying pan and heat gently until it caramelizes. Don't stir, just shake the pan if necessary. Once the sugar turns a dark caramel colour, remove from the heat immediately and drop 2 tablespoons of the butter into it.

2 Place the peaches cut-side up on top of the caramel, packing them as close together as possible and tucking the preserved ginger pieces into any gaps. Dot with the remaining butter and drizzle with the ginger syrup.

3 Return to gentle heat while you roll out the pastry in a circle larger than the frying pan you are using. Drape the pastry over the peaches and tuck it in well round the edges, brush with the beaten egg and bake in a preheated oven, 190°C/375°F/Gas Mark 5, for 20–25 minutes or until the pastry is browned and puffed up. Remove from the oven and rest for 5 minutes, then invert onto a serving plate and serve with thick cream or ice cream.

paper-thin fruit pies

ingredients

SERVES 4

1 eating apple

1 ripe pear

2 tbsp lemon juice

4 sheets filo pastry,
    thawed if frozen

4 tbsp melted butter

2 tbsp apricot jam

1 tbsp unsweetened
    orange juice

1 tbsp finely chopped
    pistachios

2 tsp icing sugar, for dusting

custard, to serve

method

1 Core and thinly slice the apple and pear and immediately toss them in the lemon juice to prevent them from turning brown.

2 Cut each sheet of pastry into 4 and cover with a clean, damp tea towel. Brush a 4-cup muffin pan (cup size 10 cm/4 inches in diameter) with a little of the butter.

3 Brush 4 small sheets of pastry with melted butter. Press a sheet of pastry into the base of 1 cup. Arrange the other sheets of pastry on top at slightly different angles. Repeat with the other sheets of pastry to make another 3 pies.

4 Arrange alternate slices of apple and pear in the centre of each pastry case and lightly crimp the edges of the pastry.

5 Stir the jam and orange juice together until smooth and brush over the fruit. Bake in a preheated oven, 200°C/400°F/Gas Mark 6, for 12–15 minutes. Sprinkle with the pistachios, dust lightly with icing sugar and serve hot straight from the oven with custard.

warm fruit nests

ingredients

SERVES 4

2–3 tbsp lemon-infused
  olive oil
8 sheets of frozen filo
  pastry, thawed
250 g/9 oz blueberries
250 g/9 oz raspberries
250 g/9 oz blackberries
3 tbsp caster sugar
1 tsp ground allspice
sprigs of fresh mint,
  to decorate
double cream, to serve

method

1 Brush 4 small muffin tins with oil. Cut the filo pastry into 16 squares measuring about 12 cm/4^1/$_2$ inches across. Brush each square with oil and use to line the muffin tins. Place 4 sheets in each tin, staggering them so that the overhanging corners make a decorative star shape. Transfer to a baking sheet and bake in a preheated oven, 180°C/350°F/Gas Mark 4, for 7–8 minutes or until golden. Remove from the oven and set aside.

2 Meanwhile, warm the fruit in a saucepan with the caster sugar and allspice over medium heat until simmering. Lower the heat and continue simmering, stirring, for 10 minutes. Remove from the heat and drain. Using a perforated spoon, divide the warm fruit between the tartlet cases. Garnish with sprigs of fresh mint and serve warm with double cream.

walnut pastries

ingredients

MAKES 12

100 g/3^1/$_2$ oz butter

350 g/12 oz walnut pieces,
   finely chopped

55 g/2 oz caster sugar

1 tsp ground cinnamon

^{1}/$_2$ tsp ground cloves

225 g/8 oz filo pastry (work
   with one sheet at a time
   and keep the remaining
   sheets covered with a
   damp tea towel)

225 g/8 oz Greek honey

2 tsp lemon juice

150 ml/5 fl oz water

method

1 Melt the butter and use a little to grease
a deep 25 x 18-cm/10 x 7-inch baking tin.

2 To make the filling, put the walnuts, sugar,
cinnamon and cloves in a bowl and mix well.

3 Cut the pastry sheets in half widthways. Take
1 sheet of pastry and use to line the tin. Brush
the sheet with a little of the melted butter.
Repeat until half of the pastry is used, then
sprinkle with the walnut filling. Top with the
remaining pastry sheets, brushing each with
butter and tucking down the edges. Using a
sharp knife, cut the top layers of the pastry into
12 diamond or square shapes.

4 Bake in a preheated oven, 220°C/425°F/
Gas Mark 7, for 10 minutes, then reduce the
oven temperature to 180°C/350°F/Gas Mark 4
and bake for another 20 minutes or until
golden brown.

5 Just before the pastries have cooked, make
the honey syrup. Put the honey, lemon juice
and water in a pan and simmer for about
5 minutes or until combined. Set aside.

6 When the pastries are cooked, remove them
from the oven and pour over the honey syrup.
Set aside to cool. Before serving, cut the
pastries along the marked lines again to divide
into pieces.

creamy mango brûlée

ingredients

SERVES 4

2 mangoes

250 g/9 oz Mascarpone
    cheese

200 ml/7 fl oz thick
    natural yogurt

1 tsp ground ginger

grated rind and juice of 1 lime

2 tbsp light brown sugar

8 tbsp demerara sugar

method

1 Slice the mangoes on either side of the stone. Discard the stone and peel the fruit. Slice and then chop the fruit and divide it between 4 ramekins.

2 Beat the Mascarpone cheese with the yogurt. Fold in the ginger, lime rind and juice and light brown sugar. Divide the mixture between the ramekins and level off the tops. Chill for 2 hours.

3 Sprinkle 2 tablespoons of demerara sugar over the top of each dish, covering the creamy mixture. Place under a hot grill for 2–3 minutes or until melted and browned. Cool completely, then chill in the refrigerator.

spanish-style rice pudding

ingredients

SERVES 4

1 large orange

1 lemon

1 litre/1³/₄ pints milk

250 g/9 oz Spanish short-grain
   rice

100 g/3¹/₂ oz caster sugar

1 vanilla pod, split

pinch of salt

125 ml/4 fl oz double cream

brown sugar, to serve
   (optional)

method

1 Finely grate the rinds from the orange and lemon and set aside. Rinse a heavy-based saucepan with cold water and do not dry it.

2 Put the milk and rice in the pan over medium–high heat and bring to the boil. Reduce the heat and stir in the caster sugar, vanilla pod, orange and lemon rinds and salt and simmer, stirring frequently, until the pudding is thick and creamy and the rice grains are tender: this can take up to 30 minutes, depending on how wide the pan is.

3 Remove the vanilla pod and stir in the cream. Serve at once, sprinkled with brown sugar, if desired, or cool completely, cover and chill until required. (The pudding will thicken as it cools, so stir in a little extra milk if necessary.)

white chocolate mousse

ingredients

SERVES 6

250 g/9 oz white chocolate,
    broken into pieces
100 ml/3½ fl oz milk
300 ml/10 fl oz double cream
1 tsp rose water
2 egg whites
115 g/4 oz plain chocolate,
    broken into pieces
candied rose petals,
    to decorate

method

1 Place the white chocolate and milk in a saucepan and heat gently until the chocolate has melted, then stir. Transfer to a large bowl and cool.

2 Whip the cream and rose water in a separate bowl until soft peaks form. Whisk the egg whites in a separate large, spotlessly clean, grease-free bowl until stiff but not dry. Gently fold the whipped cream into the chocolate, then fold in the egg whites. Spoon the mixture into 6 small dishes or glasses, cover with clingfilm and chill for 8 hours, or overnight, to set.

3 Melt the plain chocolate and cool, then pour evenly over the mousses. Set aside until the chocolate has hardened, then decorate with rose petals and serve.

chocolate mousse

ingredients

SERVES 4–6

225 g/8 oz plain chocolate,
  chopped

2 tbsp brandy, Grand Marnier
  or Cointreau

4 tbsp water

1 oz/30 g unsalted
  butter, diced

3 large eggs, separated

1/4 tsp cream of tartar

55 g/2 oz sugar

125 ml/4 fl oz double cream

method

1 Place the chocolate, brandy and water in a small saucepan over low heat and melt, stirring, until smooth. Remove the pan from the heat and beat in the butter. Beat the egg yolks into the chocolate mixture, one after another, until blended, then cool slightly.

2 Meanwhile, using an electric mixer on low speed, beat the egg whites in a spotlessly clean bowl until frothy, then gradually increase the mixer's speed and beat until soft peaks form. Sprinkle the cream of tartar over the surface, then add the sugar, tablespoon by tablespoon and continue beating until stiff peaks form. Beat several tablespoons of the egg whites into the chocolate mixture to loosen.

3 In another bowl, whip the cream until soft peaks form. Spoon the cream over the chocolate mixture, then spoon the remaining whites over the cream. Use a large metal spoon or rubber spatula to fold the chocolate into the cream and egg whites.

4 Either spoon the chocolate mousse into a large serving bowl or divide between 4 or 6 individual bowls. Cover with clingfilm and chill the mousse for at least 3 hours before serving.

chocolate trifle

ingredients

SERVES 4

280 g/10 oz ready-made
 chocolate loaf cake
3–4 tbsp seeded raspberry
 jam
4 tbsp Amaretto liqueur
250 g/9 oz frozen mixed
 berries, thawed

custard

6 egg yolks
55 g/2 oz golden caster sugar
1 tbsp cornflour
500 ml/18 fl oz milk
55 g/2 oz plain chocolate,
 melted

topping

225 ml/8 fl oz double cream
1 tbsp golden caster sugar
1/2 tsp vanilla essence

to decorate

ready-made chocolate truffles
fresh fruit, such as cherries
 and strawberries

method

1 Cut the cake into slices and make 'sandwiches' with the raspberry jam. Cut the sandwiches into cubes and place in a large serving bowl. Sprinkle with the Amaretto liqueur. Spread the berries over the cake.

2 To make the custard, place the egg yolks and sugar in a heatproof bowl and whisk until thick and pale, then stir in the cornflour. Place the milk in a saucepan and heat until almost boiling. Pour onto the egg yolk mixture, stirring. Return the mixture to the pan and bring just to the boil, stirring constantly, until it thickens. Remove from the heat and cool slightly. Stir in the melted chocolate. Pour the custard over the cake and berries. Cool, then cover and chill in the refrigerator for 2 hours, or until set.

3 To make the topping, whip the cream until soft peaks form, then beat in the sugar and vanilla essence. Spoon over the trifle. Decorate with the truffles and fruit and chill until ready to serve.

tiramisù

ingredients

SERVES 4

200 ml/7 fl oz strong black
   coffee, cooled to room
   temperature
4 tbsp orange liqueur,
   such as Cointreau
3 tbsp orange juice
16 sponge fingers
250 g/9 oz Mascarpone
   cheese
300 ml/10 fl oz double cream,
   lightly whipped
3 tbsp icing sugar
grated rind of 1 orange
60 g/2¼ oz plain chocolate,
   grated

to decorate
chopped toasted almonds
crystallized orange peel
chocolate shavings

method

1 Pour the cooled coffee into a jug and stir in the orange liqueur and orange juice. Place 8 of the sponge fingers in the bottom of a serving dish, then pour over half of the coffee mixture.

2 Place the Mascarpone cheese in a separate bowl together with the cream, icing sugar and orange rind and mix well. Spread half of the Mascarpone mixture over the coffee-soaked sponge fingers, then arrange the remaining sponge fingers on top. Pour over the remaining coffee mixture then spread over the remaining Mascarpone mixture. Sprinkle over the grated chocolate and chill in the refrigerator for at least 2 hours.

3 Serve decorated with the chopped toasted almonds, crystallized orange peel and chocolate shavings.

mascarpone creams

ingredients

SERVES 4

115 g/4 oz Amaretti biscuits,
    crushed

4 tbsp Amaretto or
    Maraschino

4 eggs, separated

55 g/2 oz caster sugar

225 g/8 oz Mascarpone
    cheese

toasted flaked almonds,
    to decorate

method

1 Place the Amaretti crumbs in a bowl, add the Amaretto or Maraschino and soak.

2 Meanwhile, beat the egg yolks with the caster sugar until pale and thick. Fold in the Mascarpone and soaked biscuit crumbs.

3 Whisk the egg whites in a separate, spotlessly clean bowl until stiff, then gently fold into the cheese mixture. Divide the Mascarpone cream among 4 serving dishes and chill for 1–2 hours. Sprinkle with toasted flaked almonds just before serving.

coffee panna cotta with chocolate sauce

ingredients

SERVES 6

oil, for brushing
600 ml/1 pint double cream
1 vanilla pod
55 g/2 oz golden caster sugar
2 tsp instant espresso coffee
    granules, dissolved in
    4 tbsp water
2 tsp powdered gelatine
chocolate-covered coffee
    beans, to serve

chocolate sauce
150 ml/5 fl oz single cream
55 g/2 oz plain chocolate,
    melted

method

1 Lightly brush 6 x 150-ml/5-fl oz moulds with oil. Place the cream in a saucepan. Split the vanilla pod and scrape the black seeds into the cream. Add the vanilla pod and the sugar, then heat gently until almost boiling. Sieve the cream into a heatproof bowl and reserve. Place the coffee in a small heatproof bowl, sprinkle on the gelatine and leave for 5 minutes or until spongy. Set the bowl over a saucepan of gently simmering water until the gelatine has dissolved.

2 Stir a little of the reserved cream into the gelatine mixture, then stir the gelatine mixture into the remainder of the cream. Divide the mixture between the prepared moulds and cool, then chill in the refrigerator for 8 hours, or overnight.

3 To make the sauce, place a quarter of the cream in a bowl and stir in the melted chocolate. Gradually stir in the remaining cream, reserving 1 tablespoon. To serve the panna cotta, dip the base of the moulds briefly into hot water and turn out onto 6 dessert plates. Pour the chocolate cream around. Dot drops of the reserved cream onto the sauce and feather it with a skewer. Decorate with chocolate-covered coffee beans and serve.

summer pudding

ingredients

SERVES 6

675 g/1 lb 8 oz mixed summer berries, such as redcurrants, blackcurrants, raspberries and blackberries

140 g/5 oz caster sugar

2 tbsp crème de framboise liqueur (optional)

6–8 slices of good day-old white bread, crusts removed

double cream, to serve

method

1 Place the fruits in a large saucepan with the sugar. Over a low heat, very slowly bring to the boil, stirring carefully to ensure that the sugar has dissolved. Cook over low heat for only 2–3 minutes until the juices run but the fruit still holds its shape. Add the liqueur if using.

2 Line a 850-ml/1¹/2-pint pudding bowl with some of the slices of bread (cut them to shape so that the bread fits well). Spoon in the cooked fruit and juices, setting aside a little of the juice for later.

3 Cover the fruit with the remaining bread. Place a plate on top of the pudding and weight it down for at least 8 hours or overnight in the refrigerator.

4 Turn out the pudding and pour over the reserved juices to colour any white bits of bread that might be showing. Serve with the double cream.

chocolate brandy torte

ingredients

SERVES 12

base

100 g/3½ oz butter, plus extra
    for greasing
250 g/9 oz ginger biscuits
75 g/2¾ oz plain chocolate

filling

225 g/8 oz plain chocolate
250 g/9 oz Mascarpone
    cheese
2 eggs, separated
3 tbsp brandy
300 ml/10 fl oz double cream
4 tbsp caster sugar

to decorate

100 ml/3½ fl oz double cream
chocolate-covered coffee
    beans

method

1 Grease the bottom and sides of a 23-cm/ 9-inch springform cake tin. Place the ginger biscuits in a plastic bag and crush with a rolling pin. Transfer to a bowl. Place the chocolate and butter in a small pan and heat gently until melted, then pour over the biscuit crumbs. Mix well, then press into the prepared tin. Chill while preparing the filling.

2 To make the filling, place the chocolate in a heatproof bowl set over a saucepan of simmering water and heat, stirring, until melted. Remove from the heat and beat in the Mascarpone cheese, egg yolks and brandy.

3 Whip the cream until just holding its shape. Fold in the chocolate mixture.

4 Whisk the egg whites in a spotlessly clean, grease-free bowl until soft peaks form. Add the sugar, a little at a time, and whisk until thick and glossy. Fold into the chocolate mixture, in 2 batches, until just mixed.

5 Spoon the mixture into the prepared base and chill in the refrigerator for at least 2 hours. Carefully transfer to a serving plate. To decorate, whip the cream and pipe onto the cheesecake, add the chocolate-covered coffee beans and serve.

irish cream cheesecake

ingredients

SERVES 12

oil, for brushing

175 g/6 oz chocolate chip
    cookies

55 g/2 oz butter

filling

225 g/8 oz plain chocolate

225 g/8 oz g milk chocolate

55 g/2 oz golden caster sugar

250 g/9 oz cream cheese

425 ml/15 fl oz double cream,
    whipped

3 tbsp Irish cream liqueur
    crème fraîche and fresh
    fruit, to serve

method

1 Line the base of a 20-cm/8-inch springform tin with foil and brush the sides with oil. Place the biscuits in a polythene bag and crush with a rolling pin. Place the butter in a saucepan and heat gently until just melted, then stir in the crushed biscuits. Press the mixture into the base of the tin and chill in the refrigerator for 1 hour.

2 To make the filling, melt the plain and milk chocolate together, stir to combine and leave to cool. Place the sugar and cream cheese in a large bowl and beat together until smooth, then fold in the whipped cream. Fold the mixture gently into the melted chocolate, then stir in the Irish cream liqueur.

3 Spoon the filling over the chilled biscuit base and smooth the surface. Cover and chill in the refrigerator for 2 hours, or until quite firm. Transfer to a serving plate and cut into small slices. Serve with a spoonful of crème fraîche and fresh fruit.

banana-stuffed crêpes

ingredients

SERVES 4

225 g/8 oz plain flour

2 tbsp soft light brown sugar

2 eggs

450 ml/16 fl oz milk

grated rind and juice of
    1 lemon

55 g/2 oz butter

3 bananas

4 tbsp golden syrup

method

1 Combine the flour and sugar and beat in the eggs and half the milk. Beat together until smooth. Gradually add the remaining milk, stirring constantly to make a smooth batter. Stir in the lemon rind.

2 Melt a little butter in a 20-cm/8-inch frying pan and pour in one-quarter of the batter. Tilt the pan to coat the bottom and cook for 1–2 minutes, until set. Flip the crêpe over and cook the second side. Slide out of the pan and keep warm. Repeat to make 3 more crêpes.

3 Slice the bananas and toss in the lemon juice. Pour the syrup over them and toss together. Fold each crêpe in half and then in half again and fill the centre with the banana mixture. Serve warm.

exotic fruit chocolate crêpes

ingredients

SERVES 4

100 g/3¹/₂ oz plain flour
2 tbsp cocoa powder
pinch of salt
1 egg, beaten
300 ml/10 fl oz milk
oil, for frying
icing sugar, for dusting

filling

100 g/3¹/₂ oz thick plain yogurt
250 g/9 oz Mascarpone
　　cheese
icing sugar (optional)
1 mango, peeled and diced
225 g/8 oz strawberries, hulled
　　and quartered
2 passion fruit

method

1 To make the filling, place the yogurt and Mascarpone cheese in a bowl and sweeten with icing sugar, if you like. Place the mango and strawberries in a bowl and mix together. Cut the passion fruit in half, scoop out the pulp and seeds and add to the mango and strawberries. Stir together, then set aside.

2 To make the crêpes, sift the flour, cocoa powder and salt into a bowl and make a well in the centre. Add the egg and whisk with a balloon whisk. Gradually beat in the milk, drawing in the flour from the sides, to make a smooth batter. Cover and stand for 20 minutes. Heat a small amount of oil in an 18-cm/7-inch crêpe pan or frying pan. Pour in just enough batter to coat the bottom of the pan thinly. Cook over medium–high heat for 1 minute, then turn and cook the other side for 30–60 seconds or until cooked through.

3 Transfer the crêpe to a plate and keep hot. Repeat with the remaining batter, stacking the cooked crêpes on top of each other with waxed paper in between. Keep warm in the oven while cooking the remainder. To serve, divide the filling between the crêpes, then roll up and dust with icing sugar.

pears in honey syrup

ingredients

SERVES 4

4 medium-ripe pears
200 ml/7 fl oz water
1 tsp sugar
1 tbsp honey

method

1 Peel each pear, leaving the stem intact. Wrap each pear in foil and place in a saucepan with the stems resting on the side of the pan. Add enough water to come at least half way up the pears. Bring to the boil and simmer for 30 minutes. Remove the pears and carefully remove the foil, reserving any juices. Set aside to cool.

2 Bring the measured water to the boil. Add any pear juices, the sugar and the honey and boil for 5 minutes. Remove from the heat and cool a little.

3 Place each pear in an individual dish. Pour a little syrup over each and serve just warm.

baked apricots with honey

ingredients

SERVES 4

butter, for greasing

4 apricots, each cut in half
    and stoned

4 tbsp flaked almonds

4 tbsp honey

pinch ground ginger or
    grated nutmeg

vanilla ice cream, to serve
    (optional)

method

1 Lightly butter an ovenproof dish large enough to hold the apricot halves in a single layer.

2 Arrange the apricot halves in the dish, cut sides up. Sprinkle with the almonds and drizzle the honey over. Dust with the spice.

3 Bake in a preheated oven, 200°C/400°F/Gas Mark 6, for 12–15 minutes until the apricots are tender and the almonds golden. Remove from the oven and serve at once, with ice cream on the side, if desired.

grilled bananas

ingredients

SERVES 4

55 g/2 oz block creamed
    coconut, chopped
150 ml/5 fl oz double cream
4 bananas
juice and rind of 1 lime
1 tbsp vegetable or peanut oil
50 g/1³/₄ oz dry unsweetened
    coconut

method

1 Put the creamed coconut and double cream in a small saucepan and heat gently until the coconut has dissolved. Remove from the heat and set aside to cool for 10 minutes, then whisk until thick but floppy.

2 Peel the bananas and toss in the lime juice and rind. Lightly oil a preheated griddle pan and cook the bananas, turning once, for 2–3 minutes, until soft and browned.

3 Toast the dry unsweetened coconut on a piece of foil under a grill until lightly browned. Serve the bananas with the coconut cream, sprinkled with the toasted coconut.

toffee bananas

ingredients

SERVES 4

70 g/2¹/₂ oz self-raising flour
1 egg, beaten
5 tbsp iced water
4 large, ripe bananas
3 tbsp lemon juice
2 tbsp rice flour
vegetable oil, for deep-frying

caramel

115 g/4 oz caster sugar
4 tbsp iced water, plus an
    extra bowl of iced water
    for setting
2 tbsp sesame seeds

method

1 Sift the flour into a bowl. Make a well in the centre, add the egg and the 5 tablespoons of iced water and beat from the centre outwards, until combined into a smooth batter.

2 Peel the bananas and cut into 5-cm/2-inch pieces. Gently shape them into balls with your hands. Brush with lemon juice to prevent discoloration, then roll them in rice flour until coated. Pour oil into a saucepan to a depth of 6 cm/2¹/₂ inches and preheat to 190°C/ 375°F. Coat the balls in the batter and cook in batches in the hot oil for about 2 minutes each, until golden. Lift them out and drain on kitchen paper.

3 To make the caramel, put the sugar into a small saucepan over low heat. Add 4 tablespoons of iced water and heat, stirring, until the sugar dissolves. Simmer for 5 minutes, remove from the heat and stir in the sesame seeds. Toss the banana balls in the caramel, scoop them out and drop into the bowl of iced water to set. Lift them out and divide between individual serving bowls. Serve hot.

toffee apple slices

ingredients

SERVES 4

4 apples, peeled, cored and
each cut into thick slices
vegetable or peanut oil, for
deep-frying

batter

115 g/4 oz plain flour
1 egg, beaten
125 ml/4 fl oz cold water

toffee syrup

4 tbsp sesame oil
225 g/8 oz sugar
2 tbsp sesame seeds, toasted

method

1 To prepare the batter, sift the flour and stir in the egg. Slowly add the water, beating to form a smooth and thick batter. Dip each apple slice in the batter.

2 Heat enough oil for deep-frying in a wok, deep-fat fryer, or large heavy-based saucepan until it reaches 180–190°C/350–375°F, or until a cube of bread browns in 30 seconds. Deep-fry the apple slices until golden brown. Drain and set aside.

3 To make the toffee syrup, heat the sesame oil in a small, heavy-based saucepan and, when beginning to smoke, add the sugar, stirring constantly, until the mixture caramelizes and turns golden. Remove from the heat, then stir in the sesame seeds and pour into a large flat saucepan.

4 Over very low heat, place the apple slices in the syrup, turning once. When coated, dip each slice in cold water. Serve immediately.

mixed fruit salad

ingredients

SERVES 4

1 papaya, halved, peeled, and
  deseeded

2 bananas, sliced thickly

1 small pineapple, peeled,
  halved, cored and sliced

12 lychees, peeled if fresh

1 small melon, deseeded and
  cut into thin wedges

2 oranges

grated rind and juice of 1 lime

2 tbsp caster sugar

method

1 Arrange the papaya, bananas, pineapple, lychees and melon on a serving platter. Cut off the rind and pith from the oranges. Cut the orange slices out from between the membranes and add to the fruit platter. Grate a small quantity of the discarded orange rind and add to the platter.

2 Combine the lime rind and juice and the sugar. Pour over the salad and serve.

steamed spiced exotic fruits

ingredients

SERVES 4

2 kiwi fruit, peeled and halved

4 rambutan or lychees, peeled, halved and stoned

2 passion fruit, the flesh scooped out

8 Cape gooseberries (physalis), papery leaves removed and fruit halved

85 g/3 oz mango, cut into 2-cm/¾-inch cubes

1 sharon fruit, cut into 2-cm/¾-inch slices

85 g/3 oz fresh raspberries

2 vanilla pods, split in half lengthways

2 cinnamon sticks, broken in half

4 star anise

4 fresh bay leaves

4 tbsp freshly squeezed orange juice

method

1 Cut 4 x 40-cm/16-inch squares of baking parchment and 4 foil squares of the same size. Put each baking parchment square on top of a foil square and fold them diagonally in half to form a triangle. Open up again.

2 Divide the fruits into 4 and arrange each portion neatly in the centre of each opened square. Add a vanilla pod half, a cinnamon stick half, a star anise, a bay leaf and 1 tablespoon of orange juice to each triangle.

3 Close each triangle over the mixture, fold in the corners and crumple the edges together to form airtight triangular bags. Transfer the bags to a baking sheet and bake in a preheated oven, 200°C/400°F/Gas Mark 6, for 10–12 minutes or until they puff up with steam.

4 To serve, put each bag on a serving plate and snip open at the table.

chocolate fondue

ingredients

SERVES 6

1 pineapple

1 mango

12 Cape gooseberries
   (physalis)

250 g/9 oz fresh strawberries

250 g/9 oz seedless green
   grapes

fondue

250 g/9 oz plain chocolate,
   broken into pieces

150 ml/5 fl oz double cream

2 tbsp brandy

method

1 Using a sharp knife, peel and core the pineapple, then cut the flesh into cubes. Peel the mango and cut the flesh into cubes. Peel back the papery outer skin of the Cape gooseberries and twist at the top to make a 'handle'. Arrange all the fruit on 6 serving plates and chill in the refrigerator.

2 To make the fondue, place the chocolate and cream in a fondue pot. Heat gently, stirring constantly, until the chocolate has melted. Stir in the brandy until it is thoroughly blended and the chocolate mixture is smooth.

3 Place the fondue pot over the burner to keep warm. To serve, allow each guest to dip the fruit into the sauce, using fondue forks or bamboo skewers.

chocolate temptations

ingredients

MAKES 24

90 g/3¹/4 oz unsalted butter,
  plus extra for greasing
365 g/12¹/2 oz plain chocolate
1 tsp strong coffee
2 eggs
140 g/5 oz soft brown sugar
185 g/6¹/2 oz plain flour
¹/4 tsp baking powder
pinch of salt
2 tsp almond essence
85 g/3 oz Brazil nuts, chopped
85 g/3 oz hazelnuts, chopped
40 g/1¹/2 oz white chocolate

method

1 Preheat the oven to 180°C/350°F/Gas Mark 4. Grease 1–2 large baking sheets. Put 225 g/8 oz of the plain chocolate with the butter and coffee into a heatproof bowl set over a saucepan of gently simmering water and heat until the chocolate is almost melted.

2 Meanwhile, beat the eggs in a bowl until fluffy. Gradually whisk in the sugar until thick. Remove the chocolate from the heat and stir until smooth. Add to the egg mixture and stir until combined.

3 Sieve the flour, baking powder and salt into a bowl, then stir into the chocolate mixture. Chop 85 g/3 oz of the remaining plain chocolate into pieces and stir into the mixture. Stir in the almond essence and chopped nuts.

4 Put 24 tablespoonfuls of the mixture onto the baking sheet, transfer to the preheated oven and bake for 16 minutes. Remove from the oven and transfer to a wire rack to cool. To decorate, melt the remaining chocolate (plain and white) in turn as in step 1, then spoon into a piping bag and pipe thin lines onto the biscuits.

double chocolate chip cookies

ingredients

MAKES 24

115 g/4 oz unsalted butter, softened, plus extra for greasing

55 g/2 oz golden granulated sugar

55 g/2 oz light muscovado sugar

1 egg, beaten

1/2 tsp vanilla essence

115 g/4 oz plain flour

2 tbsp cocoa powder

1/2 tsp bicarbonate of soda

115 g/4 oz milk chocolate chips

55 g/2 oz walnuts, roughly chopped

method

1 Preheat the oven to 180°C/350°F/Gas Mark 4, then grease 3 baking sheets. Place the butter, granulated sugar and muscovado sugar in a bowl and beat until light and fluffy. Gradually beat in the egg and vanilla essence.

2 Sift the flour, cocoa and bicarbonate of soda into the mixture and stir in carefully. Stir in the chocolate chips and walnuts. Drop dessertspoonfuls of the mixture onto the prepared baking sheets, spaced well apart to allow for spreading.

3 Bake in the oven for 10–15 minutes, or until the mixture has spread and the cookies are beginning to feel firm.

4 Remove from the oven, leave on the baking sheets for 2 minutes, then transfer to wire racks to cool completely.

oat & pecan cookies

ingredients

MAKES 15

115 g/4 oz unsalted butter, softened, plus extra for greasing

85 g/3 oz light muscovado sugar

1 egg, beaten

55 g/2 oz pecan nuts, chopped

85 g/3 oz plain flour

1/2 tsp baking powder

55 g/2 oz porridge oats

method

1 Preheat the oven to 180°C/350°F/Gas Mark 4, then grease 2 baking sheets. Place the butter and sugar in a bowl and beat until light and fluffy. Gradually beat in the egg, then stir in the nuts.

2 Sieve the flour and baking powder into the mixture and add the oats. Stir together until well combined. Drop dessertspoonfuls of the mixture onto the prepared baking sheets, spaced well apart to allow for spreading.

3 Bake in the preheated oven for 15 minutes, or until pale golden. Remove from the oven, leave to cool on the baking sheets for 2 minutes, then transfer to wire racks to cool completely.

gingernuts

ingredients

MAKES 30

350 g/12 oz self-raising flour
pinch of salt
200 g/7 oz caster sugar
1 tbsp ground ginger
1 tsp bicarbonate of soda
125 g/4$\frac{1}{2}$ oz butter,
    plus extra for greasing
75 g/2$\frac{3}{4}$ oz golden syrup
1 egg, beaten
1 tsp grated orange zest

method

1 Sift the self-raising flour, salt, sugar, ginger and bicarbonate of soda into a mixing bowl.

2 Melt the butter and golden syrup together in a saucepan over low heat. Remove the pan from the heat and cool the butter and syrup mixture slightly, then pour it onto the dry ingredients. Add the egg and orange zest and mix thoroughly to form a dough.

3 Using your hands, carefully shape the dough into 30 even-sized balls. Place the balls well apart on several baking sheets lightly greased with butter, then flatten them slightly with your fingers.

4 Bake in a preheated oven, 160°C/325°F/Gas Mark 3, for 15–20 minutes or until golden. Carefully transfer the biscuits to a wire rack to cool.

butter biscuits

ingredients

MAKES ABOUT 36

175 g/6 oz butter

140 g/5 oz caster sugar

1 egg

280 g/10 oz self-raising flour

finely grated rind of 1 lemon

3 tbsp flaked almonds
     (optional)

method

1 Put the butter and sugar in a bowl and whisk until light and fluffy. Whisk in the egg, then fold in the flour and lemon rind.

2 Turn out the dough onto a lightly floured work surface and knead gently until smooth. Form the mixture into rolls the thickness of a finger, then cut into 10-cm/4-inch lengths. Shape each roll into an S-shape and place on baking sheets, allowing room for spreading. If desired, stud with a few flaked almonds.

3 Bake the biscuits in a preheated oven, 180°C/350°F/Gas Mark 4, for about 15 minutes or until lightly browned. Cool on a wire rack. Store the biscuits in an airtight tin.

almond biscotti

ingredients

MAKES 20–24

250 g/9 oz plain flour, plus
    extra for dusting
1 tsp baking powder
pinch of salt
150 g/5$\frac{1}{2}$ oz golden
    caster sugar
2 eggs, beaten
finely grated rind of
    1 unwaxed orange
100 g/3$\frac{1}{2}$ oz whole blanched
    almonds, lightly toasted

method

1 Sift the flour, baking powder and salt into a bowl. Add the sugar, eggs and orange rind and mix to a dough, then knead in the almonds.

2 Using your hands, roll the dough into a ball, cut in half and roll each portion into a log about 4 cm/1$\frac{1}{2}$ inches in diameter. Place on a baking sheet lightly dusted with flour and bake in a preheated oven, 180°C/350°F/Gas Mark 4, for 10 minutes. Remove from the oven and cool for 5 minutes.

3 Using a serrated knife, cut the logs into 1-cm/$\frac{1}{2}$-inch thick diagonal slices. Arrange the slices on the baking sheet and return to the oven for 15 minutes or until slightly golden. Transfer to a wire rack to cool and crisp up.

cherry & sultana rockies

ingredients

MAKES 10

250 g/9 oz self-raising flour

1 tsp ground allspice

6 tbsp butter, plus extra
　　for greasing

85 g/3 oz golden caster sugar

55 g/2 oz glacé cherries,
　　quartered

55 g/2 oz sultanas

1 egg

2 tbsp milk

demerara sugar, for sprinkling

method

1 Sift the flour and allspice into a bowl. Add the butter and rub it in until the mixture resembles breadcrumbs. Stir in the sugar, cherries and sultanas.

2 Break the egg into a bowl and whisk in the milk. Pour most of the egg mixture into the dry ingredients and mix with a fork to make a stiff, coarse dough, adding the rest of the egg and milk, if necessary.

3 Using 2 forks, pile the mixture into 10 rocky heaps on a greased baking sheet. Sprinkle with demerara sugar. Bake in a preheated oven, 200°C/400°F/Gas Mark 6, for 10–15 minutes or until golden and firm to the touch. Cool on the baking sheet for 2 minutes, then transfer to a wire rack to cool completely.

hazelnut chocolate crunch

ingredients

MAKES 12

115 g/4 oz unsalted butter, plus extra for greasing

200 g/7 oz rolled oats

55 g/2 oz hazelnuts, lightly toasted and chopped

55 g/2 oz plain flour

85 g/3 oz light muscovado sugar

2 tbsp golden syrup

55 g/2 oz plain chocolate chips

method

1 Preheat the oven to 180°C/350°F/Gas Mark 4. Grease a 23-cm/9-inch shallow, square baking tin. Mix the oats, nuts and flour in a large bowl.

2 Place the butter, sugar and syrup in a large saucepan and heat gently until the sugar has dissolved. Pour in the dry ingredients and mix well. Stir in the chocolate chips.

3 Turn the mixture into the prepared tin and bake in the preheated oven for 20–25 minutes, or until golden brown and firm to the touch. Using a knife, mark into 12 rectangles and leave to cool in the tin. Cut the hazelnut chocolate crunch bars with a sharp knife before carefully removing them from the tin.

caramel chocolate shortbread

ingredients

MAKES 12

115 g/4 oz unsalted butter,
   plus extra for greasing
175 g/6 oz plain flour
55 g/2 oz golden caster sugar

filling and topping
175 g/6 oz butter
115 g/4 oz golden caster sugar
3 tbsp golden syrup
400 ml/14 fl oz canned
   condensed milk
200 g/7 oz plain chocolate,
   broken into pieces

method

1 Preheat the oven to 180°C/350°F/Gas Mark 4. Grease and line the base of a 23-cm/9-inch shallow square cake tin. Place the butter, flour and sugar in a food processor and process until they begin to bind together. Press the mixture into the prepared tin and smooth the top. Bake in the preheated oven for 20–25 minutes, or until golden.

2 Meanwhile, make the filling. Place the butter, sugar, syrup and condensed milk in a saucepan and heat gently until the sugar has dissolved. Bring to the boil and simmer for 6–8 minutes, stirring constantly, until the mixture becomes very thick. Remove the shortbread base from the oven, pour over the filling and chill in the refrigerator until firm.

3 To make the topping, melt the chocolate in a heatproof bowl set over a saucepan of gently simmering water. Remove from the heat, leave to cool slightly, then spread over the caramel. Chill in the refrigerator until set. Cut it into 12 pieces with a sharp knife and serve.

chocolate coconut layers

ingredients

MAKES 9

75 g/2³/₄ oz unsalted butter or margarine, plus extra for greasing

225 g/8 oz plain chocolate digestive biscuits

200 ml/7 fl oz canned evaporated milk

1 egg, beaten

1 tsp vanilla essence

2 tbsp caster sugar

40 g/1¹/₂ oz self-raising flour, sieved

125 g/4¹/₂ oz grated coconut

50 g/1³/₄ oz plain chocolate (optional)

method

1 Preheat the oven to 190°C/375°F/Gas Mark 5. Grease a shallow 20-cm/8-inch square cake tin and line the bottom with baking paper.

2 Crush the biscuits in a polythene bag with a rolling pin or process them in a food processor. Melt the butter in a saucepan and stir in the crushed biscuits thoroughly. Remove from the heat and press the mixture into the bottom of the prepared cake tin.

3 In a separate bowl, beat together the evaporated milk, egg, vanilla and sugar until smooth. Stir in the flour and grated coconut. Pour over the biscuit layer and use a palette knife to smooth the top.

4 Bake in the preheated oven for 30 minutes, or until the coconut topping has become firm and just golden. Remove from the oven, leave to cool in the tin for about 5 minutes, then cut into squares. Leave to cool completely in the tin.

5 Carefully remove the squares from the tin and place them on a chopping board. Melt the plain chocolate (if using) and drizzle it over the squares to decorate them. Leave the chocolate to set before serving.

pecan brownies

ingredients

MAKES 20

225 g/8 oz unsalted butter,
    plus extra for greasing
70 g/2¹/₂ oz plain chocolate
125 g/4¹/₂ oz plain flour
³/₄ tsp bicarbonate of soda
¹/₄ tsp baking powder
55 g/2 oz pecan nuts
100 g/3¹/₂ oz demerara sugar
¹/₂ tsp almond essence
1 egg
1 tsp milk

method

1 Preheat the oven to 180°C/350°F/Gas Mark 4. Grease a large baking dish and line it with baking paper.

2 Put the chocolate in a heatproof bowl set over a saucepan of gently simmering water and heat until it is melted. Meanwhile, sieve together the flour, bicarbonate of soda and baking powder into a large bowl.

3 Finely chop the pecan nuts and set aside. In a separate bowl, cream together the butter and sugar, then mix in the almond essence and the egg. Remove the chocolate from the heat and stir into the butter mixture. Add the flour mixture, milk and chopped nuts to the bowl and stir until well combined.

4 Spoon the mixture into the prepared baking dish and smooth it. Transfer to the preheated oven and cook for 30 minutes, or until firm to the touch (it should still be a little soft in the centre). Remove from the oven and leave to cool completely. Cut into 20 squares and serve.

carrot bars

ingredients

MAKES 14–16

corn oil, for oiling

175 g/6 oz unsalted butter

85 g/3 oz brown sugar

2 eggs, beaten

55 g/2 oz self-raising
     wholewheat flour, sifted

1 tsp baking powder, sifted

1 tsp ground cinnamon, sifted

115 g/4 oz ground almonds

115 g/4 oz carrot, coarsely
     grated

85 g/3 oz sultanas

85 g/3 oz no-soak dried
     apricots, finely chopped

55 g/2 oz toasted chopped
     hazelnuts

1 tbsp flaked almonds

method

1 Lightly oil and line a shallow 25 x 20-cm/ 10 x 8-inch/ baking tin with non-stick baking parchment.

2 Cream the butter and sugar together in a mixing bowl until light and fluffy, then gradually beat in the eggs, adding a little flour after each addition.

3 Add all the remaining ingredients, except the flaked almonds. Spoon the mixture into the prepared tin and smooth the top. Sprinkle with the flaked almonds.

4 Bake in a preheated oven, 180°C/350°F/Gas Mark 4, for 35–45 minutes or until the mixture is cooked and a skewer inserted into the centre comes out clean.

5 Remove from the oven and cool in the tin. Remove from the tin, discard the lining paper, and cut into bars.

apple & cinnamon muffins

ingredients

MAKES 6

85 g/3 oz plain wholewheat
    flour
70 g/2½ oz plain white flour
1½ tsp baking powder
pinch of salt
1 tsp ground cinnamon
40 g/1½ oz golden caster
    sugar
2 small eating apples, peeled,
    cored and finely chopped
125 ml/4 fl oz milk
1 egg, beaten
4 tbsp butter, melted

topping

12 brown sugar lumps,
    roughly crushed
½ tsp ground cinnamon

method

1 Place 6 muffin paper cases in a muffin pan.

2 Sift both flours, baking powder, salt and cinnamon together into a large bowl and stir in the sugar and chopped apples. Place the milk, egg and butter in a separate bowl and mix. Add the wet ingredients to the dry ingredients and gently stir until just combined.

3 Divide the mixture evenly between the paper cases. To make the topping, mix the crushed sugar lumps and cinnamon together and sprinkle over the muffins. Bake in a preheated oven, 200°C/400°F/Gas Mark 6, for 20–25 minutes or until risen and golden. Remove the muffins from the oven and serve warm or place them on a wire rack to cool.

banana pecan muffins

ingredients

MAKES 8

150 g/5¹/₂ oz plain flour

1¹/₂ tsp baking powder

pinch of salt

70 g/2¹/₂ oz golden caster
    sugar

115 g/4 oz shelled pecan nuts,
    roughly chopped

2 large ripe bananas, mashed

5 tbsp milk

2 tbsp butter, melted

1 large egg, beaten

¹/₂ tsp vanilla essence

method

1 Place 8 muffin paper cases in a muffin pan. Sift the flour, baking powder and salt into a bowl, add the sugar and pecan nuts and stir to combine.

2 Place the mashed bananas, milk, butter, egg and vanilla essence in a separate bowl and mix together. Add the wet ingredients to the dry ingredients and gently stir until just combined.

3 Divide the mixture evenly between the paper cases and bake in a preheated oven, 190°C/ 375°F/Gas Mark 5, for 20–25 minutes or until risen and golden. Remove the muffins from the oven and place them on a wire rack to cool.

doughnut muffins

ingredients

MAKES 12

175 g/6 oz butter, softened,
    plus extra for greasing
200 g/7 oz caster sugar
2 large eggs, lightly beaten
375 g/13 oz plain flour
3/4 tbsp baking powder
1/4 tsp bicarbonate of soda
pinch of salt
1/2 tsp freshly grated nutmeg
250 ml/9 fl oz milk

topping

100 g/3 1/2 oz caster sugar
1 tsp ground cinnamon
2 tbsp butter, melted

method

1 Grease a deep 12-cup muffin pan. In a large bowl, beat the butter and sugar together until light and creamy. Add the eggs, a little at a time, beating well between additions.

2 Sift the flour, baking powder, bicarbonate of soda, salt and nutmeg together. Add half to the creamed mixture with half of the milk. Gently fold the ingredients together before incorporating the remaining flour and milk. Spoon the mixture into the prepared muffin pan, filling each hole to about two-thirds full. Bake in a preheated oven, 180°C/350°F/Gas Mark 4, for 15–20 minutes or until the muffins are lightly brown and firm to the touch.

3 For the topping, mix the sugar and cinnamon together. While the muffins are still warm from the oven, brush lightly with melted butter, and sprinkle over the cinnamon and sugar mixture. Eat warm or cold.

fudge nut muffins

ingredients

MAKES 12

250 g/9 oz plain flour

4 tsp baking powder

85 g/3 oz caster sugar

6 tbsp crunchy peanut butter

1 large egg, beaten

4 tbsp butter, melted

175 ml/6 fl oz milk

150 g/5½ oz vanilla fudge, cut
    into small pieces

3 tbsp roughly chopped
    unsalted peanuts

method

1 Line a 12-cup muffin pan with double muffin paper cases. Sift the flour and baking powder into a bowl. Stir in the caster sugar. Add the peanut butter and stir until the mixture resembles breadcrumbs.

2 Place the egg, butter and milk in a separate bowl and beat until blended, then stir into the dry ingredients until just blended. Lightly stir in the fudge pieces. Divide the mixture evenly between the muffin paper cases.

3 Sprinkle the chopped peanuts on top and bake in a preheated oven, 200°C/400°F/Gas Mark 6, for 20–25 minutes or until well risen and firm to the touch. Remove the muffins from the oven and cool for 2 minutes, then place them on a wire rack to cool completely.

chocolate chip muffins

ingredients

MAKES 12

3 tbsp soft margarine

200 g/7 oz caster sugar

2 large eggs

150 ml/5 fl oz whole plain
   yogurt

5 tbsp milk

300 g/10½ oz plain flour

1 tsp bicarbonate of soda

115 g/4 oz plain chocolate
   chips

method

1 Line a 12-cup muffin pan with muffin cases.

2 Place the margarine and sugar in a mixing bowl and beat with a wooden spoon until light and fluffy. Beat in the eggs, yogurt and milk until combined.

3 Sift the flour and bicarbonate of soda into the mixture. Stir until just blended.

4 Stir in the chocolate chips, then divide the mixture evenly between the paper cases and bake in a preheated oven, 200°C/400°F/Gas Mark 6, for 25 minutes or until risen and golden. Remove the muffins from the oven and cool in the pan for 5 minutes, then place them on a wire rack to cool completely.

moist walnut cupcakes

ingredients

MAKES 12

85 g/3 oz walnuts
4 tbsp butter, softened
100 g/3^1/$_2$ oz caster sugar
grated rind of ^{1}/$_2$ lemon
70 g/2^1/$_2$ oz self-raising flour
2 eggs
12 walnut halves, to decorate

frosting

4 tbsp butter, softened
85 g/3 oz icing sugar
grated rind of ^{1}/$_2$ lemon
1 tsp lemon juice

method

1 Put 12 paper baking cases in a muffin pan, or place 12 double-layer paper cases on a baking sheet.

2 Put the walnuts in a food processor and, using a pulsating action, blend until finely ground, being careful not to overgrind, which will turn them to oil. Add the butter, cut into small pieces, along with the sugar, lemon rind, flour and eggs, then blend until evenly mixed. Spoon the mixture into the paper cases.

3 Bake the cupcakes in a preheated oven, 190°C/375°F/Gas Mark 5, for 20 minutes or until well risen and golden brown. Transfer to a wire rack to cool.

4 To make the frosting, put the butter in a bowl and beat until fluffy. Sift in the icing sugar, add the lemon rind and juice, and mix well.

5 When the cupcakes are cold, spread a little frosting on top of each cupcake and top with a walnut half to decorate.

frosted peanut butter cupcakes

ingredients

MAKES 16

4 tbsp butter, softened,
    or soft margarine
225 g/8 oz brown sugar
115 g/4 oz crunchy
    peanut butter
2 eggs, lightly beaten
1 tsp vanilla essence
225 g/8 oz plain flour
2 tsp baking powder
100 ml/3½ fl oz milk

frosting
200 g/7 oz full-fat soft
    cream cheese
2 tbsp butter, softened
225 g/8 oz icing sugar

method

1 Put 16 muffin paper cases in a muffin pan.

2 Put the butter, sugar and peanut butter in a bowl and beat together for 1–2 minutes, or until well mixed. Gradually add the eggs, beating well after each addition, then add the vanilla essence. Sift in the flour and baking powder and then, using a metal spoon, fold them into the mixture, alternating with the milk. Spoon the mixture into the paper cases.

3 Bake the cupcakes in a preheated oven, 180°C/350°F/Gas Mark 4, for 25 minutes or until well risen and golden brown. Transfer to a wire rack to cool.

4 To make the frosting, put the cream cheese and butter in a large bowl and, using an electric hand whisk, beat together until smooth. Sift the icing sugar into the mixture, then beat together until well mixed.

5 When the cupcakes are cold, spread a little frosting on top of each cupcake, swirling it with a round-bladed knife. Store the cupcakes in the refrigerator until ready to serve.

chocolate butterfly cakes

ingredients

MAKES 12

8 tbsp soft margarine

100 g/3½ oz caster sugar

150 g/5½ oz self-raising
flour

2 large eggs

2 tbsp cocoa powder

25 g/1 oz plain chocolate,
melted

icing sugar, for dusting

filling

6 tbsp butter, softened

175 g/6 oz icing sugar

25 g/1 oz plain chocolate,
melted

method

1 Put 12 paper baking cases in a muffin pan, or put 12 double-layer paper cases on a baking sheet.

2 Put the margarine, sugar, flour, eggs and cocoa in a large bowl and, using an electric hand whisk, beat together until just smooth. Beat in the melted chocolate. Spoon the mixture into the paper cases, filling them three-quarters full.

3 Bake the cupcakes in a preheated oven, 180°C/350°F/Gas Mark 4, for 15 minutes or until springy to the touch. Transfer to a wire rack to cool completely.

4 To make the filling, put the butter in a bowl and beat until fluffy. Sift in the icing sugar and beat together until smooth. Add the melted chocolate and beat until well mixed.

5 When the cupcakes are cold, use a serrated knife to cut a circle from the top of each cake and then cut each circle in half. Spread or pipe a little of the buttercream into the centre of each cupcake and press the 2 semicircular halves into it at an angle to resemble butterfly wings. Dust with a little sifted icing sugar before serving.

marbled chocolate cupcakes

ingredients

MAKES 21

175 g/6 oz soft margarine
175 g/6 oz caster sugar
3 eggs
175 g/6 oz self-raising flour
2 tbsp milk
55 g/2 oz plain chocolate,
    melted

method

1 Put 21 paper baking cases in a muffin pan, or place 21 double-layer paper cases on a baking sheet.

2 Put the margarine, sugar, eggs, flour and milk in a large bowl and, using an electric hand whisk, beat together until just smooth.

3 Divide the mixture between 2 bowls. Add the melted chocolate to one bowl and stir together until well mixed. Using a teaspoon, and alternating the chocolate mixture with the plain mixture, put 4 half-teaspoons into each paper case.

4 Bake the cupcakes in a preheated oven, 180°C/350°F/Gas Mark 4, for 20 minutes or until well risen and springy to the touch. Transfer to a wire rack to cool.